FAMOUS BOMBERS OF THE SECOND WORLD WAR

Second Series

Famous Bombers

of the Second World War

Volume Two

WILLIAM GREEN

Illustrated by G. W. HEUMANN and
PETER ENDSLEIGH CASTLE, A.R.Ae.S.

DOUBLEDAY & COMPANY, INC.

GARDEN CITY, NEW YORK

Doubleday edition, 1960

MADE AND PRINTED IN GREAT BRITAIN

INTRODUCTION

The amazing metamorphosis in bomber design which took place during the world conflict which began twenty-one years ago is perhaps better illustrated by this second volume of *Famous Bombers of the Second World War* than by its predecessor. Whereas the first volume was devoted largely to the bombers that reached maturity during the conflict, the pages that follow relate primarily to those which, already mature when war began, were among the first to see action, and also to the machines which, evolved during the war years, saw action during the closing stages of the conflict. The radical character of the transformation in design can be perceived by comparing the maximum speed of 266 m.p.h. at 11,800 feet of the Bristol Blenheim, the first aircraft described in this volume, with that of the Arado Blitz which attained more than 460 m.p.h. at twice the altitude; by comparing the R.A.F.'s heaviest bomber at the beginning of the war, the Whitley, with its normal gross weight of 28,200 lb. and defensive armament of five rifle-calibre machine guns, with the Superfortress which, normally weighing in at 120,000 lb. and carrying twelve half-inch guns plus a 20-mm. cannon, had a short-range bomb load of no less than two-thirds the earlier "heavy" bomber's loaded weight !

Fame is the condition of being much talked about, and a warplane did not have to be entirely successful to enjoy fame during the Second World War. Indeed, there were many aircraft of that period whose fame owed more to the colourful imaginations of the propagandists than to intrinsic qualities or operational exploits. Many wildly inaccurate claims made years ago to boost public morale have been repeated so frequently since that they have come to be accepted as fact, and the totally distorted picture that they present may well confuse the historians of the future.

Blenheim, Hampden, Whitley—all honourable names which graced bombers commanding a healthy respect at the beginning of the Second World War; machines claimed to be among the world's most potent offensive weapons and upon which Britain's claim to leadership in international bomber development largely rested. Yet, although admirable machines in many ways, they possessed serious shortcoming which were soon revealed in the hard school of war, for, the pace of aircraft development had increased so rapidly in the space of a few short years, that they were already bordering upon the obsolescent when they took-off on their first operational sorties. Not that British bombers were alone in this respect. Their principal failings were in their lack of defensive armament and armour protection for crew and fuel tanks, and German and Japanese bombers, relying on experience gained during the Spanish Civil War and the Chinese "incident", suffered similar deficiences.

In the United Kingdom as elsewhere, the build-up of the bomber forces was one of expediency; a period in which reliance had to be placed on increased production of existing types despite the fact that their shortcomings were manifestly obvious. Then came the period of adaptation and improvisation in which these aircraft were modified and their operational tasks reassessed, providing the props and mainstays of the bomber squadrons while a newer generation of bombing machines was emerging. In the R.A.F., the Stirling, much vaunted by propagandists of the period, represented the first stage in the revitalisation of Bomber Command with four-engined "heavies". Yet, owing to certain short-sighted aspects of the specification which gave it birth, this bomber could not be developed to keep pace with changing requirements and, a disappointment, its operational career was relatively brief. The R.A.F.'s second four-engined "heavy", the Halifax, also suffered a full share of trials and tribulations; teething troubles which cost much in lives and time before they were finally eradicated.

In Germany, bomber development was fraught with even greater difficulties. Short sightedness on the part of the German High Command had led to the virtual discontinuation of four-engined long-range bomber development, necessitating one of the most remarkable adaptations of the war years; the transformation of the lightly constructed Condor commercial airliner as a reconnaissance bomber. The only German heavy bomber to see operational service, Heinkel's He 177 Greif, suffered a seriously protracted gestatory period which cost the Luftwaffe dear. The Japanese, among the first exponents of true strategic bombing, learned the lessons of operational experience too late to have any serious effect on the course of the air war in the Pacific, although with such machines as the Hiryu they proved their ability to produce bombers comparing favourably with the best of those evolved by the Allies. The American aircraft industry was a late starter but, with remarkable drive, caught up with the industries of other countries and produced such superlative machines as the Boeing Superfortress which literally delivered the *coup de grace* against Japan.

The bombers described and illustrated in this volume varied widely in appearance and operational efficiency, but successful or otherwise, they *were* famous, and all played their part in the overall pattern of bomber development.

As in previous volumes in this series, I wish to record my thanks to Gert W. Heumann who, together with Peter Endsleigh Castle, has contributed the general arrangement tone drawings of the bombers, and to those many friends who have assisted me with information and photographs.

August 1960   WILLIAM GREEN

CONTENTS

(*Above*) *The first Blenheim off the assembly line (K7033)
and (right) the original Type 142 "Britain First".*

THE BRISTOL BLENHEIM

When, in the summer of 1936, the Bristol Blenheim made its début, it was immediately hailed as a major step forward in combat aircraft design which placed the British aircraft industry in the forefront of fast day-bomber development. It was the first modern all-metal cantilever monoplane of stressed-skin construction to be placed in production for the Royal Air Force and, as such, it denoted the beginning of a new era in the equipment of that air arm. For several years acute uneasiness had existed concerning the obsolescence of the R.A.F's operational equipment; uneasiness accentuated by developments abroad. The emergence of the Blenheim, representing such a tremendous technical advance over the aircraft which it superseded, did much to still this disquiet. More than any other aeroplane it sounded the death knell of the fighting biplane; it set a pattern in light-bomber design which other nations were not slow to follow, yet the Blenheim was fated never to fulfil the very high hopes that were placed in it.

One of the key types selected by the Air Ministry for the re-equipment of the rapidly expanding R.A.F. of the late 'thirties, the Blenheim, at the time of its service introduction, was possessed of a performance which enabled it to outpace most contemporary service fighters. Yet, such was the pace of combat aircraft evolution during those last two years of peace in Europe that, when the R.A.F. went to war, in September 1939, it soon discovered that the Blenheim was not the redoubtable weapon that it had supposed. Its shortcomings soon manifested themselves in the hard school of aerial combat; it was to prove

The first Type 142M Blenheim (below) made its initial flight on June 25, 1936, and, together with the second machine off the assembly line, served as a test and trials aircraft. It flew initially with Mercury VI-S.2 engines.

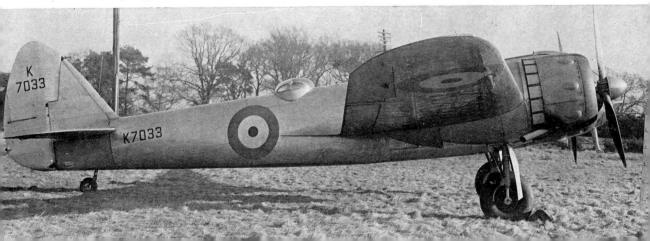

The fifth Blenheim I off the production line, K7037 (above) was issued to No. 114 Squadron which, by March 1937, had become the first unit to be equipped with the new bomber. K7037 was the first Blenheim produced to full production standards.

woefully vulnerable to fighter attack; it was to be found deficient in both defensive armament and armour. Nevertheless, it was to bear the brunt of much of the fighting on every front to which the R.A.F. was committed for the first three years of the Second World War, and, despite its limitations, it was to serve valorously. A parallel might be drawn between the Blenheim and the Curtiss P-40. Like the American fighter, it was praised and abused, lauded and vilified, but it was all that was available, and however divergent were views of the effectiveness of the Blenheim as a weapon, it was one of the truly historic aircraft of the war.

In the years immediately preceding the war, the Blenheim had been more in the news, it had been more widely discussed and, in foreign aviation circles, it had aroused greater controversy than any other British bomber, and to the Blenheim was to go the distinction of being the first British warplane to cross the enemy's frontier after Britain's declaration of war on Germany, on September 3, 1939. At 12.01 hours on that day, one minute after the declaration took effect, a Blenheim IV (N6215) of No. 139 Squadron took-off from Wyton on a reconnaissance sortie. Its task was to photograph the German fleet at Kiel and, on a flight lasting 4 hr. 49 min., it took seventy-five photographs from an altitude of 24,000 ft.

On the following day, ten Blenheim IVs drawn from Nos. 107 and 110 Squadrons based at Wattisham undertook R.A.F. Bomber Command's first bombing sortie of the war by attacking German warships in the Schillig Roads. Blenheims were subsequently active with the Advanced Air Striking Force and the Air Component of the British Expeditionary Force in France until the time of that country's capitulation; they made many low-level daylight raids over Occupied Europe until late in 1941; they fought against appalling odds in the defence of Burma and Malaya; they served conspicuously in the Western Desert; they were active against enemy shipping from Norway to the Bay of Biscay; they were among the very few types to serve with *all* R.A.F. Commands—Bomber, Fighter, Coastal, Training and Army Co-operation, and they served with many foreign air forces, both Allied *and* enemy! Indeed, one of the Blenheim's chief claims to fame was its ubiquity.

The Blenheim's progenitor, the original Type 142, had been instrumental in disrupting Air Ministry

The export of Blenheim Is began in 1937, and the photograph below depicts one of two machines supplied to Yugoslavia in the spring of 1938. The Blenheim I was manufactured under licence by the Ikarus factory at Zemun, the first licence-built machine flying in March 1939, fifty-nine being in service with the Royal Yugoslav Air Force at the time of the German attack.

Turkey received twelve Blenheim Is between October 1937 and July 1938, and a further eighteen were purchased before the end of 1938. Later, the Turkish Air Force received small quantities of Blenheim Vs.

complacency with, what was for its time, a phenominal performance. This performance, which revolutionized official thinking, bested by a handsome 40 m.p.h. the highest speeds attained by fighters then in service with the R.A.F. In some respects, the Blenheim may be compared, therefore, with the Mosquito which came after. There was, however, one vital difference between the development backgrounds of the two aircraft: Whereas the Mosquito was born of a conviction that the high-speed, unarmed bomber had a future as a military machine, the Blenheim was born casually—almost accidentally—from some work on high-speed commercial aircraft. The first of these, and, therefore, the *real* forefather of the Blenheim and the Bristol twins which followed it, was, oddly enough, never built. This was the Bristol Type 135, a small, low-wing cabin monoplane designed to carry six to eight passengers at a cruising speed of 180 m.p.h.

As no suitable engines were available for the Type 135 with the required power of about 350 h.p., Bristol developed the sleeve-valve Aquila nine-cylinder single-row air-cooled radial specifically for their projected aircraft. Among the advanced features embodied by the

Type 135 was all-metal, stressed-skin construction, and a good deal of favourable comment was aroused when a mock-up fuselage of the project was displayed at the *Salon International de i'Aéronautique* in Paris in 1934. The project was the work of Bristol's chief designer, Captain Frank Barnwell, who had been responsible for the majority of Bristol designs since the First World War. Among those interested in the project was the newspaper proprietor, Lord Rothermere, who informed the Bristol Aeroplane Company that he would be prepared to purchase an aeroplane of about this size and performance, capable of making non-stop flights between the principal cities of Europe. The Type 135 lacked the range to fulfil this task, and so Captain Barnwell laid out a new aeroplane—the Type 142—which, based on the earlier design, was specifically intended to fulfil Lord Rothermere's requirements.

The aircraft was designed around two 640 h.p. Bristol Mercury VI nine-cylinder air-cooled radial engines, and the original project drawings were dated April 27, 1934. At that time, the aircraft, with eight passengers, was expected to offer a maximum speed of

The Blenheim I (L1348) illustrated below was used for early photographic reconnaissance experiments at Heston. With boosted engines, reduced wing span, a special "camotint" finish, and the dorsal turret removed, this Blenheim achieved a speed of 296 m.p.h. at 8,000 ft. The lower glazed nose panels were removed, and cameras were installed in small bulges in the fuselage belly.

9

The Blenheim I was manufactured under licence in Finland by the Government Aircraft Factory at Tampere, the first batch of fifteen being delivered in 1941. Finnish Blenheims featured an enlarged bomb-bay, and were sometimes operated with skis (see left).

the order of 250 m.p.h. Simultaneously, a parallel scheme was drawn up for a less advanced and less expensive aircraft to succeed the original Type 135 project, and this was allocated the Type number 143. Lord Rothermere ordered a prototype of the Type 142 in mid-1934, and the Bristol company themselves financed construction of the Type 143.

Carrying the identification "R-12" on its fuselage sides—the registration G-ADCZ was later allocated to the aircraft—the Type 142 made its first flight at Filton on April 12, 1935, piloted by Captain Cyril Uwins, the company's chief test pilot. Retaining the basic wing design of the Type 135 project, the Type 142 featured a fuselage of reduced cross section which resulted in an exceptionally slim, all-metal monocoque structure accommodating six passengers, a "bay window" in the nose providing the pilot with an excellent field of vision. The main undercarriage members retracted into the engine nacelles, and the two 640 h.p. Mercury VI radials drove fixed-pitch, four-blade wooden airscrews. These airscrews were replaced by Hamilton Standard controllable-pitch, three-blade metal units for the Certificate of Airworthiness trials at Martlesham Heath, and the performance of the prototype exceeded the most sanguine expectations.

The official report of the trials conducted with the Type 142 at Martlesham Heath, in June 1935, indicated that the aircraft achieved 285 m.p.h. when flying at maximum loaded weight. This was 30 m.p.h. faster than the maximum speed of the fighter which, but a short time previously, had won the protracted

contest for the F.7/30 specification—the Gloster Gladiator—and which was about to be ordered into production for the R.A.F. It was hardly surprising, therefore, that the Air Ministry should approach Lord Rothermere for permission to make further tests. He went one better, and presented his aeroplane to the Air Council, naming it the "Britain First".

Trials with the Type 142—now bearing R.A.F. insignia and the serial number K7557—continued while Barnwell turned his thoughts to ways and means of translating the basic design into a useful military aeroplane. As it happened, military roles had already been considered for the parallel Type 143. There had been, for instance, a proposal in December 1934 to use a variant of this type for coastal and general reconnaissance duties, and in January 1935 had come the Type 143F project—a fighter-bomber for the Finnish Air Force with Mercury VI engines replacing the Aquila IIIs, a 20-mm. Madsen cannon in the nose, and a dorsal gunner's position. Although neither of these projects materialized, and the Type 143 itself was not to fly until January 20, 1936, they were links in the chain which led, in the summer of 1935, to a proposal for the Type 142M, a bomber based on the design of the "Britain First".

Initially, the Type 142M project envisaged a crew of two with a pair of Aquila or Mercury engines. A 1,000-lb. warload was to be carried over a range of 1,000 miles. A major difference from the "Britain First" was the raising of the wing on the fuselage by sixteen inches in order to provide space in the fuselage below the main wing spars for a bomb-bay capable of housing four 250-lb. or two 500-lb. bombs. The design retained the curiously short nose of the "Britain First", but an incidental disadvantage resulting from the raising of the wing from low to mid position was the restriction placed on the pilot's view to the side by the high-placed engine nacelles. The tailplane was increased in span and raised on the

Although few Blenheim Is remained in service with home-based bomber squadrons at the outbreak of World War II, a night fighting version, the Blenheim IF (above) saw fairly extensive service. The machine illustrated belonged to No. 614 (County of Glamorgan) Squadron.

fuselage; the adjustable incidence gear was removed, resulting in an increase in elevator chord and the introduction of trim tabs; the tailwheel was made retractable—linked to the main undercarriage members by cable to avoid hydraulics at the rear end of the fuselage; structural strength was increased; a 0.303-in. Browning machine gun and a bomb-aiming station were provided in the fuselage nose, and provision made for a semi-retractable gun turret in the dorsal position.

On July 9, 1935, the first design conference on the project was held between the Bristol design team and Air Cdre. Verney, Director of Technical Development at the Air Ministry. In view of the fact that the results of trials with the "Britain First" were indisputable, it was to be expected that the Air Ministry would move swiftly, and by August specification B.28/35 had been drawn up to cover detail design of the Type 142M proposal, a contract had been placed for 150 machines "off the drawing board", and the name "Blenheim" had been bestowed upon the type. With this order in hand, the Bristol company had no need to bother with prototypes—in any case, the "Britain First" had furnished a pretty good idea of the characteristics to be expected in the bomber—and, therefore, the first two Blenheims off the assembly line at Filton served as test and trials aircraft. The first of these (K7033) made its initial flight on June 25, 1936, but before this milestone had been attained, the Bristol design office had already commenced the study of a variety of projects based upon the Blenheim.

During 1935, while detail design of the Blenheim was the principal activity, Bristol prepared at least three designs based on or developed from the Type 142M. These designs included a 37,500-lb. four-engined bomber which, submitted in December 1935, and possessing no Type number, employed a standard Blenheim cockpit married to a new, slim fuselage, a 96-ft. span wing, and four Mercury IX engines. Three years later, this project was to be revived to form the basis of the Bristol tender to the B.1/39 specification for a medium-heavy bomber which, in the event, was not proceeded with. The Type 149 was a slightly modified Blenheim intended for the general-purpose role to specification G.24/35, two Aquila AE-3M engines stretching the range, and the Type 150 was a torpedo-bomber with internal stowage for one torpedo, and two Bristol Perseus VI engines to specification M.15/35. In April 1935 a further Blenheim variant was evolved, the Type 152. This combined in one machine the requirements of both G.24/35 and M.15/35 with the only exception that the torpedo could not be housed wholly within the bomb-bay. This development was later to see production as the Beaufort. Meanwhile, the Type 149 project had been revised to incorporate a forward navigation table, as in the Type 152, and in this form the aircraft was also adopted by the Air Ministry which ordered 150 in November 1936. The type was named Bolingbroke, and production was covered by specification 11/36. Interest in this type was expressed by the air forces of both Canada and Australia.

By this time, however, as already noted, the Blenheim was already in the air, and in December 1936 the Bristol company had been instructed to proceed with production with all possible speed—a year later, twenty-four Blenheims were being delivered from the Filton factory each month, and Rootes Securities and A. V. Roe factories were being brought into the production programme. The initial production model was the Blenheim I powered by two 840 h.p. Mercury VIII engines, although the first example (K7033) was initially flown with Mercury VI-S.2s. At the Martlesham trials, this aircraft achieved 281 m.p.h. at 12,000 ft., despite its loaded weight of 11,000 lb. compared with the 9,000 lb. of the "Britain First". A few small changes were made on later aircraft. For instance, the landing lamp in the starboard wing was deleted; the shape of the side cockpit windows was modified, and controllable gills were

THE BRISTOL BLENHEIM

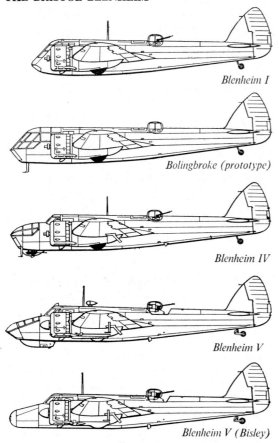

Blenheim I

Bolingbroke (prototype)

Blenheim IV

Blenheim V

Blenheim V (Bisley)

added to the engine cowlings. A little later, airscrew spinners were abandoned, together with the retractable tailwheel, as unnecessary luxuries.

In service form the Blenheim I carried a crew of three, comprising a pilot, navigator-bombardier, and wireless-operator-gunner, and armament comprised one forward-firing 0.303-in. Browning machine gun in the port wing, and one Vickers "K" gun in a Bristol hydraulically-operated dorsal turret. A 1,000-lb. bomb load was carried internally. The fuselage, which was built in three sections, was a light alloy monocoque built up of formers and open-section stringers, with Alclad skin riveted to the flanges of the formers and stringers. The wings, which were also built in three sections, comprised spars built up of two heavy high-tensile steel flanges with a light, single-plate Alclad web, reinforced with vertical stringers, between them. The ribs were made from Alclad sheet, the whole being covered by an Alclad stressed-skin. Bristol-Frise mass-balanced ailerons and split trailing-edge flaps were carried, and small trim tabs in the

ailerons were adjustable on the ground. The construction of the tail assembly was similar to that of the wings. A servo-tab was fitted in the rudder, and rudder and elevators were aerodynamically and statically balanced. All moveable control surfaces were fabric covered.

Fully equipped, the loaded weight of the Blenheim I rose to 12,500 lb., but a maximum speed of 285 m.p.h. was attained at 15,000 ft., speeds at 10,000 and 20,000 ft. being 269 and 277 m.p.h. respectively. Range, fully loaded at 220 m.p.h., was 1,250 miles, endurance was 5.65 hrs., initial climb rate was 1,540 ft./min., and service ceiling was 27,280 ft.

The first aircraft to go to a squadron, the third machine off the line (K7035), arrived at Wyton early in 1937, and by March of that year No. 114 Squadron had become the first Blenheim-equipped unit. The appearance of the Blenheim at the Hendon Display of that year caused a considerable stir, and the type was soon equipping R.A.F. squadrons in Iraq and India. In service it was giving an excellent account of itself, and some exceptionally fast flights, both by single machines and formations, were recorded. A Blenheim squadron flew from Dhibban to Aboukir, a distance of 811 miles, in 3.25 hours, the average speed being 250 m.p.h., while one machine flew from Abbotsinch to Upavon against a head wind and in poor visibility yet covered the 335 miles in seventy minutes, giving an average speed of 280 m.p.h.

Production of the Blenheim I by Bristol, A. V. Roe and Rootes Securities totalled 1,552 machines, and these served with the following home and overseas bomber squadrons of the R.A.F. from March 1937 onwards: Nos. 8, 11, 21, 30, 34, 39, 44, 45, 55, 57, 60, 61, 67, 82, 84, 90, 101, 104, 107, 108, 110, 113, 114, 139, 144 and 211. Few Blenheim Is remained in service with home-based bomber squadrons by the outbreak of war, having been superseded by the later Mk. IV, although a few Blenheim Is saw operational service in the bombing role during the early stages of the fighting in the Western Desert. As the Blenheim IF, however, the type did see fairly extensive operational service in the night-fighting role, some two hundred being converted from bombers by the attachment of a pack housing four 0.303-in. Brownings under the forward fuselage. Blenheims of this type undertook the first night-intruder sorties of the war, on December 21-22, 1939, and largely pioneered airborne interception radar, scoring their first success with this revolutionary development on July 22, 1940.

One Blenheim I (L1348) was the subject of an interesting experiment in the early days of photographic reconnaissance activities at Heston. This aircraft had its wing span reduced by 3ft., the dorsal turret re-

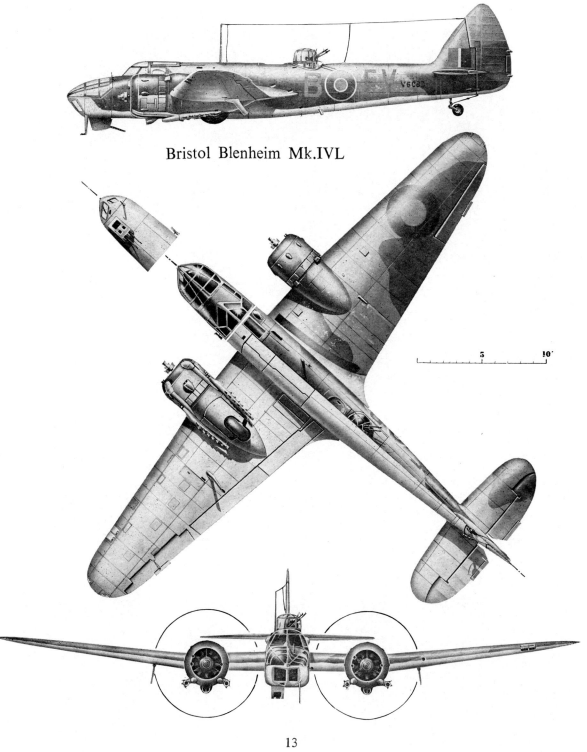

Bristol Blenheim Mk.IVL

(Above and left) This early production Blenheim I (K7072) was set aside in 1937 as the prototype Bolingbroke. Initially, the whole windscreen was moved forward by three feet, but before the aircraft flew the forward panelling was lowered below the pilot's line of vision. This was later "scalloped" on the portside (as seen lower left), and the aircraft shipped to Canada. This aircraft was not designated Blenheim III, an error first perpetrated during the war years which has persisted until now.

moved, the engines boosted, a special "camotint" finish applied, the lower nose panels filled-in, and cameras installed in small bulges in the fuselage belly. The refinements served to increase the speed of this aircraft at 8,000 ft. from 274 m.p.h. to 296 m.p.h.

It was to be expected that the performance of the Blenheim, with all its attendant publicity, would not escape unnoticed abroad, and several batches of the Mk.I version were exported, while manufacturing licences for the type were acquired by Finland and

Yugoslavia. Twelve Blenheim Is were delivered to the Turkish Air Force between October 1937 and July 1938, followed by a further eighteen before the end of 1938. Two were purchased by the Yugoslav government, and licence manufacture was initiated by the Ikarus factory at Zemun, Belgrade, the first Ikarus-built Blenheim flying in March 1939. An additional twenty-two Blenheim Is were diverted from the R.A.F. to Yugoslavia as part of the British government's policy of strengthening the Balkan *Entente* against possible attack by Germany. At the same time fourteen were delivered to Rumania. When Germany attacked Yugoslavia on April 6, 1941, the Royal Yugoslav Air Force possessed fifty-nine Blenheims (twenty-three with each of the 1st and 8th Bomber Regiments, and thirteen with the 11th Independant Group). Blenheims of the 1st Bomber Regiment made extremely valorous low-level

The Fairchild-built Bolingbroke IVW (below) was fitted with 1,200 h.p. Pratt and Whitney Wasp R-1830 fourteen-cylinder radials, and fifteen aircraft of this type were delivered.

The first eighteen aircraft built by Fairchild were essentially replicas of the Bolingbroke prototype (K7072) and were known as Bolingbroke Is, but the standard Canadian production model was the Mercury XV-powered Bolingbroke IV, one of which (9048) is illustrated above. The Bolingbroke IV was redesigned extensively to U.S. standards and for U.S. and Canadian equipment. One machine completed with 990 h.p. Wright Cyclone R-1820-G3B radial engines (right) was designated Bolingbroke IVC. This aircraft bore the serial number 9074.

attacks on German armoured columns invading Yugoslavia from Bulgaria, during which the Regimental Commander was killed by fragments from his own bombs, and those of the 8th Regiment were employed against targets in Hungary and Austria, and made attacks on Graz and Vienna. Many Yugoslav Blenheims were destroyed on the ground, and those that survived the onslaught were incorporated in the Croat Air Force.

Another country to order the Blenheim I was Finland, who received eighteen between July 1937 and June 1938. Finland also acquired a manufacturing licence for the bomber, which was placed in production at the Government Aircraft Factory at Tampere, the Mercury engines being produced at the Tampella Machine Works. The Finnish Blenheim Is had an enlarged bomb-bay capable of accommodating both Swedish and American bombs, and sometimes operated with fixed skis in place of the normal wheel

One Bolingbroke I (717) was fitted with twin Edo floats and redesignated Bolingbroke III (below). Although the possibility of having interchangeable wheel, ski or float undercarriages was considered, only one machine was tested with floats.

The first sixty-eight Blenheim IVs produced were actually Mk.I airframes, and to distinguish true production aircraft from these hybrids later machines were designated Blenheim IVL. A late production Blenheim IVL (V5382) is illustrated above.

undercarriage. The first batch of fifteen Blenheim Is was delivered by the Tampere factory in 1941, and production continued until 1944, a further forty machines being built. In addition to the Blenheim Is, the Finnish Air Force received twenty-four Blenheim IVs from the United Kingdom prior to the second Russian assault.

An early production Blenheim I (K7072) was set aside, in 1937, for conversion as a prototype for the Bolingbroke, the Type, 149 of which 150 had been ordered. The unusually short nose which had characterized the Blenheim gave place to a lengthened structure which, in the first place, retained the contours of the Blenheim I, the whole windscreen and bombardier's window assembly being moved forward bodily by about 3 ft. Before the aircraft had flown it was realised that the pilot's view—the position of his seat being unchanged—was inadequate, to say the least! The windscreen was, therefore, moved back to its original position, with the forward transparent hooding lowered below the pilot's line of vision. In this form, K7072 flew for the first time on September 24, 1937, but the view for landing still left something to be desired. The forward hooding on the portside was, therefore, "scalloped" to produce what was later to become the characteristic nose of the Blenheim IV.

In this form the Bolingbroke was now adopted by the Royal Canadian Air Force, and negotiations commenced with a view to producing the bomber in Canada. Plans for producing the Bolingbroke for the R.A.F. at Filton, Bristol, were cancelled, however, in favour of maintaining the supply of Blenheims to re-equip R.A.F. squadrons overseas. The prototype Bolingbroke, K7072, was shipped to Canada in due course to assist in the production of Bolingbrokes by Fairchild Aircraft Limited at Longueuil. The first batch of eighteen Bolingbrokes were built to Bristol drawings, and were essentially replicas of K7072, with Mercury VIII engines. These were designated Bolingbroke Is. The standard Canadian version, redesigned extensively to U.S. standards and for U.S. and Canadian equipment, was the Bolingbroke IV with Mercury XV engines, and 125 examples of this model were built. The Bolingbroke II was a Mk.I rebuilt to Mk.IV standards after a crash, and the Bolingbroke III was another Mk.I completed as a float-plane with twin Edo floats and Mercury XV engines. One Bolingbroke IV completed with 990 h.p. Wright Cyclone R1820-G3B nine-cylinder air-cooled radials was designated Mk.IVC, and fifteen delivered with 1,200 h.p. Pratt and Whitney Twin Wasp R-1830 fourteen-cylinder two-row air-cooled radials were designated Mk.IVW. Finally, following production of the Bolingbroke IVs, a batch of IVT trainers were built, equipped for bombing and gunnery training, flying training, and drogue target towing, etc.

In 1938—the year in which Frank Barnwell was killed when making the second flight in a light monoplane that he had built privately—Air Ministry interest in the Bolingbroke revived, and it was decided to put a generally similar aircraft in production at Filton until the Type 152 Beaufort became available. The Type number 149 was retained, but the aircraft was designated Blenheim IV, and this variant differed from the preceding production version of the Blenheim in only two major respects—a new forward fuselage with the lengthened nose, a stepped windscreen introduced on the Bolingbroke, and long-range tanks in the wings. The first sixty-eight Blenheim IVs were actually Mk.I airframes, and did not have the long-range wing, and to distinguish the true production aircraft from these hybrids, the later machines were usually designated Blenheim IVL, or, when carrying the gun tray beneath the fuselage (which, containing four 0.303-in. Brownings with 500 r.p.g., was similar to that carried by the Blenheim IF) as the Blenheim IVF.

There was no prototype of the Blenheim IV, and production had begun to switch from the Mk.I to the later type before the end of 1938. The Blenheim II and III did not reach fruition, and it is no longer certain which variants were covered by these designations. Some documents suggest that the Blenheim II was intended to be the Blenheim I with a long-range wing, and the Blenheim III was basically the Blenheim IV with a short-range wing. This cannot now be confirmed, but it *is* certain that the prototype Bolingbroke, K7072, was *not* designated Blenheim III, an error first perpetrated during the war years which has persisted until now.

All Blenheim IVs had Mercury XV engines rated at 920 h.p. for take-off—similar engines were installed retroactively in some Blenheim Is—and the initial loaded weight was increased progressively from 12,500 lb. to 13,800 lb. and, eventually, to 14,500 lb. Initially, the Blenheim IV had a single Vickers "K" gun in a Bristol B.I.Mk.III dorsal turret, and a single, forward-firing 0.303-in. Browning, but the need to increase defensive armament in order to stave off fighter attacks was rendered patently obvious at an early stage in the fighting. Various unorthodox modifications were made by squadrons in the field, and among these was one machine with two fixed guns, one in each engine nacelle, firing rearwards, while another had a fixed, rearward-firing gun in the fuselage tail. A standard modification was subsequently incorporated which comprised a single free-mounted Vickers "K" gun on a gimbal mounting in the nose and a rearward-firing Browning in a blister attached to the emergency hatch in the floor of the fuselage nose. A B.I.Mk.IIIA dorsal turret housing two Vickers "K" guns was introduced and, later, this gave place to a B.I.Mk.IV turret with twin Brownings. Later still, a Frazer-Nash controllable mounting with two rearward-firing Brownings was fitted under the nose.

At the outbreak of war, R.A.F. Bomber Command had six squadrons of Blenheim IVs forming No. 2 Group. Two of these squadrons were immediately flown to France as part of the Advanced Air Striking Force, while the Air Component of the British Expeditionary Force included a further four squadrons equipped with Blenheim IVs. Prior to the outbreak of war, twelve Blenheim IVs had been ordered by and delivered to the Royal Hellenic Air Force, although an order for eighteen aircraft of this type for the Royal Swedish Air Force was refused. As previously recounted, twenty-four Blenheim IVs were supplied to the Finnish Air Force and, early in 1940, a quantity was delivered to the Turkish Air Force to supplement the Blenheim Is previously supplied.

Within a few days of the commencement of the main German offensive, on May 10, 1940, the Blenheim squadrons attached to the A.A.S.F. had been decimated, having proved particularly vulnerable to fighter attack. Nevertheless, after the collapse of France, the Blenheim IVs of No. 2 Group continued to operate by daylight over the Continent, frequently without fighter escort, although attrition was high. The daylight activities of Bomber Command's Blenheims included many noteworthy sorties, such as the daring attack on Bremen, on July 4, 1941, for which Wing Commander H. I. Edwards was awarded the Victoria Cross, and a memorable attack on Cologne in the following month. An equally important task for the Blenheim squadrons during the early war years were strikes against enemy shipping in the Channel and the Bay of Biscay. These strikes were invariably made at altitudes of the order of 50 ft., and the aircraft suffered severely from the intense anti-aircraft fire of escorting warships, but on occasions

During the war years, the Portuguese Air Force received a number of Blenheim IVs and Vs, some having made forced landings in Portugal and others being supplied direct from the United Kingdom. The photograph below depicts Portuguese Blenheim IVs.

The prototype Blenheim V (AD657) was fitted with a ground attack nose, but the type was never produced in this form. The name "Bisley" had been allocated to this model but supplanted by that of Blenheim V before the prototype flew.

the Blenheim manifested a remarkable ability to absorb damage and remain in the air. This quality could hardly be better illustrated than by the Blenheim which, weaving violently to avoid intense fire from an enemy destroyer, actually struck the water. The impact was so violent that one of the engines was wrenched completely out of its mounting, and the tips of the airscrew of the other engine were badly bent, yet the Blenheim's pilot succeeded in nursing the crippled aircraft back to a coastal airfield! Blenheims were based on besieged Malta in 1941, accounting for a remarkable amount of enemy shipping in the Mediterranean; others played an important role in the fighting in the Western Desert, but in the Far East, Blenheims defending Singapore suffered sorely at the hands of Japanese fighters. Blenheim IVs last operated with Bomber Command on August 18, 1942, giving place to Douglas Bostons and de Havilland Mosquitoes, but overseas these aircraft fought on with the R.A.F., the S.A.A.F., and the Free French Air Force.

Like the Blenheim I, the Blenheim IV was built by A. V. Roe and Rootes Securities, in addition to the parent company, and a total of 1,930 was produced, eventually operating with the following bomber squadrons at home and overseas: Nos. 8, 11, 13, 14, 15, 18, 21, 34, 35, 39, 40, 45, 52, 55, 57, 67, 87, 88, 90, 101, 104, 107, 108, 110, 113, 114, 139, 142, 150, 162, 203, 218, 223, 226, 244, 326, 327, 342, 454, 500, 608 and 614. The Blenheim IV also flew operationally with Nos. 53 and 59 Squadrons on Army Co-operation and Coastal Command duties and, in its Mk.IVF version, with thirteen fighter squadrons.

One Blenheim was fitted with a fixed nosewheel undercarriage for taxying tests, but did not fly in this form. This was part of an investigation into tricycle undercarriages in connection with the Type 155 design in 1938, to meet specification B.18/38. The Type 155 was not unlike the Beaufort in general design, the essence of the requirement being that it

should employ materials "not in general use" for aircraft construction, and be suitable for large-scale production by sub-contractors outside the aircraft industry. This design eventually formed the basis of the A.W.41 Albemarle later produced by A. W. Hawksley at Gloucester.

In January 1940, the Bristol company suggested, in the light of experience in France, that a specialised variant of the Blenheim could serve as a direct support bomber, having a new front fuselage with a battery of machine guns. The project envisaged alternative roles of interim fighter and dual-control trainer. The Air Staff thinking on this subject was outlined in specification B.6/40, and Bristol's ideas were then consolidated into a new machine, the Type 160, to to meet this requirement. Responsibility for detail design of the Type 160 was delegated to Rootes Securities, a large-scale producer of Blenheims, and the name Bisley was selected for the new development. The principal difference from the Blenheim IV was the provision of a new nose section housing four 0.303-in. Browning machine guns with 1,000 r.p.g. An improved, armoured windscreen was provided, the cockpit was armoured, and a Bristol B.X dorsal turret, with two Brownings and a gyro gunsight, was installed. For the low-altitude close-support role, the Bisley was to have had a pair of Mercury XVI engines with cropped impellers and operating on 100 octane fuel.

Before the prototypes of this new design were completed, the specification was revised to include high-altitude bombing as an alternative role. This new demand was met, in the case of the Bisley, by the development of a new, interchangeable front fuselage, the high-altitude version having a bombardier's station with offset aiming panels, and a faired "bath" underneath to serve as a foot-well for the bombardier when navigating, and as a housing for a Frazer-Nash mounting carrying two Browning guns for rearward

The Blenheim V had a very short service life as its performance left much to be desired. It served in the Middle and Far East, but when Blenheim V-equipped units reached Italy losses were such that they were hurriedly re-equipped.

defence. The engines became Mercury XVs or XXVs, and the gross weight was raised to 17,000 lb.

Two prototypes were built, and the name Blenheim V had supplanted that of Bisley before either of these flew. The first Blenheim V prototype (AD657) with the ground-attack nose flew at Filton on February 24, 1941, and was followed by the second prototype (AD661) with the high-altitude nose. All production of the Blenheim V was undertaken by Rootes Securities Limited at Speke and Stoke-on-Trent, 940 machines being built in all. Deliveries of the Blenheim V three-seat high-altitude bomber with the semi-glazed unsymmetrical nose commenced in the summer of 1942, the two-seat close-support variant having been abandoned, and No. 18 Squadron was the first unit to receive the new equipment. This squadron, together with Nos. 13, 114, 244, 454 and 614, flew Blenheim Vs in the Middle East, and Nos. 11, 42, 113 and 211 employed the type in the Far East. First mention of the Blenheim V on operations was made in November 1942, when the Allied landings were proceeding in North Africa, and Acting Wing Commander H. G. Malcolm was awarded a post-humous Victoria Cross for his gallantry when leading a formation of No. 18 Squadron's Blenheim Vs during the following month. However, the service life of the Blenheim V was destined to be a short one, for the performance of the type left much to be desired, and with a loaded weight of 17,000 lb., the two 830 h.p. Mercury engines left the Blenheim V decidedly under-powered. Losses on operations were such that, on reaching Italy, the squadrons equipped with this type were re-equipped with Martin Baltimores and Lockheed Venturas. Production ceased in June 1943, and the Blenheim V remained operational in the Far East until the end of that year.

Many Blenheim Vs were converted for use as dual-control trainers, being among the first R.A.F. aircraft to employ two-stage amber night simulation filters, and these were flown by Fighter Command operational training units. In 1942 a number of Blenheim Vs in the Middle East were transferred to the Turkish Air Force, and a number were received by the Portuguese Air Force which already operated several Blenheim IVs which had made forced landings in Portugal and been "interned".

While the exploits of the Blenheim during wartime operations were overshadowed by those of other types, this aircraft made a significant contribution to the development of the R.A.F. The Blenheim was one of a handful of types on which Bomber Command cut its teeth; with it the R.A.F. learned much of daylight operations over enemy territory which was to prove of inestimable value later in the war. Again, the Bristol company's experience in designing and building the Blenheim found expression in a whole series of successful types, such as the Beaufighter. Thus, the Blenheim, although not the most effective of weapons, is fully deserving of its place among the truly historic aircraft of the Second World War.

Bristol Blenheim IV

Dimensions : Span, 56 ft. 4 in. ; length, 42 ft. 7 in. ; height, 9 ft. 10 in. ; wing area, 469 sq. ft.

Armament : One fixed forward-firing 0.303-in. Browning machine gun with 400 rounds ; twin 0.303-in. Browning guns with 600 r.p.m. in B.I.Mk.IV dorsal turret, and two remotely-controlled Browning guns on rearward-firing Frazer-Nash mounting under the nose, with 1,000 r.p.g. Normal bomb capacity, 1,000 lb.

Power Plants : Two Bristol Mercury XV nine-cylinder air-cooled radial engines rated at 905 h.p. at 2,750 r.p.m. for take-off, and (maximum for five minutes) 995 h.p. at 2,750 r.p.m. at 9,250 ft.

Weights : Empty, 9,790 lb. ; normal loaded, 13,500 lb. ; maximum loaded, 14,400 lb. ; normal service load, 3,710 lb.

Performance : Maximum speed, 266 m.p.h. at 11,800 ft., 259 m.p.h. at 15,000 ft. ; initial climb rate, 1,500 ft./min. ; time to 5,000 ft., 3.7 min., to 10,000 ft., 7.2 min. ; service ceiling, 27,260 ft. ; maximum range, 1,460 miles at 169 m.p.h. ; normal cruising speed, 198 m.p.h.

The first Mitsubishi Ki.21-Ia Type 97 Model 1a bombers reached the J.A.A.F. early in 1938, and were immediately assigned to units operating over China. Operational experience dictated an increase in defensive armament, the result being the Ki.21-Ib, a formation of which bombers is illustrated above over the Chinese mainland.

THE MITSUBISHI KI.21 TYPE 97

The Mitsubishi Type 97 Heavy Bomber was, in its heyday, the backbone of the strongest air arm in the Far East; the Japanese Army Air Force. Entering service in 1937, it was a formidable bomber by any standard. It fought the Russians at Changkufeng and Nomonhan; it was in action throughout the "Chinese Incident", and at the commencement of the Pacific War it was the mainstay of the J.A.A.F. heavy bomber force. By the time the Pacific War reached the Japanese home islands, the Type 97 was totally obsolete, but it had remained a standard first-line type until late in 1943, and had earned the distinction of serving operationally with the J.A.A.F. longer than any other Japanese combat aircraft.

The Ki.21-Ib (below) enjoyed relatively clean lines. It was used as a tactical bomber over Mongolia but was withdrawn soon after the beginning of the Pacific War.

The last operational task of this venerable bomber, which, for several years had served as a symbol of Japanese aerial domination in Asia and the Orient, was typical of the desperation with which Japan greeted the Pacific War's twelfth hour. The American invasion of Okinawa in April 1945 had placed B-29 Superfortress bombers a mere few hundred miles from Japan's principal cities, presaging final victory for the Allies. In a daring but hopeless attempt to destroy the American installations and aircraft on Okinawa, nine Type 97 bombers, converted for use as assault transports, were assembled on an airfield in Southern Kyushu. On May 24, 1945, loaded with specially-trained demolition troops, the aircraft took-off for Okinawa. Flying low over the water, seven of the aircraft succeeded in reaching the target area where they encountered American interceptors which destroyed all but one of the intruders. The surviving machine crash-landed on the American-held Yontan Airfield, and the twelve Japanese troops that it carried immediately set about their appointed task. Before they were overwhelmed by American marines, the Japanese destroyed seven aircraft, damaged two others, burned 2,600 drums of fuel and blew up a vast quantity of ammunition, putting the American base out of commission for ten hours. But this suicidal effort gave Japanese cities only a few hours' respite, and a few weeks later when the Mitsubishi Type 97 was again encountered by the Allies it was painted white overall and carried green surrender crosses.

The Type 97, eventually to become known to the Allies as *Sally*, was the result of an Army specification

Numerically the most important J.A.A.F. bomber when the Pacific War began, the Ki.21-IIa Type 97 Model 2a, was essentially similar to the Ki.21-Ib but employed 1,490 h.p. Mitsubishi Ha.101 engines in place of the original Nakajima Ha.5-Kai Zuisei radials with a consequent improvement in overall performance.

issued in February 1936. The Japanese High Command was dedicated to the "theoretical enemy" concept, and the specification called for a bomber suitable for long-range overland operations, Russian installations north and west of Japan's Manchurian hinterland being its potential target areas. Russian ambitions in the Far East, being directly opposed to those of Japan, rendered the Soviet Union the principal potential enemy. With the continued growth of Russian power, Japan's expanding area of military responsibility on the Asiatic mainland, and the J.A.A.F.'s obvious inability to retain control in the air and maintain an air offensive against pressure from the north, a programme of J.A.A.F. revitalization was called for, and the new bomber specification was an integral part of this programme.

For an aircraft industry that had produced few aircraft of modern configuration by international standards appertaining at the time, the requirements of the specification were stiff, demanding as they did a modern twin-engined monoplane with a retractable undercarriage, capable of a maximum speed in excess of 250 m.p.h. at 10,000 feet, and the ability to carry a 1,650-lb. bomb load for five hours at 190 m.p.h. The specification also stipulated the use of either the Nakajima Zuisei Ha.5 or Mitsubishi Kinsei Ha.6 power plant, both newly-designed fourteen-cylinder two-row radial air-cooled engines at that time in the experimental stage; a crew of four; a loaded weight of less than 14,000 lb.; a take-off run of less than 330 yards; and the ability to attain an altitude of 10,000 feet in eight minutes.

Only two manufacturers entered the competition, both having enjoyed some measure of success in the multi-engined aircraft field. The Nakajima company,

armed with a background of experience provided by the licence manufacture of the Douglas DC-2, the development of the small AT-2 transport, as well as the DC-2-inspired 9-*Shi* LB-2 experimental Naval bomber, entered a mid-wing monoplane powered by two 950 h.p. Nakajima Ha.5 engines and designated Ki.19. The Mitsubishi company's design team of Nakata and Ozawa developed an aircraft entirely different to any previously evolved by the firm and bearing no relationship to the successful G3M1 9-*Shi* Naval bomber which was also a twin-engined all-metal monoplane with a retractable undercarriage. The design team was an experienced one. Nakata was well-known for his 1931 adaptation of the Junkers K-51—a bomber variant of the massive G-38

The cowlings of the Ha.101 engines employed by the Ki.21-IIa were very much cleaner than those of the Ha.5-Kai engines of the Ki.21-Ib illustrated on the opposite page.

The early production Ki.21-Ia illustrated above carried a crew of seven and a defensive armament of three 7.7-mm. machine guns. The first two prototypes of the Ki.21 (left) featured angular nose contours and a "stepped" rear fuselage for the ventral gun.

transport—as the Ki.20 Type 92 heavy bomber for the J.A.A.F., and both Nakata and Ozawa had assisted in the design of Mitsubishi's Ki.2 Type 93 Light Bomber based on the Junkers K-37. Their project was assigned the designation Ki.21, and work was initiated on four Ki.19 and five Ki.21 prototypes for exhaustive comparative tests and evaluation trials.

The first two prototypes of the Ki.21 were completed at Mitsubishi's 5th Airframe Works in November and December 1936. They were large, blunt-nosed mid-wing monoplanes with nose armament, a dorsal turret, and a stepped rear fuselage providing a ventral gun position. Power was provided by the Mitsubishi Kinsei Ha.6 of 850 h.p., and although performance more than met the demands of the specification, it was patently obvious that the defensive armament was ineffective. The nose-mounted 7.7-mm. machine gun could be moved on a vertical axis only; the traverse of the dorsal turret was strictly limited, and the ventral gun was virtually useless. Three further prototypes were therefore completed, each differing in defensive armament. Dorsal gun positions of semi-exposed, spherical, cylindrical, oval and flush type were tested, and the contours of the fuselage were revised and improved. The ventral step was removed from the rear fuselage, a hand-held 7.7-mm. gun being mounted above a flush sliding panel, and the lines of the nose were refined, terminating in a hemispherical glazed nose

cap containing a 7.7-mm. gun on a ball-and-socket mount. Lateral gun positions were proposed and rejected, and the fifth prototype embodied an innovation in the form of a remotely-controlled 7.7-mm. gun in the extreme tail, a device to be employed by later production models of the Ki.21.

The five Ki.21 prototypes were extensively tested against the four Nakajima Ki.19 prototypes throughout the spring and summer of 1937, with ultimate J.A.A.F. selection of the Ki.21 with the proviso that the Mitsubishi bomber utilize the Nakajima Ha.5 power plant. The production model was allocated the designation Ki.21-Ia Type 97 Heavy Bomber Model 1a, and as deliveries of the new bomber began to reach the J.A.A.F. early in 1938, Japanese military stature grew considerably in importance. The rapid spread of fighting in China necessitated a rapid build-up of production, and Mitsubishi's 5th Airframe Works soon reached saturation point. Production orders for the Type 97 were, therefore, also assigned to Nakajima who began deliveries in August 1938.

Mitsubishi had completed three production aircraft by the end of 1937, and had delivered a further 163 machines by the end of 1938, subsequent production reaching an average of more than fifteen aircraft per month. In its original form, the Ki.21-Ia carried a crew of seven and defensive armament consisted of three 7.7-mm. machine guns. The dorsal gun position was covered by a long "greenhouse" enclosure, the hand-held machine gun being mounted at its rear end. Power was provided by two Zuisei Ha.5-Kai radials, production versions of the original Ha.5 and rated at 850 h.p. With its 1,650-lb. bomb load and 269 m.p.h. maximum speed the Ki.21-Ia bomber did much to change the balance of air power in the Far East.

Operational experience dictated numerous changes

The Ki.21-IIa (above) carried a defensive armament of five or six 7.7-mm. machine guns, one of which was mounted as a remotely-controlled "stinger" in the extreme tail. This "stinger" gun is shown in close-up on the right.

as production gained momentum. The bomb-bays were enlarged, the landing flaps were increased in area, the fuel tanks were provided with partial leak protection by rubber laminated covering, light armour protection was fitted for the crew, and defensive armament was increased to five and, on some machines, six 7.7-mm. machine guns. One of these was mounted as a remotely-controlled "stinger" in the extreme tail, this having been tested on the fifth prototype. The modified aircraft was known as the Ki.21-Ib Type 97 Model 1b, this becoming numerically the most important Army bomber in service over the Chinese mainland, and it soon appeared over Chungking and Lanchow, far inland. It also served as a tactical bomber over Outer Mongolia in the Khalkhiin Gol fighting, and during the opening days of the Pacific War bombers of this type raided Hong Kong, the Philippines and Burma.

In addition to the bomber models, the Ki.21-I was produced in several versions for the training and transport roles, the first transport model being a modified Ki.21-Ia with armament removed and the bomb-bays covered over. This was employed by the J.A.A.F., but a number were also built as civil freighters for use by the Japan Air Transport Company under the designation MC-21-I. The first of these commercial models, which served on domestic and overseas routes from the early 'forties throughout the war years, was J-BFOA *Hiei* which pioneered routes for a civil passenger transport derived from the Ki.21 series. This aircraft utilized the standard engines and nacelles, wings and tail surfaces of the Ki.21-Ia, these being married to an entirely new fuselage which accommodated four crew members and eleven passengers. The prototype was completed in the summer of 1940 as the Mitsubishi MC-20, and immediately began route-proving trials with J.A.T. Sales of the MC-20 were solicited in several Asian

and South American countries, and the type was subsequently used widely by J.A.T., also being accepted for service with the J.A.A.F. as the Ki.57-I Type 100 Transport Model 1, and the J.N.A.F. as the Type O Transport.

Increased opposition over China revealed certain defensive and performance deficiencies in the Ki.21-I, and in November 1939, work was initiated on an improved model, the Ki.21-II. The modified bomber used the basic Ki.21-I airframe but switched to 1,490 h.p. Mitsubishi Ha.101 fourteen-cylinder two-row radials which were housed in aerodynamically cleaner cowlings. The overall span of the tailplane was increased by four feet and, as the Ki.21-IIa Type 97 Model 2a, it was numerically the most important J.A.A.F. bomber when the Pacific War began. In spite of the improvements incorporated in the Ki.21-IIa, the bomber proved an easy target for the Hawker Hurricane fighters by which it found itself opposed over Burma and India, and the J.A.A.F. bomber squadrons suffered heavy casualties when unprotected by escort fighters. One of the chief disadvantages was the limited traverse of the dorsal gun, and the long "glasshouse" enclosure was, therefore, removed and replaced by a large conical turret containing a single 12.7-mm. machine gun. This turret was a marvel of inconvenience for it was operated by

The final major production version of the Type 97 heavy bomber was the Ki.21-IIb illustrated above. This featured increased armour protection for the crew and a large conical dorsal turret housing a single 12.7-mm. machine gun.

bicycle pedals with a chain drive for gun traverse. Some 16-mm. armour plate was mounted aft of the dorsal turret to protect the gunner, 12.5-mm. armour was mounted fore and aft of the pilot, and all fuel tanks were protected. To provide additional range, an auxiliary fuel tank could be installed in the bomb-bay, having a capacity of 110 Imp.gal., and when

The late production Ki.21-IIb bombers (illustrated below) carried four 100-lb. bombs externally when an auxiliary tank was fitted in the bomb-bay.

carried four 110-lb. bombs were usually mounted externally.

With the dorsal turret fitted, the bomber was designated Ki.21-IIb Type 97 Model 2b, but when first encountered by the Allies it was thought to be a new type and was initially given the identification name of *Gwen*. With the introduction of the Ki.21-IIb, the remaining Ki.21-Is and many Ki.21-IIa bombers were relegated to training duties, the primary assignment being to the Hamamatsu Advanced Heavy Bomber Train-

FINISH AND INSIGNIA: *Mitsubishi Type 97 bombers were frequently camouflaged to conform with the terrain over which they were operating and, in consequence, a variety of different schemes were employed. The aircraft illustrated on the opposite page is a Ki. 21-IIb operated by the 14th Heavy Bombing Squadron in the South-West Pacific. The light jungle green "zebra stripes" were applied directly to the natural metal over all upper surfaces, and the under surfaces were left natural metal. The standard white "combat stripe" for I.F.F. identification was applied to the rear fuselage, and the circular red national insignia, or Hinomaru, was outlined in white on the fuselage sides, but appeared as a plain red disc on the wing surfaces.*

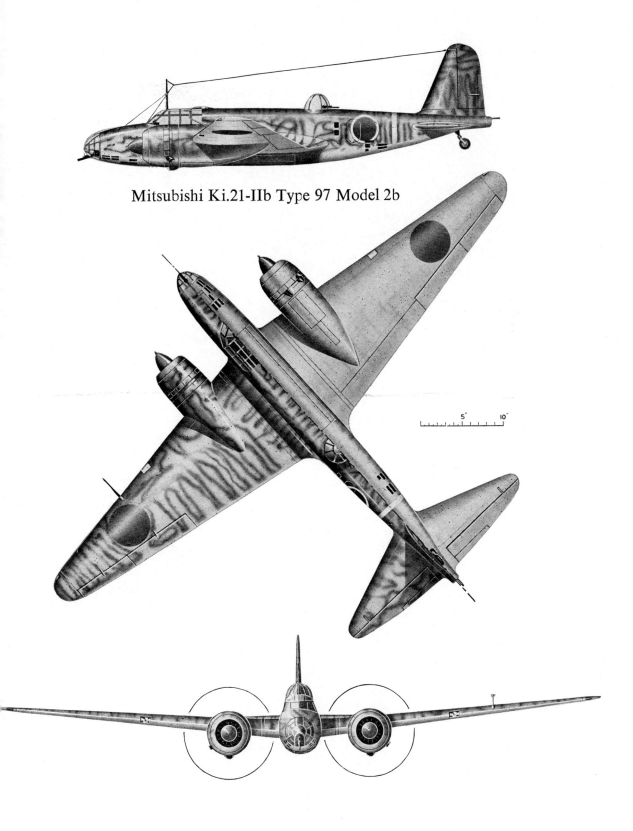

Mitsubishi Ki.21-IIb Type 97 Model 2b

5′   10′

c

Shown clearly in this photograph, the dorsal turret of the Ki.21-IIb was operated by bicycle pedals with a chain drive for gun traverse. It replaced the long "glasshouse" enclosure of the Ki.21-IIa and earlier models.

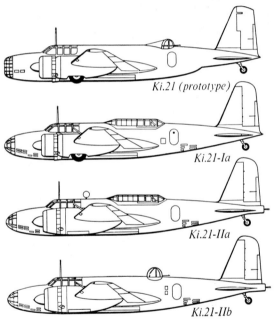

Ki.21 (prototype)

Ki.21-Ia

Ki.21-IIa

Ki.21-IIb

ing School. The Ki.21-IIb, despite its obsolescence, remained in service as a standard first-line bomber in company with the later Nakajima Ki.49-II Donryu until ultimately replaced by the Ki.67 Hiryu late in 1944. A parallel transport model was evolved as the MC-21-II, and limited production was undertaken for both civil and military use. The MC-20 transport series was also re-engined, receiving the 1,050 h.p. Mitsubishi Ha.102 Type 1 radial as the MC-20-II. One camouflaged MC-20-II was to be awarded the task of carrying the Japanese surrender delegation to Chirkiang airfield in China to arrange for the surrender of all Japanese forces in that country. The military version of the MC-20-II was built by

both Mitsubishi and Kokusai as the Ki.57-II Type 100 Transport Model 2.

The last projected version of the Type 97 bomber was the Ki.21-III which was abandoned in favour of the Ki.67 Hiryu, and production of the aircraft finally terminated at Mitsubishi's 5th Airframe Works in September 1944. The basic aircraft had been in continuous production for no less than eight years, and with the delivery of the last machine more than 1,800 aeroplanes of this type had been manufactured, 315 of these having been built by Nakajima who completed production in February 1941. Hopelessly outclassed during the last two years of the war, it had, nevertheless, served long and well on every Japanese battlefront, and can probably lay claim to the title of the most famous Japanese bomber of the Second World War.

Mitsubishi Ki.21-IIb Type 97 Model 2b

Dimensions: Span, 72 ft. 9¾ in.; length, 52 ft. 6 in.; height, 15 ft. 11 in.; wing area, 749.167 sq. ft.

Armament: One 12.7-mm. Type 1 (Browning) machine gun with 600 rounds in dorsal turret, and five 7.7-mm. Type 89 machine guns with 600 r.p.g. in hand-held nose, lateral and ventral positions, and remotely-controlled tail position. Maximum bomb load, 2,200 lb. Alternative loads: Sixteen 110-lb. bombs; nine 220-lb. bombs, four 550-lb. bombs, or two 1.100-lb. bombs.

Power Plants: Two Mitsubishi Ha.101 Type 100 fourteen-cylinder radial air-cooled engines rated at 1,490 h.p. at 2,450 r.p.m. for take-off, 1,445 h.p. at 2,350 r.p.m. at 8,550 ft., and 1,360 h.p. at 2,350 r.p.m. at 15,100 ft.

Weights: Empty, 13,382 lb.; normal loaded, 21,407 lb.

Performance: Maximum speed, 297 m.p.h. at 13,120 ft.; cruising speed, 236 m.p.h. at 16,400 ft.; initial climb rate, 1,660 ft./min.; time to 10,000 ft., 6.5 min., to 19,685 ft., 13.15 min.; service ceiling, 32,800 ft.; endurance. 7 hrs.; range (with maximum bomb load). 1.350 mls. at 176 m.p.h. at 1,500 ft. (with 440-lb. bomb load and auxiliary bomb-bay tank), 1,595 mls.

26

The Whitley, frequently referred to as the "Grand Old Lady of Bomber Command", dropped the first bombs on German soi and undertook the first attacks on Italy, being finally retired from Bomber Command in the spring of 1942.

THE ARMSTRONG WHITWORTH WHITLEY

The angularly ugly Armstrong Whitworth Whitley— the "Flying Barn Door"—heading into the gathering dusk *en route* to a nocturnal rendezvous over enemy territory was a familiar sight to dwellers on Britain's east coast during the early war years. With its characteristic nose-down flying attitude and unmistakable, rather irritating note variation of its twin Merlin engines which could rarely be synchronized for more than a few seconds at a time, the Whitley was the prop and mainstay of the Royal Air Force's night offensive during those first two years of war in which the seeds of strategic night bombing's future pattern were being sown. To this grand old lady of Bomber Command went the distinction of being the first British bomber to appear in the skies of Berlin; the first to drop bombs on German soil, and the first to attack targets in Italy—"firsts" which succeeded others of equal importance in the field of technical development.

With its ponderous, slab-sided fuselage, and thick, broad wings, the Whitley was aesthetically the least appealing of the bombers with which the R.A.F. went to war. Its wings and fuselage gave the impression that they were travelling along different paths, and in flight its attitude was disconcertingly nose down, but it was as sturdy as a rock; a docile, matronly aeroplane which enjoyed the affection of its crews, although, as one pilot put it, "The Whitley, like the old lady she was, never did quite what she was told to do, but the things that she did were for the most part reasonable and comfortable."

The Whitley represented an important landmark in the history of the R.A.F.'s offensive capability. Prior to its service début, the heavy-bombing squadrons were equipped for the most part with the Handley Page Heyford biplane, and the Whitley, which was then still classified as a "heavy" and the R.A.F.'s first bomber to feature turreted defensive armament and a retractable undercarriage, offered tremendous advances over its predecessor in both performance and load-carrying ability. Whereas the Hampden and the Wellington, the compatriots with

(Above and below) The first prototype Whitley (K4586) was flown for the first time at Baginton on March 17, 1936, by which time a contract for eighty machines had already been placed.

THE ARMSTRONG WHITWORTH WHITLEY

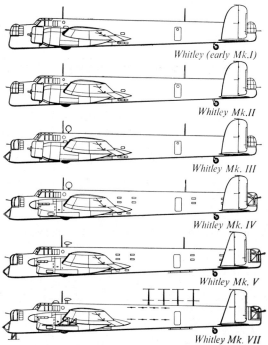

Whitley (early Mk.I)

Whitley Mk.II

Whitley Mk. III

Whitley Mk. IV

Whitley Mk. V

Whitley Mk. VII

of No. 10 Squadron, based at Dishforth, Yorks., and three months later, this squadron was to come under the command of No. 4 Bomber Group which, ultimately equipped entirely with Whitleys and commanded by Air Commodore A. T. Harris (later Air Marshal Sir Arthur "Bomber" Harris and Commander-in-Chief of R.A.F. Bomber Command), was to become the only specialist night-bombing group possessed by any air arm at the outbreak of the Second World War.

The Whitley I differed little from the prototypes. It possessed an empty weight of 14,275 lb., and normal and maximum loaded weights of 21,660 lb. and 23,500 lb. respectively. Defensive armament comprised a single 0.303-in. Vickers machine gun in each of the manually-operated Armstrong Whitworth nose and tail turrets, and a total bomb load of 3,365 lb. could be carried. At an early stage in the bomber's production life it was found desirable to introduce dihedral on the outboard wing panels to improve overall stability, and this modification was applied on the production line after the completion of the first few machines, these being retroactively modified. The twenty-sixth production Whitley I (K7208) was modified to permit it to operate at an all-up weight of 33,500 lb.—10,000 lb. above the normal maximum loaded weight—with which it had a maximum range of 1,940 miles. This aircraft, together with the

twenty-seventh Whitley I (K7209), was eventually converted as a prototype of the Merlin-engined Whitley IV, while the twenty-ninth Whitley I (K7211) was successively modified as a prototype Mk.III and then as a prototype Mk.IV.

Only thirty-four Whitley I bombers were completed before production gave place to the Whitley II which entered squadron service in January 1938. The Whitley II, around which specification B.21/35 was framed, differed from the initial production model in having 920 h.p. Tiger VIII engines equipped with two-speed superchargers which markedly improved the bomber's performance. Maximum speed at 15,000 feet was raised to 215 m.p.h., and cruising speed at the same altitude was 177 m.p.h. Maximum range was 1,315 miles, service ceiling was boosted to 23,000 feet, and an altitude of 15,000 feet was reached in 23.5 minutes.

While development of the Whitley was proceeding, Armstrong Whitworth's design team was also engaged in work on the A.W.39, a proposed heavy bomber to specification B.1/35. Derived from the Whitley, the A.W.39 was to have had two 1,185 h.p. Armstrong Siddeley Deerhound twenty-one cylinder three-row radial air-cooled engines with two-stage superchargers buried in its wings, and although no development contract for this bomber was received by the company, a pair of Deerhounds were eventually installed for air tests in the twenty-seventh production Whitley II (K7243). In the event, the Deerhound was abandoned owing to difficulties associated with the adequate cooling of the rear row of cylinders, but the Deerhound-Whitley test-bed was eventually flown on several occasions by Eric Greenwood during 1940, but nearly every flight terminated in an emergency landing as a result of the engines overheating.

With the delivery of the forty-sixth Whitley II (K7262) in the summer of 1938, thus completing the initial production order, work commenced on the improved Whitley III under a second contract for eighty aircraft placed with the company in 1936. The twenty-ninth Whitley I (K7211) served as a prototype for the Mk.III around which specification B.20/36 was prepared. The most important innovation in the Whitley III from the defensive viewpoint was the replacement of the manually-operated Armstrong Whitworth nose turret with its single Vickers gun by a similarly armed Nash and Thompson powered turret. The old Armstrong Whitworth manually-operated tail turret was retained, but to afford some measure of protection from attacks outside the traverse of its gun, a ventral "dustbin", retractable and rotatable through a full 360° and mounting twin

FINISH AND INSIGNIA: The Armstrong Whitworth Whitley Mk.V (Z6635) illustrated on the opposite page was operated by No. 51 (York) Squadron and was finished matt black overall. However, part of the black finish had worn away along the top of the fuselage, the original dark green and dark earth camouflage showing through. The B.T.R. de-icers on wing, tailplane and tail fin leading edges were putty-chrome yellow in colour. The squadron code letters ("MH") and individual aircraft letter ("O") were painted in grey, as was also the serial number. Slightly modified "A.2" type roundels appeared on the fuselage sides, the yellow outline being thicker than the outer blue circle, and the white circle being darkened, and standard "B" type blue-red roundels appeared on the upper surfaces of the wings.

Armstrong Whitworth Whitley Mk.V

The Whitley V was powered by two Merlin X engines, and deliveries commenced early in 1939 with N1345 (illustrated above). The first Whitley Vs reached the squadrons of No. 4 Group a month before the Second World War began.

0.303-in. Browning machine guns, was installed in the aft fuselage. Since this "dustbin" weighed half a ton and, when lowered, drastically reduced speed at a critical time during combat, it was never used, although its "well" was subsequently to prove useful as a dropping hatch for paratroops.

In addition to the modified defensive armament, the Whitley III had new bomb racks to accommodate bombs of larger calibre, and increased dihedral on the wing outer panels, and the first bombers of this type were delivered in August 1938. Such had been the pace of combat aircraft development in the previous three years, however, that the Whitley III was already bordering on the obsolescent. Nevertheless, to the Whitley III went the honour of undertaking Bomber Command's first operation over Germany on the first night of the War, ten Whitley IIIs from Nos. 51 and 58 Squadrons operating from Leconfield dropping thirteen tons of leaflets on Bremen, Hamburg and the Ruhr. This was the first of many similar "bumph raids", as the Whitley crews dubbed these sorties, which characterised the so-called "phoney war", but not so many months later, the Whitleys of No. 4 Group were to be carrying far less innocuous cargoes on their nocturnal visits to enemy territory.

By the time the eightieth and last Whitley III (K9015) had been delivered late in 1938, the bomber had taken on a new lease of life with the substitution of twelve-cylinder, liquid-cooled Merlin engines for the air-cooled Tigers. Three Whitley Is (K7208, K7209, and K7211) had been re-engined to serve as prototypes for the production Whitley IV which received Rolls-Royce Merlin IV engines each rated at 1,030 h.p. for take-off and 990 h.p. at 12,250 feet, and driving Rotol constant-speed airscrews. Forty Whitley IVs (K9016 to K9055) had been ordered in 1936, and the first of these reached the squadrons in May 1939. Apart from the liquid-cooled engines, the Whitley IV differed from its predecessors in several respects. From the viewpoint of defence, the most important innovation was the provision of a new power-operated Nash and Thompson tail turret mounting what was, for its time, the phenomenal armament of four 0.303-in. Browning machine guns.

These provided the Whitley IV with the most vicious tail sting of any bomber extant. A few early Whitley IVs did, however, retain the old manually-operated Armstrong Whitworth tail turret.

Fuel capacity was supplemented by the installation of two 93 Imp.gal. tanks in the wings, increasing the standard tankage to 705 Imp.gal., and another change was the fitting of a Plexiglas "chin" extension for the bombardier. This replaced the flush-fitting panel of earlier marks. With the substantial increase in power afforded by the Merlins, the Whitley IV possessed a markedly improved all-round performance. Maximum speed was 245 m.p.h. at 16,250 feet, and maximum cruising speed was 215 m.p.h. at 15,000 ft., this altitude being attained in sixteen minutes. Normal cruising range was 1,250 miles, but this could be extended to 1,800 miles with auxiliary fuel tanks in the fuselage, and empty and normal loaded weights were 17,520 lb. and 25,900 lb. respectively. The Merlin-engined Whitley retained the docility of the Tiger-engined machines in the air, although it could be something of a handful on take-off owing to a marked swing to port which could not be held satisfactorily on the rudders. This could be corrected by combinations of throttle and rudder, but the Whitley often took to the air in a crabwise fashion.

With the availability of the Merlin X engine rated at 1,075 h.p. for take-off and 1,130 h.p. at 5,250 feet, this power plant was installed in seven Whitley IV airframes which then became known as Mk.IVAs. Three Whitley IVs of No. 10 Squadron claimed the distinction of being the first British bombers to visit Berlin when they made a "bumphlet raid" on the German capital on October 1, 1939.

The largest pre-war production contract for the Whitley was placed in 1938, this calling for 302 examples of what was to prove the most important variant of the basic design, the Mk.V. Like the Whitley IVA, the Mk.V was powered by a pair of Merlin X engines, and deliveries (commencing with N1345) began early in 1939, the first bombers of this type reaching the squadrons of No. 4 Group a month before hostilities commenced. Externally, the Whitley V differed little from the Mk.IVA. In order to improve the field of fire of the tail turret, an extra section was installed aft of the rearmost fuselage frame, increasing overall length by fifteen inches, the tail fins and rudders were redesigned, and rubber de-icing boots were fitted along the wing leading edges. In general, performance differed little from that of the Mk.IVA, but normal loaded weight was increased to 28,200 lb., while maximum loaded weight rose to 33,500 lb.

When war was declared on September 3, 1939, six squadrons of Whitleys were ready for operations with Bomber Command's No. 4 Group, and, apart from No. 77 Squadron which had received the first Whitley Vs, these were equipped with Whitley IIIs and IVs. The Whitley's first wartime tasks were leaflet-dropping and security patrols over the German mine-laying seaplane bases at Borkum, Nordeney and Sylt, and it was not until the night of March 19-20, 1940, that Whitleys dropped the first bombs on German soil when thirty Whitley Vs drawn from Nos. 10, 51, 77, and 102 Squadrons, accompanied by a force of twenty Hampdens from No. 5 Group, attacked the seaplane base at Hornum. Seven weeks later, with the termination of the "phoney war" by the German offensive on the Western Front, Whitleys again joined forces with Hampdens for an attack on the railway junction at München Gladbach, dropping the first bombs on the German mainland. Soon Whitleys were visiting nearly all the important targets in Germany, and performing many noteworthy long-range missions, such as that on June 11, 1940, when Whitleys from Nos. 10, 51, 58, 77, and 102 Squadrons flew across the Alps to Turin and Genoa, becoming the first British bombers to raid targets in Italy. Whitleys penetrated deep into Austria and Czechoslovakia, and on some occasions even over Polish territory.

On May 15, 1940, representatives of the new Ministry of Aircraft Production which had been established under Lord Beaverbrook, agreed with members of the Air Staff that complete production priority should be given to five selected warplanes, and one of these was the Whitley. An order for a further 150 Whitley Vs had been placed in 1939, but no fewer than 1,170 additional machines were now ordered, and production tempo rose rapidly, reaching a peak of twelve machines a week in 1942. Plans were prepared for the production of the Whitley VI with Merlin XX "power eggs", but, in the event, this version did not materialise.

Meanwhile, the Whitley's substantial endurance had commended it for the task of maritime reconnaissance, and in the autumn of 1940 when this bomber supplanted the Ansons of No. 502 Squadron based at Aldergrove, it embarked upon a new career with R.A.F. Coastal Command, a career which had been initiated when No. 58 Squadron was temporarily loaned to Coastal Command at the end of September 1939. No. 502 Squadron initially used the standard bomber version of the Whitley, and was joined by the Whitleys of No. 612 Squadron in March 1941, the latter unit operating anti-submarine patrols from Reykjavik, Iceland. The success of the Whitley in the maritime reconnaissance role led to the appearance, by the end of 1941, of a modified version of the Whitley V intended specifically for Coastal Command use. Designated Whitley VII, this variant was first issued to No. 502 Squadron and was the first aircraft to carry the long-range A.S.V. Mk.II air-to-surface-vessel radar. The prototype (P4949) was a converted Mk.V.

The Whitley VII, which carried six crew members, undertook long and often hazardous patrols over hundreds of miles of ocean, and was frequently engaged by Arado Ar 196 floatplanes and Junkers Ju 88 fighters over the Bay of Biscay. Empty weight had risen to 19,605 lb., and its loaded weight of 33,950 lb., combined with the wealth of "Christmas trees" of its A.S.V. radar reduced its maximum speed to 215 m.p.h. at 16,400 ft., its cruising speed to 195 m.p.h. at 15,000 ft., and its ability to remain aloft on one engine. Fuel capacity was increased to 969 Imp.gal. (normal) and 1,101 Imp.gal. (maximum), resulting in a maximum range of 2,300 miles. The first definite victim of the Whitley VII was U-206 which was sunk in the Bay of Biscay on November 30, 1941, by an aircraft of No. 502 Squadron, this being Coastal Command's first A.S.V. "kill".

Whitley Vs were finally retired from Bomber Command in the spring of 1942, performing their last operation on April 29th of that year with an attack on Ostend, and a few months later, the last Whitley VIIs were retired from operational service with Coastal Command. During the Whitley's distinguished career, many of the R.A.F.'s leading bomber aces had flown this type on their first operations. Surprisingly, the Whitley was still being employed as late as the Spring of 1943 in the role with which it initiated its operational career—that of leaflet dropping. It also made notable contributions in the roles of paratroop-trainer and glider-tug with the Airborne Forces. All marks of Whitley, apart from the Mk.VII, saw service at No. 1 Parachute Training School at Ringway, Manchester, and Whitleys carried paratroops operationally during *Operation Colossus* which took place on February 10, 1941, when a raiding party destroyed an aqueduct at Tragino in Italy. A year later, on February 27-28, 1942, the Whitleys of No. 51 Squadron carried paratroops on the famous Bruneval raid in which airborne troops captured a complete *Wurzburg* radar installation. With their tail turrets removed and fitted with a metal towing yoke, Whitley Vs served as tugs for Horsa gliders at No. 21 Heavy Glider Conversion Unit at Brize Norton, and in mid-1942 fifteen Whitley Vs were converted for use as freighters by the British Overseas Airways Corporation, among their activities being the carriage of essential freight into beleaguered Malta. Three Whitleys were used by the Royal Aircraft Establishment for trials with

The Whitley V numbered among its duties those of leaflet, supply and agent dropping, and the machine illustrated (T4149) has supply containers mounted underwing.

braking parachutes, and another tested Rocket-Assisted-Take-Off packs.

The 1,824th and last Whitley (1,476 of which were Mk.Vs and 146 being Mk.VIIs) left the Baginton assembly line on July 12, 1943, this aircraft remaining at the factory as a test-bed, the last machine for the R.A.F. having been delivered on June 6, 1943. During its career, it had been operated by Nos. 7, 10, 51, 58, 76, 77, 78, 97, 102, 103 and 166 Squadrons with Bomber Command, by Nos. 77, 502 and 612 Squadrons with Coastal Command, by Nos. 295, 296 and 299 Squadrons in the transport role, and on special duties by Nos. 138 and 161 Squadrons. It had accumulated a long line of technical and operational

"firsts", and although the "Flying Barn Door" never enjoyed the popular acclaim that was to be the lot of its successors, its appearance in service was the equal in significance to that of any bomber destined to join R.A.F. Bomber Command during the years of the Second World War.

Armstrong Whitworth Whitley Mk.V

Dimensions: Span, 84 ft. 0 in.; length, 72 ft. 6 in.; height, 15 ft. 0 in.; wing area, 1,138 sq. ft.

Armament: One 0.303-in. machine gun in power-operated Frazer-Nash nose turret and four 0.303-in. machine guns in Frazer-Nash tail turret. Maximum bomb load, 7,000 lb.

Power Plants: Two Rolls-Royce Merlin X twelve-cylinder 60° Vee liquid-cooled engines each rated at 1,075 h.p. at 3,000 r.p.m. for take-off and 1,130 h.p. at 3,000 r.p.m. at 5,250 ft.

Weights: Empty, 19,350 lb.; normal loaded, 28,200 lb.; maximum overload, 33,500 lb.

Performance: Maximum speed, 228 m.p.h. at 17,750 ft.; maximum cruising speed, 210 m.p.h. at 15,000 ft.; economical cruising speed, 185 m.p.h.; normal cruising range (at economical cruising speed) at 12,000 ft., 1,500 mls.; maximum range (with auxiliary fuel tanks), 2,400 mls at 12,000 ft.; range with 3,000-lb. bomb load, 1,650 mls., with 7,000-lb. bomb load, 470 mls.; initial climb rate, 800 ft./min.; time to 15,000 ft., 16 min.; normal service ceiling, 17,600 ft.; maximum ceiling, 24,000 ft.

The Whitley VII was used extensively for maritime reconnaissance by Coastal Command. This aircraft was the first to carry the long-range A.S.V. Mk.II air-to-surface-vessel radar. Whitley VII (LA794) is illustrated below.

The Handley Page H.P.52 prototype (K4240) was flown for the first time on June 21, 1936. On one flight an airscrew and part of an engine came adrift, striking the fuselage just aft of the cockpit. Six weeks later the first flight production orders were placed.

THE HANDLEY PAGE HAMPDEN

All military aeroplanes are to a greater or lesser extent compromises between conflicting requirements, and the Handley Page Hampden was no exception. It reflected the indecision of the Air Staff who were wavering between the desire to carry a moderate offensive load quickly and a larger load at more sedate speeds over considerable distances. The Hampden represented the middle path. It lay roughly between its contemporaries, the Wellington and Whitley and the Blenheim in load-carrying ability and operational range, yet its performance compared closely with that of the last-mentioned bomber. Named appropriately enough after the 17th-century opponent of tyranny, John Hampden, the bomber was unique in several respects, not least of which being its distinctive appearance. Its fine aerodynamic form, characterized by sharply tapered, slotted and flapped wings, and a deep, slab-sided fuselage to which was appended a slim boom carrying the tail surfaces, inspired a variety of affectionate epithets during its operational career, ranging from that of

"The Frying Pan" to "The Flying Tadpole".

The Hampden was one of the world's most advanced warplanes at the time of its début, and it came of a distinguished line, tracing its ancestry from the O/100 of 1915 which, together with its successors, the O/400 and the V/1500, established the name of Handley Page in the forefront of the world's bomber manufacturers. The Hampden was the Handley Page company's first bomber monoplane, and it was fortunate in retaining many of the characteristics which had popularized its predecessors in Royal Air Force service. It was a forgiving aeroplane from the pilot's viewpoint, and its ease of control rendered it an extremely pleasant aeroplane to fly. It was small enough to be highly manoeuvrable; its cockpit offered an excellent "fighter-like" field of vision, and it possessed a remarkable speed range.

Although the Hampden's operational exploits were to be overshadowed by those of its larger successor and stablemate, the Halifax, it was one of the quartet of British twin-engined bombers which bore the brunt

The second prototype H.P.52 (L7271) was converted after initial flight trials to take Dagger XIII engines as the prototype H.P.53. It was flown with Daggers for the first time on July 1, 1937, and, with these engines, was produced as the Hereford.

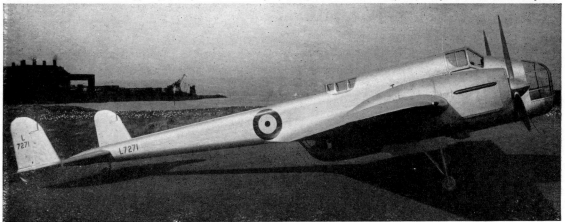

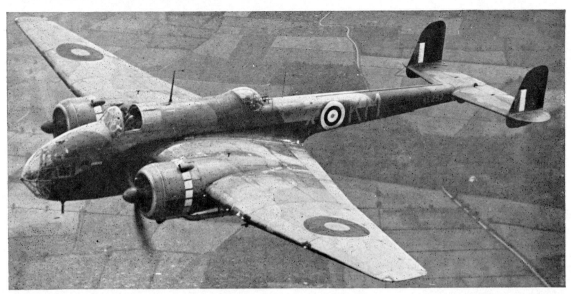

This Hampden I (AE257) was one of three hundred ordered on July 6, 1940, and was operated by No. 44 (Rhodesia) Squadron. The twin Vickers K guns in the dorsal position can just be discerned. These were introduced as part of an attempt to reduce the Hampden's vulnerability early in 1940.

of the R.A.F.'s early offensive sorties, and some ten Hampden-equipped squadrons were almost continuously in action over the Continent during the first two years of the war, apart from a brief period after the near-calamitous use of the type on daylight operations. Undeniably, the Hampden possessed its share of operational shortcomings, and these came to light at a very early stage in the air war. Its original defensive armament of a fixed forward-firing Browning and a trio of hand-held Vickers K guns with limited traverse proved woefully inadequate, leaving blind spots which were immediately ferreted out by opposing interceptors, and after early setbacks on daylight sorties, the Hampdens were fitted with heavier defensive armament and confined largely to nocturnal activities. Another shortcoming of the Hampden, one resulting from the choice of an extremely narrow fuselage to reduce drag, was the near-impossibility of removing a badly wounded pilot

from his seat so that another crew member could take over the controls. Later, when the Hampden was used for mine-laying operations and a relief pilot was carried, changing seats called for a display of extreme dexterity.

In the middle of 1932, the Air Ministry issued specification B.9/32 which called for a twin-engined day bomber offering an appreciably higher performance than any such machine previously envisaged. The Handley Page design team headed by Mr. G. R. Volkert began work on what was for that time an extremely radical machine, but it was not until mid-1934 that the Air Ministry relaxed the strict limit imposed by B.9/32 on the bomber's tare weight that an official prototype contract was awarded for Handley Page's bomber which now bore the designation H.P.52. The H.P.52 could not have been more unlike its immediate predecessor, the wire-braced Heyford biplane that had just entered service with the

The first production Hampden I (L4032), illustrated below, was flown for the first time in May 1938, and three months later, the first aircraft of this type (the third production machine—L4034) was delivered to the R.A.F.

This English Electric-built Hampden I was operated by No. 16 Operational Training Unit. The first English Electric-built Hampden flew on February 22, 1940, and the company manufactured 770 aircraft of this type.

R.A.F. It featured a highly tapered, low-drag wing incorporating the most advanced slot equipment. This was to enable the bomber to achieve a phenomenally high maximum speed without sacrifice of low speed qualities. Another outstanding feature was its exceptionally slim, compact fuselage—the maximum width of which was only 3 ft.—which carried the tail surfaces on a long boom-like extension, permitting the provision of dorsal and ventral defensive armament without incurring any serious penalty from drag.

Various power plants had been considered for the H.P.52 during its progress across the drawing boards, including the steam-cooled Rolls-Royce Goshawk highly favoured by the Air Ministry at one period, but when the first prototype (K4240) made its appearance in 1936, it was powered by two Bristol Pegasus P.E.5S(a) nine-cylinder radial air-cooled engines with single-stage blowers and driving three-bladed de Havilland controllable-pitch airscrews. This prototype was flown for the first time at Radlett on June 21, 1936, with Major J. L. H. B. Cordes, the

company's chief test pilot, at the controls. The initial success of flight trials was such that, in August 1936, within some six weeks of the prototype first taking to the air, an initial production order for 180 machines to specification 30/36 was placed by the Air Ministry, and, simultaneously, one hundred machines powered by the 24-cylinder H-type Napier Dagger air-cooled engine were ordered, the responsibility for their production being allocated to Short and Harland's Belfast factory.

The flight testing of the first prototype H.P.52 did not proceed entirely without untoward incidents. On one occasion an airscrew and part of one of the engines detached themselves in mid-air, striking the fuselage just aft of the pilot's cockpit, and on another occasion a wheels-up landing resulted from a fault in the indicator circuit which displayed a green light despite the fact that the wheels were still retracted. The observer on this flight was Mr. R. S. Stafford, who was later to succeed G. R. Volkert as the company's technical director. Seated in the extensively glazed nose, the wheels-up landing elicited from

The first production H.P.53 Hereford (L6002), illustrated below, flew for the first time late in 1939. It was powered by two Dagger VIII engines but these proved extremely temperamental, and their teething troubles were never entirely eradicated.

THE HANDLEY PAGE HAMPDEN

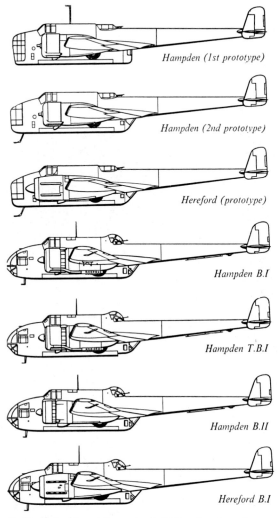

Hampden (1st prototype)

Hampden (2nd prototype)

Hereford (prototype)

Hampden B.I

Hampden T.B.I

Hampden B.II

Hereford B.I

superchargers supplanted the early P.E.5S(a) radials, the birdcage-like forward gun position was replaced by a curved perspex moulding which, incorporating an optically-flat bomb-aiming panel, was more in keeping with the Hampden's clean lines, and the angular dorsal and ventral gun positions were revised, the former having a semi-circular cupola which could be pushed back over the gunner's head.

As unconventional as its configuration were the methods employed in the Hampden's construction. While development of the H.P.52 had been proceeding, the Air Ministry had ordered the H.P.54 Harrow heavy bomber into production as an interim type due to the pressing requirements of the R.A.F. Expansion Scheme. A split-assembly method of construction had been evolved by Handley Page for Harrow production, and this technique was adapted for the Hampden. For example, the fuselage was built in two halves, just like a split lobster, and all pipelines, control runs, etc., were installed before the two halves were mated, greatly simplifying manufacture, and enabling Hampdens to flow from the assembly lines in record time. The fuselage of the Hampden was a flush-riveted stressed-skin all-metal monocoque built in three sections, the nose portion, the centre section and the tailboom, the two latter being split longitudinally for ease of manufacture. The all-metal flush-riveted stressed-skin wing was built in three sections, and was fitted with leading-edge slots and hydraulically-operated trailing-edge flaps All fuel was housed in six tanks in the wing centre section, these having a total capacity of 654 Imp.gal. Four crew members were carried, and armament comprised one fixed forward-firing 0.303-in. Browning machine gun and three hand-held Vickers K guns of similar calibre.

The first Hampden was delivered to the R.A.F. on August 8, 1938, this aircraft (L4034) going to the Central Flying School at Upavon. Manufacture proceeded rapidly, and by the end of November, No. 49 Squadron based at Scampton, one of the squadrons of the newly-formed No. 5 Group which was eventually to be equipped throughout with Hampdens, had received its full complement of machines. By the end of the year, Nos. 50 and 83 Squadrons were also re-equipping, and the R.A.F. had taken thirty-six Hampdens on strength. In the meantime, arrangements had been made for the Hampden to be built under sub-contract by the English Electric Company's Preston plant, this company being awarded its initial contract for seventy-five aircraft on August 6, 1938, while in Canada several prominent organisations had banded together to form Canadian

Stafford the impassive remark "There's a lot of grass in here!" During the spring of 1937, a second prototype H.P.52 (L7271) joined the test programme. Initially, this machine was similarly powered to its predecessor, but it was subsequently converted by Handley Page to take two Dagger XIII H-type engines and, as the H.P.53, flew with these for the first time on July 1, 1937.

The production prototype H.P.52 (L4032) flew for the first time in May 1938, and on June 24th was christened by Viscountess Hampden at an official ceremony at Radlett. The production bomber differed from the prototype in several respects. Two 1,000 h.p. Pegasus XVIII engines with two-speed

---

FINISH AND INSIGNIA: *The aircraft illustrated on the opposite page is a Canadian-built Hampden T.B.I. (AN127) of No. 489 (New Zealand) Squadron. This aircraft employed the temperate sea scheme of dark slate grey and dark sea grey camouflage on the upper surfaces and so-called sky-grey on the under surfaces. The squadron letters ("XA") and individual aircraft letter ("Y") which appeared in white on the fuselage sides read XA-Y on the starboard side and*

Y-XA on the port side. The serial number appeared in black. No national insignia appeared on the under surfaces of the wings, Type B blue and red roundels appeared on the wing upper surfaces. Type C red, white and blue roundels appeared on the fuselage sides, together with the appropriate fin flashes. No. 489's Hampden T.B.Is operated from Wick in 1942.

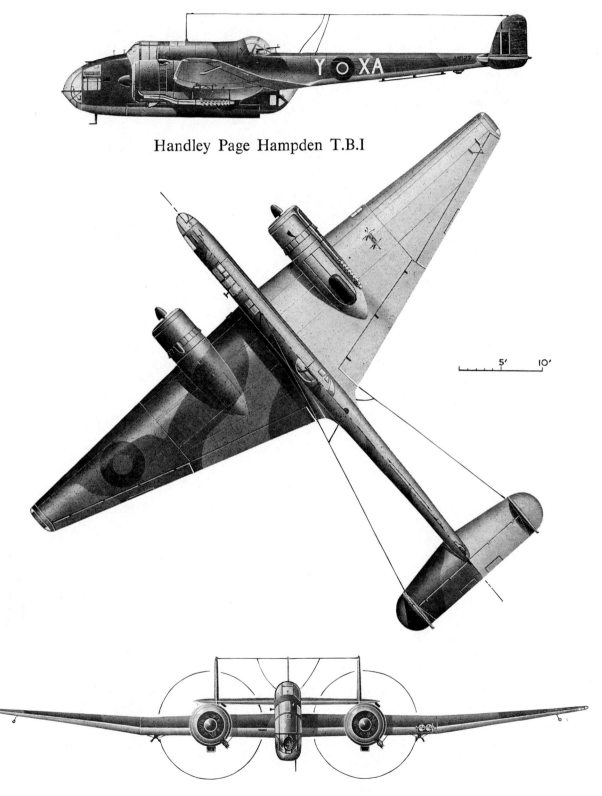

Handley Page Hampden T.B.I

5'   10'

Associated Aircraft Limited, receiving an order for eighty Hampdens for the R.A.F. During this period, one Hampden powered by 1,010 h.p. Pegasus XXIV engines was supplied to the Royal Swedish Air Force, being flown to Sweden in September 1938. At one time it was proposed to manufacture the Hampden in Sweden under licence, but this scheme was abandoned.

On September 3, 1939, there were eight Hampden squadrons in the R.A.F.'s line of battle, and on the following day Hampdens of No. 83 Squadron made a sortie against German warships in the Schillig Roads. Unfortunately, their first operation was abortive as they were unable to find their target owing to bad visibility. It was during an attack on two destroyers off Heligoland by eleven Hampdens from Nos. 61 and 144 Squadrons on September 29th that it became apparent that the bomber's defensive armament was inadequate to fend off any determined fighter attack, five of the Hampdens being lost. Shortly afterwards, Bomber Command tacitly abandoned the belief that medium bombers could successfully operate in small formations by day in the face of German fighter opposition, and after December 18, 1939, the Hampden ceased to undertake daylight sorties. The Hampdens were hastily withdrawn from service to undergo a programme of modification designed to reduce their vulnerability. Armour protection for the crew was fitted, twin Vickers K guns were mounted in the dorsal and ventral positions, and flame-damping exhaust pipes were fitted for night operations.

During the early months of 1940, the Hampden was awarded its full share of "bumphlet" sorties—dropping propaganda leaflets, and during the German invasion of Norway, in the spring of 1940, the bomber embarked upon a new career—that of aerial minelaying. Many long and hazardous minelaying sorties were flown during the Norwegian campaign, the Hampden being the first Bomber Command aircraft to engage in these activities. The squadrons became particularly skilled in planting their mines

under the noses of German defence units, but the Hampden was to find its true forté in night bombing and, despite its frail appearance, prove itself capable of absorbing a surprising amount of battle damage. On the night of March 19-20, 1940, Hampdens had dropped their first bombs on German soil with an attack on the seaplane hangars and slipways at Hornum, and on the night of May 11-12th, Hampdens, in concert with a force of Whitleys, dropped the first bombs on the German mainland.

In the late summer of 1940, Hampdens played a leading part in the attacks on the German barges concentrated at Antwerp and other occupied ports in preparation for the invasion of the British Isles. It was during one of these attacks on Antwerp, on the night of September 15-16th, that a member of a Hampden crew performed the deed for which he was to be awarded the Victoria Cross. During the attack, Hampden P1355 of No. 83 Squadron received a direct hit. Fuel tanks in both wings were holed, and fire rapidly enveloped the navigator's and rear gunner's cockpits, forcing the rear gunner to bale out. The whole of the bomb-bay, the flames fanned by the inrush of air through holes blown in the fuselage, was such an inferno that the aluminium floor of the gunner's cockpit melted in the heat. Sergeant John Hannah, the wireless operator/air gunner, forced his way aft and, despite severe burns, extinguished the flames after which, crawling forward, he discovered that the navigator had also baled out. Despite his serious condition he assisted the pilot to bring the crippled bomber safely back to its base.

This was not the first Victoria Cross to be awarded to a member of a Hampden crew, however, for the first of these very signal honours bestowed so sparingly to be gained by a Bomber Command pilot was that won by Flt. Lieut. R. A. B. Learoyd of No. 49 Squadron. On the night of August 12-13, 1940, five Hampdens drawn from Nos. 49 and 83 Squadrons attacked an aqueduct forming part of the Dortmund-Ems Canal. Heavy anti-

The second production Hereford (L6003) is illustrated below. A total of 150 Herefords was ordered but many were converted to Hampden configuration either before or after leaving the production line at Belfast.

The Hampden T.B.I (above) differed from the standard Hampden bomber in having a slightly deeper bomb-bay to accommodate an 18-in. torpedo. Hampden T.B.Is continued to operate until December 1943.

aircraft defences were disposed so as to form a lane down which attacking aircraft were forced to fly to reach their target. At intervals of two minutes the Hampdens went in from the North, and two of the first four aircraft were shot down and the other two seriously damaged. The fifth Hampden, P4403 piloted by Flt. Lieut. Learoyd, dived to 150 feet, despite the fact that the anti-aircraft guns were firing at point blank range, pressed home an attack and successfully blocked the canal. Many holes were shot in the Hampden's wings and the hydraulic system was put out of action, but the pilot nursed the seriously damaged bomber back to base, waited for the dawn and landed, despite lack of flaps or under-carriage, without injury to his crew.

The parent company completed its 500th and last Hampden in July 1940, and of the initial production order for 180 machines, four (L4208-4211) had been sent to Canada to serve as prototype aircraft for Canadian Associated Aircraft's Hampden produc-tion, and another, L4207, was delivered to the English Electric Company at Preston for the same purpose. One machine, P4285, was used for experi-ments with balloon cable cutters, and P4290 was employed on overload tests. Prior to the completion of the last Handley Page-built Hampden, deliveries from English Electric's assembly line had com-menced, the first of these, P2062, flying on February 22, 1940. By this time, the initial production order placed with English Electric for seventy-five machines had been supplemented on April 21st and December 20, 1939, by orders for 150 and 125 machines respec-tively, and by January 31, 1941, no fewer than 300 Hampdens had been delivered from Preston, the grand total of English Electric-built Hampdens reaching 770 by the time the last aircraft (AE439) left the line on March 15, 1942.

The first Canadian-built Hampden (P5298) flew on August 9, 1940, a delivery rate of fifteen aircraft per month being attained by Canadian Associated Air-craft by the following October. These aircraft were ferried over to the United Kingdom, the total

Hampden production in Canada reaching 160 machines when the last was delivered at the end of 1941. At one time it was envisaged that Canadian Hampdens would be fitted with 1,100 h.p. Wright Cyclone GR1820-G105A radials, but this proposal did not see fruition. However, two Hampdens were fitted with Cyclones for test purposes, these being known as the H.P.62 Hampden II. One Cyclone-powered Hampden II (X3115) actually served with No. 415 (Canadian) Squadron from 1940 until the end of 1943.

The version of the Hampden fitted with Dagger engines built by Short and Harland at Belfast had been designated H.P.53 by the parent company and named Hereford. Built to specification 44/36, the first production Hereford (L6002) flew late in 1939, powered by twenty-four-cylinder Napier Dagger VIII engines each offering 955 h.p. at 4,200 r.p.m. at sea level and 1,000 h.p. at 4,200 r.p.m. at 8,750 ft. The Hereford weighed 11,700 lb. tare and 17,800 lb. loaded. Performance was slightly higher than that of the Hampden, maximum speed being 265 m.p.h. at 15,500 ft., and cruising speed being 172 m.p.h. The astonishingly noisy Dagger engines with their remarkably high revs proved, to say the least, temperamental, and their teething troubles were never satisfactorily eradicated. The original production order for one hundred Herefords had been increased to 150 machines, but only one machine of this type is known to have reached operational service—with No. 185 Squadron which was to have operated a Hereford flight alongside two Hampden flights. Many of the Herefords were converted to Hampden configuration either before or after leaving the assembly line, and others were employed as crew trainers by No. 16 Operational Training Unit at Upper Heyford, as well as other training units, the first Hereford being delivered to No. 16 O.T.U. on May 7, 1940.

As Bomber Command's night offensive increased in tempo, Hampdens attacked all parts of Germany. Twelve Hampdens of Nos. 61 and 144 Squadrons

D
41

Two Hampdens were fitted with 1,100 h.p. Wright Cyclone GR1820-G105A radials, these being known by the designation H.P.62 Hampden II, and one of these (X3115) is illustrated here.

took part in the R.A.F.'s first bombing raid on Berlin on the night of August 25-26, 1940, and on the night of May 30-31, 1942, a small force of Hampdens was present on the occasion of Bomber Command's first 1,000-bomber raid which was made against Cologne. But by this time, the Hampden's days as an operational night bomber were numbered, and on the night of September 14-15, 1942, they operated with Bomber Command for the last time. During its years of service with that Command, the Hampden had operated with Nos. 7, 44, 49, 50, 61, 76, 83, 97, 106, 144, 185, 207 and 408 Squadrons.

Although no longer operated by Bomber Command, the Hampden was still to continue in action for, during the previous summer, it had gained a new lease on life as a torpedo-bomber with R.A.F. Coastal Command, and following experiments with six Hampdens at the Torpedo Development Unit at Gosport, three Hampden squadrons were detached from No. 5 Group for anti-shipping duties with Coastal Command. The torpedo-bombing variant was designated Hampden T.B.I, differing from the standard Hampden B.I in having a slightly deeper bomb-bay to accommodate an 18-in. torpedo internally, and racks under the wings for two 500-lb. bombs.

Two of the Hampden torpedo-bombing squadrons, Nos. 144 and 455, flew to Russian bases to attack German supply ships off the Norwegian coast north of Bergen and in the Barents Sea. The outward journey proved extremely hazardous, and one of the Hampdens was shot down by a Russian fighter while coming in over a prohibited area. As one of the Hampden pilots subsequently put it, they reached Russia "without wireless, in very bad weather, with very poor maps, and having as our only means of identification the undercarriage which we put down as a friendly gesture when the quick-fingered Russians started to shoot." The Hampdens forced the Germans to provide both escort vessels and air cover for their convoys, and after completing their operations, the two squadrons handed over the fourteen remain-ing serviceable Hampdens to the Russians. What use the Russians made of these is unknown. No. 144 Squadron re-equipped with Beaufighters at the end of 1942, and No. 408 Squadron re-equipped with Halifaxes and returned to Bomber Command, but not before the two squadrons had given a good account of themselves with their torpedo-carrying Hampdens. No. 455 Squadron retained its Hampden T.B.Is until December 1943 when the operational career of Handley Page's first bomber monoplane finally drew to a close.

A grand total of 1,580 Hampdens (including a few Herefords) during the six years in which the bomber was in production played no small part in what were for the Allies the most difficult years of the war. It may be said that the Hampden did not entirely live up to its designer's more sanguine expectations in the stern test of war, but whatever its operational shortcomings, it played an important role in raising Allied air power to the pre-eminent position which it was eventually to enjoy.

Handley Page H.P.52 Hampden B.I.

Dimensions: Span, 69 ft. 2 in.; length, 53 ft. 7 in.; height, 14 ft. 11 in.; wing area, 668 sq. ft.

Armament: One fixed and one movable 0.303-in. machine gun in the nose and twin 0.303-in. machine guns in dorsal and ventral positions Maximum internal bomb load, 4,000 lb.

Power Plants: Two Bristol Pegasus XVIII nine-cylinder radial air-cooled engines each rated at 965 h.p. at 2,475 r.p.m. for take-off and 1,000 h.p. at 2,600 r.p.m. at 3,000 ft.

Weights: Empty, 11,780 lb.; normal loaded, 18,756 lb.; maximum permissible, 21,000 lb.

Performance: Maximum speed (at 18,756 lb.), 265 m.p.h. at 15,500 ft., 254 m.p.h. at 13,800 ft.; maximum cruising speed, 217 m.p.h. at 15,000 ft.; economical cruising speed, 167 m.p.h. at 15,000 ft.; initial climb rate, 980 ft./min.; time to 15,000 ft., 18.9 min.; service ceiling, 22,700 ft.; range (at 21,000 lb. with maximum bomb load of 4,000 lb.), 870 mls. at 172 m.p.h. at 15,000 ft.; maximum range (with 2,000-lb. bomb load), 1,990 mls.

The Stirling I was the first of the R.A.F.'s four-engined "heavies" to see combat, but as the war progressed it was limited by its altitude performance.

THE SHORT STIRLING

The Short Stirling was not merely the first of the Royal Air Force's true "heavies" of the Second World War, it was the *only* British four-engined bomber designed from the outset to take four power plants to see operational service during the conflict, the Lancaster and Halifax having both stemmed from twin-engined designs. Carrying bomb loads far greater than any previously contemplated, the Stirling proved one of the most important landmarks in the history of the R.A.F., for it was the first bomber to be received by that service capable of giving tangible expression to the Air Staff's beliefs in strategic bombing, and delivering, in Winston Churchill's words, "the shattering strokes of retributive justice" with which Germany's industry was to be crippled; the first of the great four-motor bombers which were to play a primary role in the defeat of the Axis powers. Yet the official history of the R.A.F. in the Second World War was to refer to the Stirling as "a disappointment."

This may appear an unfair comment on a warplane which more than fulfilled the requirements of the specification to which it had been designed, but if the Stirling *was* a disappointment, it was also a revealing example of the rapidity with which operational

requirements can change under the exigencies of war. The Stirling's shortcomings could, for the most part, be laid at the doorstep of the short-sighted limitations imposed upon its design by the official specification. This insisted that the wing span should be less than the 100-ft. door opening of standard R.A.F. hangars, and in order to keep the wing loading within reasonable limits, the Stirling's designers were forced to employ a wing of low aspect ratio and high induced drag with, in consequence, an adverse effect on performance. Undoubtedly, had they had a free hand they would have selected a wing of greater span and higher aspect ratio, but in the event, the chosen wing, although endowing the Stirling with outstanding manoeuvrability for an aircraft of its size, severely restricted the bomber's operational ceiling. This shortcoming increasingly handicapped the Stirling's operations as more effective anti-aircraft defences forced the bomber higher, and proved particularly serious during attacks on Italian targets when its pilots frequently found it necessary to fly *through* the Alps rather than over them! While the hangar door opening dictated the wing span, the size of the fuselage cross section was dictated by the size of

The first prototype Stirling (L7600), above and left, was written off during its first landing when the undercarriage collapsed as a result of the binding of a wheel brake. The undercarriage was extensively modified for the second prototype.

standard packing cases!

Another unfortunate feature of the Stirling was its inability to carry really large bombs. At the time of the bomber's conception, prevalent ideas on strategic bombing demanded the saturation of the target area with large quantities of 500-lb. and 1,000-lb. bombs. The Stirling could carry twenty-four 500-pounders, but its 42 ft. 7 in. bomb-bay, being divided into three longitudinal cells by two girders which gave the fuselage its structural stiffness, could not accommodate the very much larger weapons that became available soon after the Stirling's service introduction, thus imposing strict limitations on the bomber's usefulness.

In view of the restrictive specification, the Stirling was perhaps more of a compromise than most war-planes. Aerodynamic and operational consideration dictated a mid-mounted wing, but the price paid for the advantages offered by this wing position was an exceptionally tall undercarriage of extraordinary geometry which proved necessary in order to obtain a satisfactory ground angle. This tended to result in a dangerous swing on take-off if the pilot was not adept with the throttles; a problem aggravated by the provision of armour protection and additional armament and equipment which boosted the design gross weight of 52,000 lb. to 70,000 lb., rendering take-offs somewhat marginal operations, especially when being effected from muddy grass fields. The Stirling suffered its full share of take-off accidents and was therefore considered by many to be dangerous.

The Air Staff requirement for a heavy bomber possessing a range and bomb load far in excess of any previously envisaged was formulated in July 1936, and embodied in Air Ministry Specification B.12/36.

The S.31 half-scale flying model of the S.29 Stirling was first flown in 1938 with 90 h.p. Niagara III engines. These were later replaced by 115 h.p. Niagara IVs.

The second prototype Stirling (L7605), above and right, flew shortly after the outbreak of World War II. The undercarriage was modified and spinners were temporarily fitted.

Short and Harland Limited, the Supermarine Aviation Works, and Sir W. G. Armstrong Whitworth Aircraft Limited submitted proposals to meet the demands of the specification, and the two first-mentioned companies were awarded development contracts. Supermarine's contender for the specification—known as the Type 317 with Bristol Hercules engines and as the Type 318 with Rolls-Royce Merlins—was the last design of R. J. Mitchell of Spitfire fame, but the prototypes were destroyed during an attack on the Southampton factory where they were nearing completion and, owing to the company's other commitments, further development of the bomber was abandoned. Meanwhile, Short's contender, then known as the S.29, had been completed and flown.

Because of the relatively advanced nature of the S.29 bomber's design, it was considered advisable to build an aerodynamically similar half-scale flying model to provide information on the flying qualities and handling characteristics to be expected from the full-scale bomber. The wing of the Short Scion Senior which spanned 50 ft. was essentially similar in planform to that of the proposed bomber, and roughly half size, so modified Scion Senior wing components and engine mounts were employed for the S.31 model when construction of this began in 1937. When first flown in 1938, the S.31 was powered by four 90 h.p. Pobjoy Niagara III seven-cylinder engines, but in the following year these were replaced by 115 h.p. Niagara IVs. The two-seat S.31 was a fairly faithful model of the bomber and weighed 5,700 lb. The engines and their airscrews were roughly half the size of those to be employed by the bomber, representing the slipstream effects to be expected quite well, and bomb doors were fitted so that some idea of the effect of opening and closing the

On the ground one of the most noticeable characteristics of the Stirling was its exceptionally tall undercarriage which is well portrayed by this photograph of an early production Stirling I without dorsal turret.

THE SHORT STIRLING

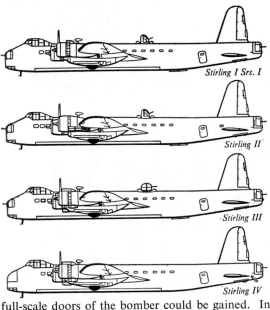

Stirling I Srs. I

Stirling II

Stirling III

Stirling IV

full-scale doors of the bomber could be gained. In fact, as the S.31's pilot, Mr. Lankester Parker, said afterwards, he was the only item not to scale.

Flight trials with the S.31 had given the design team a pretty good idea of what they might expect from the S.29 when, in May 1939, the first full-scale prototype (L7600) took-off on its maiden flight. Unfortunately, during its first landing, the prototype's undercarriage collapsed as a result of the binding of a wheel brake, and the machine was a total write-off. This mishap inevitably delayed the flight test programme at a critical period, and the second prototype (L7605), which, like the ill-fated first machine, was powered by four 1,375 h.p. Bristol Hercules II fourteen-cylinder sleeve-valve engines, did not fly until shortly after the outbreak of the war by which time the Stirling heavy bomber had already entered quantity production.

In October 1938, the Air Ministry had been working to "Programme L" which involved 3,500 heavy bombers to be delivered by April 1942. This quantity was to comprise 1,500 Stirlings, 1,500 Manchesters, and 500 Halifaxes—although, in the event, deliveries were to be about a year behind the target set by this programme—and the scheme led to the concept of so-called "quantity groups". This meant introducing a limited number of new types of aircraft and dividing the total production of each type between several companies. The "Stirling Group", which initially comprised Short Brothers, the Rootes Group, and the Austin Motor Company, had been formed in

January 1939. The group had a team of nearly 600 skilled engineers and draughtsmen which was to become one of the most travelled supervisory bodies ever to serve the British aircraft industry. Under its supervision, an organised system of dispersal was established whereby the primary components of the Stirling were built in more than twenty different factories, and a large sub-contracting scheme for smaller components arranged.

Production deliveries of the bomber were disappointingly slow in getting under way, some of the delays being the result of enemy attacks which destroyed a number of early Stirling Is (N3645 and N3647 to N3651) at the Rochester works. Five Stirling Is were also destroyed at the Belfast works, and although the first production Stirling I (N3635) appeared in May 1940, no more than three of these bombers were delivered during the second quarter of that year, with six in each of the third and fourth quarters. Nevertheless, although fewer than half a dozen production Stirling Is were available, the new bomber began to replace the Wellington in No. 7 Squadron, a member of No. 3 Group, during August 1940, this unit thereby gaining the distinction of becoming the first four-engined bomber squadron of the Second World War.

The large, flat-sided fuselage of the Stirling, married to what appeared to be inordinately small wings and an unusually tall undercarriage, gave an impression of lanky ungainliness which was entirely belied by the bomber's manoeuvrability. On one occasion, a Short test pilot demonstrating the Stirling to an R.A.F. crew, pulled up the nose of the large bomber until it stood vertically on its tail and then stalled it in that position. The bomber dropped its nose and returned easily to level flight after a brief dive, but the tail gunner, who had not been warned of this violent manoeuvre, had attempted to bale out! Fortunately, he stuck in the escape hatch and succeeded in clambering back into the bomber when it regained its normal attitude. These powers of manoeuvre were to prove particularly useful when the Stirling appeared on daylight operations, and the belief that the heavy bomber could "look after itself", current during 1941, was the direct result of a combination of this agility and effective turreted defensive armament.

The structure of the Stirling offered much evidence of its flying boat ancestry, and the wing construction in particular followed closely that of the earlier Short flying boats, and possessed a tapered planform typical of the wings employed by the Empire and Sunderland. The wing was basically a two-spar

---

FINISH AND INSIGNIA: *The Stirling B.Mk.III of No. 75 "New Zealand" Squadron illustrated on the opposite page was finished in the standard R.A.F. Bomber Command scheme comprising a dark earth and dark green camouflage pattern over the upper surfaces, and matt black over all wing, tail and fuselage under surfaces, extending up the fuselage sides and including the vertical tail surfaces. The* "C" *type roundels with yellow outline appeared on the fuselage sides with corresponding "flashes" on the fin. Blue and red* "B" *type roundels appeared on the upper wing surfaces, and the code letters indicating the squadron (i.e., AA) and the individual aircraft (i.e., K) were painted dull red as was also the serial number.*

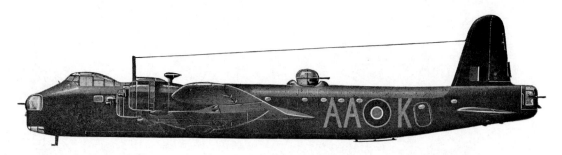

Short Stirling B.III

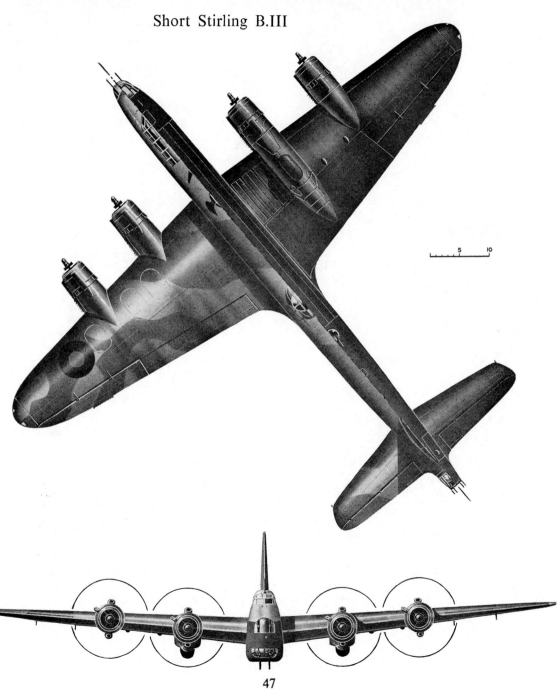

(Above) The eighth production Stirling I (N3642) from Rochester fitted with a twin-Browning dorsal turret, and (left) the Stirling II. Two Stirling Is (N3657, left, and N3711, bottom left) were fitted with Wright Cyclone engines as prototypes for the Stirling II.

carried in each of the two bays to bring total fuel capacity to 2,692 Imp.gal. Gouge-type trailing edge flaps with a chord equal to forty-eight per cent of the main wing chord were used, these being generally similar to Fowler flaps but having no gaps between them and the main wings, worked solely by the increase in area and angle of incidence.

The fuselage also employed a form of construction similar to that of Short's flying boats, and was of rectangular section with rounded corners built up of transverse frames with aluminium alloy skinning. Two longitudinal beams supported the bombs in a tremendous bay stretching from beneath the flight deck to a point well aft of the wings. The bomb-bay could accommodate seven 2,000-lb. or eighteen 500-lb. bombs, but with the heavier bombs the supplementary wing bomb cells were not used. The defensive armament initially comprised twin 0.303-in. Browning machine guns in a power-operated nose turret, four similar guns in a power-operated tail turret, and two further Brownings in a retractable ventral turret. The last-mentioned turret was only fitted to the prototypes and the first few production aircraft, and this was never employed operationally as it was realised that its extension would reduce speed at a critical moment. Another disadvantage of the ventral turret was its tendency to creep down into the fully-extended position during taxying and take-off, the guns sometimes fouling the ground. After the first few Stirling Is had been delivered, an oddly-shaped Boulton Paul power-operated dorsal turret with twin Brownings was added. The port inner engine was fitted with a twin pump to operate the

structure covered by aluminium alloy sheet flush-riveted to the spars and rib members. The leading edges were armoured and provided with balloon cable cutters, and outboard of the engines most of the space between the spars was occupied by fuel tanks. Seven tanks were installed in each wing with a total capacity of 2,254 Imp.gal., and all but two of the tanks (No. 7 in each wing) were self-sealing, the No. 7 tanks not being used unless maximum range was essential in which case their contents were used first. Inboard of the engines were bomb cells which, each containing three 500-lb. bombs, supplemented the immense fuselage bay and could also be used to house auxiliary fuel tanks, 219 Imp.gals. being

(Above) The Stirling III (BF509) differed from the Mk.I principally in having its engines installed as "power eggs". Two Stirling Is were converted as prototypes for the Mk.III, one of these (BK649) being illustrated (right), and others were converted to Mk.III standards on the assembly line, such as R9309 (below, right).

nose and dorsal turret, the starboard inner engine having a pump for the tail turret. Later, the turreted defensive armament was augmented in the Stirling I Series II production model by a pair of hand-held 0.303-in. beam guns.

The crew of the Stirling I normally comprised seven members—pilot and co-pilot, navigator/bombardier, radio-operator, engineer/gunner and two gunners—and power was provided by four 1,595 h.p. Hercules XI engines. The outboard engines were mounted centrally on the wing profile, but the inner pair were set lower in order to provide sufficient room for the main undercarriage members to retract into their nacelles. Because of its length and the need to accommodate the wheels between the main wing spars, the design of the undercarriage structure was rather complex, and made use of a system of double-jointed struts.

During the working up period with No. 7 Squadron many teething troubles were encountered, as was perhaps to be expected with such a radically new aircraft. The characteristics of the Stirling I met with general approval. The controls were good, the ailerons being relatively light for such a large aircraft, although the elevator control had a slightly heavy and sluggish initial movement. The aircraft was extremely stable directionally and laterally, and it was reasonably stable longitudinally, except when fully loaded with the C.G. in the most aft position. With any one engine out of action, the aircraft could maintain height at any weight, although with two

engines out it was difficult to maintain altitude at any weight over 50,000 lb. The maximum permissible take-off weight was 70,000 lb. at which the Stirling I would clear a 50-ft. obstacle within 1,400 yards. The recommended climbing speed from sea level to 10,000 ft. was 150 m.p.h. (I.A.S.), and from 10,000 to 15,000 ft. was 145 m.p.h., this altitude being attained in forty-two minutes.

The production build-up of the Stirling was extremely slow, only fifteen having been delivered by the end of 1940, but the tempo began to increase from the beginning of 1941 with twenty-one machines being delivered in the first quarter of that year. The Stirling was introduced into operational service as

49

rapidly as possible, and on February 10, 1941, three Stirlings of No. 7 Squadron, each carrying sixteen 500-lb. bombs, took-off from Oakington for a night sortie against Rotterdam oil storage tanks, marking the début of "the first of the heavies" over enemy occupied territory. In the following month, No. 7's Stirlings undertook night attacks on the German battlecruisers *Scharnhorst* and *Gneisenau* laying in Brest, but in April some unpleasant tasks fell to the lot of the Stirlings when they commenced daylight sorties. The first of these took place against Emden on April 27th, and no fighter escort was provided, but the Stirlings provided the defending interceptors with a formidable opponent. One of the most famed of their daylight sorties was that made in July 1941 against the *Scharnhorst* which, by this time, was laying in La Pallice. During this month new tactics were evolved, and the Stirling participated in combined "circus" operations, a fighter force accompanying the bomber formation in an attempt to draw the Luftwaffe into battle. During this period of R.A.F. Bomber Command's offensive, the guns of the Stirling accounted for a substantial number of Messerschmitt Bf 109 and Bf 110 fighters, but Luftwaffe fighters had discovered that a burst of fire in the vicinity of the fuselage roundels put the tail turret out of action, and the whole system had to be modified.

Throughout 1941, production deliveries of the Stirling I from Short's Rochester, Belfast and Swindon factories, and from the Austin Motor Company at Birmingham, had been steadily increasing, and by the end of the year 153 machines had been produced, and additional squadrons of No. 3 Group had re-equipped with the heavy bomber. By the beginning of 1942, however, the daylight attacks by Stirlings were petering out as German defences were making such sorties extremely hazardous, and the bombers were forced to contain themselves to nocturnal activities, much to the relief of their crews.

Stirlings had previously visited Berlin by night, their first attack on the German capital having taken place on April 17, 1941, and on May 30, 1942, Stirlings participated in the first thousand-bomber raid on Germany. By this time, the Stirling had been joined on operations by the higher-performing Lancaster and Halifax, but although outshone in speed and altitude capability, the Stirling proved time and time again its ability to absorb an immense amount of battle damage and stay in the air. One Stirling of No. 75 Squadron even survived a collision with a Bf 109 fighter, regaining its base less four feet of the starboard wing. Another Stirling from the same squadron succeeded in returning on three engines with the complete rudder shot away, while a No. 218 Squadron Stirling raiding Turin was hit in three of its four engines but succeeded in staying in the air for five hours, eventually landing at Bone, in North Africa. The pilot of this Stirling, Flight Sergeant Arthur Aaron, performed this feat after having his jaw smashed, part of his face torn away,

an arm broken and a lung perforated. He was the second Stirling pilot to be awarded a posthumous Victoria Cross, the first being Flight Sergeant Rawdon Middleton of No. 149 Squadron. Despite the fact that a shell splinter had destroyed Flt. Sgt. Middleton's right eye and he had suffered wounds in the body and legs during an attack on Turin, he personally directed the hazardous re-crossing of the Alps and remained at the controls until his Stirling had reached the British coast.

To safeguard against a possible shortage of Hercules engines, in 1941 two Stirlings (N3657 and N3711) were fitted with 1,600 h.p. Wright R-2600-A5B Cyclone 14 engines to serve as prototypes for the Stirling II, but no shortage of the British power plants arose, and only three production Stirling IIs were produced, one by the Rochester factory and two by the Swindon factory. As a result of operational maintenance experience, the next version of the Stirling to reach the assembly lines was the Mk.III. This differed from the Mk.I principally in having 1,635 h.p. Hercules VI or XVI engines which were installed as "power-eggs", considerably easing maintenance. A new twin-Browning dorsal turret was fitted, and various internal changes were made. Maximum speed was increased to 270 m.p.h. at 14,500 feet but, by the early months of 1943, the Stirling was already out-dated. While the Lancasters and Halifaxes were flying at altitudes approaching 20,000 ft., a fully laden Stirling was hard put to reach 12,000 feet. Two Stirling Is (BK648 and 649) served as prototypes for the Mk.III, and another Stirling I (R9254) was used in the development of H2S radar, and was one of the first aircraft to sport the characteristic ventral radome which was to appear on Lancasters and Halifaxes.

As early as 1941, Short's design team had submitted a proposal for an improved version of the basic Stirling in which the wing span was increased to 135 ft. 9 in. and the wing area to 2,145 sq.ft. This, the Short S.34 to specification B.8/41, was to have been powered by four Bristol Centaurus engines and, with an all up weight of 104,000 lb., carry a 10,000-lb. bomb load over 4,000 miles at 300 m.p.h. However, despite the promise of vastly superior characteristics, the S.34 development of the Stirling was not proceeded with.

Peak production of the Stirling was reached in the second quarter of 1943 during which the bomber was being delivered at the rate of eighty machines per month, but by that time, the Stirling squadrons were attacking only the less well-defended targets, and the last aircraft of this type to be built for the bombing role were delivered during the third quarter of 1944, when they were retained mainly for use against fringe targets and flying-bomb sites in Northern France. The Stirling had served operationally with Nos. 7, 15, 75, 90, 101, 149, 166, 199, 214, 218, 513, 622, 623 and 624 Squadrons, as well as by Nos. 138 and 161 (Special Duties) Squadrons who operated

A Stirling I (R9254), illustrated above, was employed in the development of H2S radar, and was one of the first aircraft to feature the ventral radome later to appear on Halifaxes and Lancasters.

them from Tempsford during 1942-43 for dropping saboteurs and supplies to partisans in occupied territories. The last sortie undertaken by Bomber Command Stirlings took place on September 8, 1944.

Apart from bombing, the Stirling had also been used for mine-laying and radio-countermeasures, but its primary role from the beginning of 1944 was that of transport, this version being known as the Stirling IV. The prototype Stirling IV (LJ512) was converted from a Mk.III, and flew for the first time in 1943. The nose turret was supplanted by a transparent plastic fairing, the dorsal turret was deleted, and only some machines retained their tail turret. Glider-towing equipment was installed in the rear fuselage, and twelve Stirling IVs were delivered in the last quarter of 1943, transport Stirlings subsequently being delivered at a rate of 30-35 machines per month until mid-1945. Many of the bomber variants were also converted for use as transports in service, and on D-Day, June 6, 1944, Stirling IVs of Nos. 190, 196, 299 and 622 Squadrons towed Airspeed Horsas during their operational début as glider tugs. Stirling IVs also towed gliders during the Arnhem landing, and were subsequently employed to supply fuel to the squadrons of the 2nd Tactical Air Force on the Continent.

The last production variant was also a transport, the Stirling V which differed from the Mk.IV principally in having a lengthened and redesigned nose, the prototype Mk.V being LJ530. When Stirling production finally terminated in November 1945 with the 160th Mk.V, the grand production total had reached 2,375 machines. Of these, 756 were Mk.Is and 875 were Mk.IIIs, although many were subsequently converted for the transport role.

The Short Stirling possibly was "a disappointment", but this was hardly the fault of the design team or manufacturers for what other first-line operational bomber was designed to meet the requirements of hangar door openings and packing cases! There can be no doubt that, at the time the Stirling's specification was framed, the operational conditions and requirements that were to exist six years later were not foreseen, and the design of the Stirling was such that it could not be modified to meet the new demands. In consequence, its career as a first-line heavy bomber was relatively brief. Nevertheless, as the R.A.F.'s first four-engined "heavy" of the Second World War, the Stirling occupies a particularly important place in the history of that air arm.

Short Stirling Mk.I Series I

Dimensions: Span, 99 ft. 1 in.; length, 87 ft. 3 in.; height, 22 ft. 9 in.; wing area, 1,460 sq. ft.

Armament: Two 0.303-in. Browning machine guns with 1,000 r.p.g. in nose and dorsal power-operated turrets and four 0.303-in. Browning machine guns with 1,000 r.p.g. in power-operated tail turret. Reserve ammunition, 5,750 rds. Maximum bomb loads: Seven 2,000-lb. bombs in fuselage bay (14,000 lb.), or eighteen 500-lb. bombs in fuselage bay and six 500-lb. bombs in wing cells (12,000 lb.).

Power Plants: Four Bristol Hercules XI fourteen-cylinder sleeve-valve double-row radial air-cooled engines each rated at 1,590 h.p. at 2,900 r.p.m. for take-off, 1,460 h.p. at 2,800 r.p.m. at 9,500 ft. maximum power for five minutes, and 1,020 h.p. at 2,500 r.p.m. at 7,500 ft. maximum economical cruising power.

Weights: Tare, 44,000 lb.; empty equipped 46,900 lb.; normal loaded, 59,400 lb.; maximum permissible, 70,000 lb.

Performance: Maximum speed, 245 m.p.h. at sea level, 260 m.p.h. at 10,500 ft.; economical cruising speed, 200 m.p.h. at 15,000 ft.; maximum weak mixture cruising speed, 215 m.p.h. at 15,000 ft.; range (with 980 Imp. gal. and 14,000-lb. bomb load), 740 mls. (with 2,254 Imp. gal. and 5,000-lb. bomb load), 1,930 mls. (with 2,694 Imp. gal. and 1,500-lb. load), 2,330 mls.; time to 15,000 ft. (maximum weight), 42 min.; service ceiling (normal loaded), 20,500 ft. (maximum loaded), 16,500 ft.

The Mitsubishi G4M1 Type 1 Model 11 began its operational career in May 1941 with attacks on Chungkung and Chengtu.

THE MITSUBISHI G4M TYPE 1

The time was 12.44 p.m. on August 19, 1945. The place was the small, torrid island of Ie Shima, and the event was possibly the most important Japanese flying mission of the entire Pacific War. At that memorable moment, two rotund Japanese bombers landed on the island airstrip, their arrival presaging the end of hostilities in the Pacific. Painted white overall, and bearing the large green "surrender crosses" on their wings, fuselages, and tails, the pair of emasculated bombers, hastily stripped to carry the Japanese surrender delegation headed by Lieut. General Torashiro Kawabe, were, appropriately enough, examples of a type that had become all too familiar to the Allies from the first day of the Pacific War.

Dubbed *Betty* by the Allies and known officially to the Japanese Naval Air Force as the Mitsubishi 1-*Rikko*, or Type 1 Land Attack Aircraft, these bombers had seen action in every Pacific theatre of operations from the Aleutian Islands to Australia; they were the instruments with which Japan gained many of her initial victories, and, for a while, they had numbered among the most feared of Japanese operational aircraft.

The Mitsubishi G4M1 Type 1 Land Attack Aircraft Model 11 was the first new twin-engined bomber to be encountered by the Allies in combat. Both the Army's Mitsubishi Ki.21 and the Navy's G3M2 had been met in numbers over China, and much information on their capabilities was, in consequence, available to Allied aircrews when combat was joined, but even though the 1-*Rikko* had also made its operational début over the Chinese mainland, its appearance in the Pacific came as a complete surprise to the Allies. When these new Mitsubishi bombers were first encountered in the air by American fighters west of the Gilberts early in 1942, far beyond the estimated range of bombers operating from known Japanese bases, they were thought to have been carrier-launched and, as such, examples of a radically new Japanese approach to long-range strategic bombing.

Subsequent encounters at Midway and Guadalcanal, and analyses of wrecked 1-*Rikko* bombers found in New Guinea revealed the secret of the bomber's phenomenal range and, thus, this new Mitsubishi product took its proper place as an example of Japanese thinking in the field of land-based strategic bombers. But it was soon to become apparent to both the Japanese Navy and the Allies that within this "thinking" lay the seeds of the bomber's destruction. Japanese insistence on maximum range at the expense of protective armour rendered the 1-*Rikko* supremely vulnerable to air and ground fire. Its immense wing tanks, designed to accommodate more than 1,100 Imp.gal. of fuel, were totally unprotected, and armour protection for the crew was confined to a pancake-sized piece of armour plate located aft of the tail gunner's ammunition storage rack. In fact, the bomber's complete inability to survive enemy fire power and its notorious inflammability rapidly earned for it the term "Type 1 Lighter" from its crews, although the more tolerant dubbed it the *Hamaki*, or "Flying Cigar".

The J.N.A.F. had blundered for, in developing a versatile heavy bomber for the Pacific War, they had based their design requirements largely on experience gained over the Chinese mainland, and the consequences of this blunder were to be exceeded in seriousness only by the strategical errors of the disastrous Midway and Guadalcanal operations. Conceived as a weapon of offence, the design did not take into account the possibility of aggressive fighter opposition. The result was that, as Allied strength in the Pacific grew, the 1-*Rikko* became totally ineffectual unless enjoying the protection of a strong fighter escort. The limits of the bomber's usefulness were soon clearly drawn, and repeated modifications and revised operational assignments were never able to keep abreast of Allied developments, or instil confidence in the 1-*Rikko*'s crews.

The 1-*Rikko* started life late in 1937 under a cloak of the strictest secrecy in the Central Engineering and Design Department of Mitsubishi Jukogyo KK., located at Oe-machi, Nagoya. Japan had already embarked upon the "China Incident", and there could be little doubt that the world was heading towards general war. An attitude of suspicion and distrust of Japan by the Western Powers led Japanese

52

The removal of the bomb doors from some G4M1 aircraft gave the bomber a distinctive "broken-back" profile.

planners to the conclusion that the days of design dependency upon foreign sources were nearing their end, and that Japan should firmly establish design self-sufficiency within her aircraft industry. An expansion programme for Mitsubishi was proposed in 1937, and actively launched in the following year with a series of secret design projects for both the Army and the Navy, the two most important of which were the 12-*Shi* Carrier Fighter, which was to enter service as the A6M2 *Zero-Sen*, and the 12-*Shi* Land Attack Aircraft, eventually to be accepted as the G4M1.

Secrecy in design and factory expansion was considered to be of the utmost importance in order to avoid alienating foreign sources of materials and tools, the principal of which was the United States. Any suggestion that the J.N.A.F. was actively developing a bomber capable of flying non-stop across the Pacific would, in all probability, have led to a trade boycott of Japan, and an end to vital imports. As long as Japan was still largely dependent on the United States for machine tools, steel billets, and forgings for aircraft and power plant production, the secrecy of the prototype programme had to remain closely guarded.

The Mitsubishi design office at Oe-machi was placed on an overtime basis early in 1938 in order to cope with the new series of indigenous designs for the Army and Navy, and to get the preliminary work on the important 12-*Shi* bomber underway. The J.N.A.F. had issued a design requirement for a heavy land-based bomber possessing a maximum range of 2,990 miles without bomb load, and 2,300 miles with a standard 1,760-lb. torpedo or an equivalent bomb load. The 12-*Shi* bomber was considered as a potential replacement for the Mitsubishi G3M2 Type 96 then entering J.N.A.F. service, and the individual members of the design staff were selected for their known creative abilities and advanced ideas. Headed by Dipl. Eng. Kiro Honjo, chief designer of the earlier Mitsubishi bomber, the team initially considered the development of a large four-engined machine, but this proposal was rejected by the J.N.A.F. which recommended that the 12-*Shi* speci-

fication be met with a large twin-engined aircraft. It was agreed that development work on the fuselage of the new bomber should be the responsibility of the 1st Naval Arsenal, the basic design and remaining assemblies continuing to remain the responsibility of Mitsubishi.

Detail design work progressed at a rapid tempo throughout 1938, and by the spring of 1939, various major components were ready for prototype assembly. J.N.A.F. insistence on a twin-engined aircraft necessitated relatively light construction for an aircraft of the 12-*Shi* bomber's size. The wings, which utilised the Mitsubishi 118 aerofoil section as did also the parallel 12-*Shi* fighter, employed a two-spar structure with flush-riveted stressed skinning, and were mid-set on a remarkably bulky, elliptical section, semi-monocoque fuselage. The very size of the fuselage belied the fact that it was intended for a *twin*-engined bomber, a comment made by Heinkel engineers visiting the factory in 1939, and the chosen power plants were a pair of the new Mitsubishi Kasei (Mars) 11 fourteen-cylinder two-row radials. This was the first modern two-row radial evolved in Japan to equal contemporary foreign models in performance, developing 1,530 h.p. at sea level in its initial form. The choice of this engine was fundamental to the performance success of the 1-*Rikko* bombers. Provision was made for seven crew members and, in September 1939, the first 12-*Shi* bomber prototype was completed.

The first flight tests were conducted in October with Mitsubishi test pilot Katsuzo Shima at the controls, and as the results of these initial trials met the design team's most sanguine expectations, it appeared that the way was clear for J.N.A.F. acceptance and quantity production of the bomber. In the event, service approval was to be withheld for

THE MITSUBISHI G4M TYPE 1

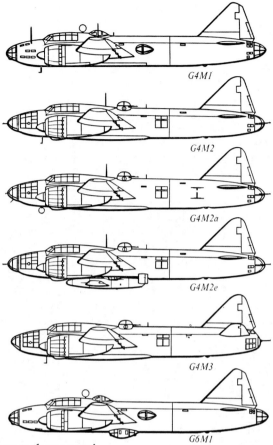

G4M1

G4M2

G4M2a

G4M2e

G4M3

G6M1

more than a year!

The delay was largely due to a proposal made late in 1938 by the Yokosuka Experimental Air Corps. This suggested the development of a heavily-armed escort aircraft which could accompany the slow-flying G3M2 Type 96 bombers operating over China beyond conventional fighter range. A small but insistent group of Naval officers forced the acceptance of the multi-gun escort fighter on the J.N.A.F. who requested that the 12-*Shi* bomber prototype be modified to fulfil this requirement. Despite the protests of the design team, the 12-*Shi* bomber became the 12-*Shi* long-range convoy fighter, and the type was awarded the designation G6M1, thereby bypassing the G4M1 designation assigned to the original bomber project.

Production of the G6M1 began in October 1939 at the 3rd Airframe Works at Nagoya on a limited

procurement basis. A total of thirty of the immense "fighters" was completed before production was terminated in March 1941. The G6M1 carried ten crew members and an armament of four 20-mm. cannon and a single 7.7-mm. machine gun. It was soon apparent that the "wingtip escort" theory was impracticable as the G6M1 possessed an entirely different performance envelope to that of the G3M2; it was seriously overloaded and therefore unwieldy, and it could not keep formation with the lightly loaded bombers returning from a mission. The whole scheme was, therefore, abandoned, late production models were completed as G6M1-K crew trainers and, ultimately, all remaining aircraft of the type were converted as transports under the designation G6M1-L2, these carrying paratroops in the South-West Pacific.

With the failure of the G6M1, the 12-*Shi* bomber was finally accepted for production as the G4M1 Type 1 Land Attack Aircraft Model 11 in April 1941. From completion of the original bomber prototype in September 1939, followed by a second bomber prototype in December 1940, through an additional thirteen prototypes delivered between January and March 1941, production was stepped up to a rate of twenty-five aircraft a month by November 1941, and somewhat over 180 machines had been delivered to the J.N.A.F. by the time Pearl Harbour was attacked during the following month. The G4M1 was rapidly assigned to operational units, making its first sortie in May 1941 with an attack on Chungking and Chengtu. This raid was undertaken by the veteran Hankow Air Wing, and was the harbinger of things to come, for it also marked the operational début of the A6M2 *Zero-Sen* fighter, then undergoing combat trials in China, in the escort role.

Before launching the Pacific War, the J.N.A.F. had assigned 120 G4M1 bombers to the 11th Air Fleet in preparation for the invasion of the Philippines, the Dutch East Indies and Malaya. The aircraft were ultimately spread in a wide arc aimed at these target areas, with fifty-four aircraft and reserves assigned to the 21st Air Flotilla's Kanoya Air Corps, and an additional fifty-four aircraft and reserves assigned to the 23rd Air Flotilla's Takao Air Corps. With the location and identification of the British battleships *Repulse* and *Prince of Wales* at Singapore in the weeks preceding the War, plans were prepared which were to render British Asiatic sea power impotent in one blow. Twenty-seven of the Kanoya Air Corps' G4M1 bombers were re-assigned to bases

---

FINISH AND INSIGNIA: *Although early wartime models of the 1-Rikko were finished sea-blue or light green land camouflage, while others employed natural metal finish, late models, such as the G4M2 Type 1 Land Attack Aircraft Model 24 illustrated on the opposite page, were painted to conform to the necessity of overland operations faced by the J.N.A.F. in 1944-45. The machine illustrated belonged to the 763rd Kokutai (Air Corps), all J.N.A.F. medium bomber units being assigned numbers in the 700 series, operating in the Philippines in October 1944. The upper surfaces were painted dark jungle green while the* under surfaces employed natural metal finish. The national insignia, the circular red Hinomaru, was outlined in white on the fuselage, and on some machines was also outlined in white on the upper wing surfaces. About ten inches of the wing leading edges to the outboard wing panels were painted yellow on many aircraft—a J.N.A.F. adaptation of the J.A.A.F. "combat stripe" which served as an identification aid. The numerals "763-12" were painted in white across the vertical tail surfaces, denoting the twelfth aircraft of the 763rd Kokutai.

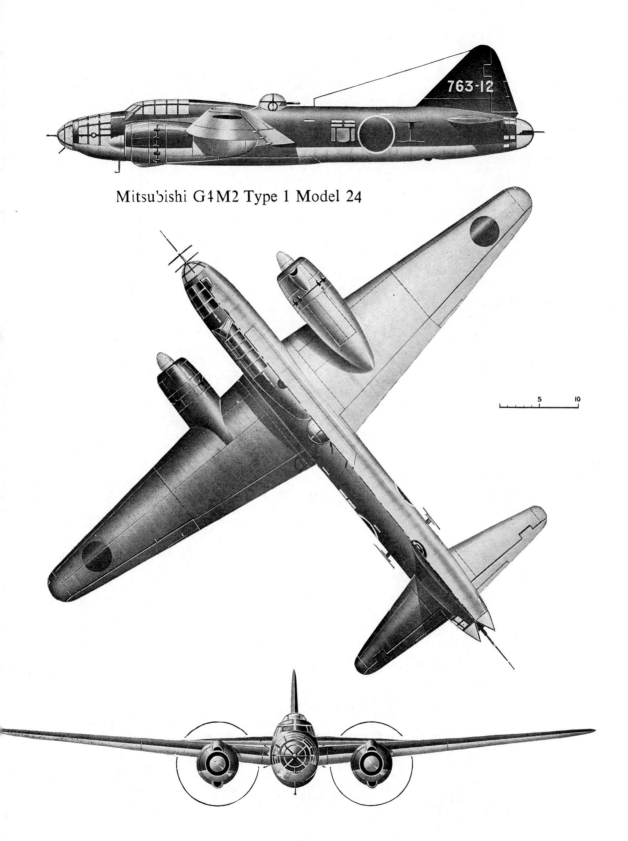

Mitsubishi G4M2 Type 1 Model 24

The G4M2 introduced a hydraulically-operated dorsal turret and protected fuel tanks.

in Indo-China which had previously been occupied by Japanese forces, and from these bases they were, subsequently, to attack and destroy the British surface vessels, scoring a tremendous victory which was to have far-reaching effects on military operations in the Pacific.

When, on the morning of December 8, 1941 (Japanese time), war enveloped the entire South-West and Central Pacific, attacks being launched against Pearl Harbour, the Philippines, Malaya, Wake and Guam, fifty-four G4M1 bombers of the 23rd Air Flotilla based on Formosa attacked Clark Field in the Philippines, virtually obliterating the American air formations based there. Two days later, G4M1s, operating from the Indo-Chinese bases to which they had been ordered by Admiral Yamamoto, found the *Repulse* and the *Prince of Wales* cruising off the coast of Malaya, and sunk both capital vessels, clearing the way for the Japanese invasion of Malaya and the East Indies. This victory, one of the major Allied reverses of the Pacific War, was accomplished without the participation of a single Japanese surface vessel, and played a major part in establishing the reputation of the 1-*Rikko* as one of Japan's most formidable offensive weapons.

During the weeks and months that followed, the G4M1 appeared ubiquitous. It was encountered in the Marianas, the Marshalls, over New Britain, New Georgia, New Guinea, Peleliu, the Solomons, and the Kuriles. Its record was impressive, and included the sinking of the U.S.S. *Langley*, night attacks in the Gilberts, high-altitude raids on Port Moresby, Australia, and daring daylight attacks against American surface units in the Guadalcanal fighting.

The characteristic "broken-back" profile of the G4M1 which resulted from the removal of the bomb-bay doors was soundly anathematized by Allied forces on the receiving end of the bomber's cargo, but during this period of apparent success, the G4M1 was also displaying its vulnerability.

Attrition was high, of the initial "available" force of 240 G3M2 and G4M1 bombers possessed by the J.N.A.F. on the day the Pacific War commenced, no fewer than 182 had been lost within three months. The Japanese aircraft industry was hard put to keep pace with this attrition which was considered to be far above the maximum practicable, and many attempts were made to improve the G4M1's performance and defence, resulting in the appearance of the G4M2. In its original service form, the G4M1 carried seven crew members, and defensive armament comprised four 7.7-mm. hand-held machine guns distributed in nose, dorsal and lateral positions, and a 20-mm. cannon in the tail. Early Model 11 aircraft had a full cone tail position, but later production aeroplanes had the tip of the cone cut away in a variety of styles to provide a wider traverse for the cannon.

The performance of the G4M1 included a maximum speed of 266 m.p.h. at 13,780 ft., and normal cruising speed was 196 m.p.h. at 9,840 ft. Service ceiling was 30,250 ft., range was 1,864 miles, and the offensive load comprised a 1,760-lb. torpedo or 2,200 lb. of bombs. Empty weight was 14,860-14,990 lb., and normal loaded and maximum permissible weights were 20,944 lb. and 28,220 lb. Some late production G4M1s had MK4E Kasei 15 engines and were designated Model 12, and others mounted two 7.7-mm. guns in the tail in place of the cannon.

The G4M2, the prototype of which was completed in November 1942, featured a new laminar flow aerofoil and MK4P Kasei 21 radials with methanol-water injection. Provision was made for an additional 330 gallons of fuel in a fuselage tank just aft of the pilot, and some attempt was at last made to protect the fuel tanks. The fuselage tank was protected by layers of rubber sheet and sponge, but the wing tanks were protected from the underside only, rubber sheet being plastered to the inside of the wing skin. In addition to the rubber leak-proofing material, the possibility of fire around the fuel tanks was further reduced by means of a carbon dioxide fire extinguisher system. No provision was made for crew armour, but the defensive armament was extensively revised. The dorsal gun blister of the G4M1 was replaced by a flush, glass-panelled entry hatch, and the first power-operated dorsal gun turret in Japanese practice was provided. This hydraulically-operated turret possessed a 360° traverse and allowed an 80° elevation of the 20-mm. Type 99 Mk.1 (Oerlikon) cannon. The lateral blisters were supplanted by flush panels, and the glazed section of the tail gun position was redesigned, a pie-shaped cut-out permitting lateral and longitudinal traverse of the cannon. The wing and tail surface tips were rounded, the fuselage nose contours were refined and the nose glazing extended, the bomb-bay was redesigned and enlarged, and a fully retractable tailwheel was provided. Variations in armament and equipment, such as the addition of two 7.7-mm. machine guns firing through small ports on either side of the nose section, led to the Models 22a and 22b. The maximum speed of the G4M2 Model 22 was boosted very slightly, but the additional fuel tankage provided a useful increment in range. Empty weight rose to 17,624 lb., and normal loaded and maximum permissible weights became 27,557 lb. and 33,070 lb.

In the meantime, production of the basic G4M1 had continued at the 3rd Airframe Works, 371 machines being delivered in 1942, but with increasing Allied domination of the air, the losses suffered by 1-*Rikko*-equipped units bordered on the disastrous. No. 751 Kokutai, formerly the Kanoya Kokutai or Air Corps, operating from Kavieng, experienced particularly heavy losses. For instance, during an attack on Port Moresby in January 1943, no fewer than ten of No. 751's G4M1 bombers failed to return of the seventeen despatched, and the unit was so weakened that it had to be temporarily withdrawn from operations. With the introduction of the improved G4M2, 660 of which were produced in 1943, the original model was retired from first-line service, subsequently being employed in the maritime reconnaissance, transport and training roles.

In May 1944, the engines of the 1-*Rikko* were again changed, the installation of MK4T Kasei 25 radials offering a useful reduction in fuel consumption and increasing range. The bomb-bay doors were bulged, and the new version entered production in the summer of 1944 as the G4M2a Type 1 Model 24. These bombers entered service rapidly, and were assigned to the 763rd Kokutai of the 2nd Air Fleet defending the Philippines, as well as units based on Formosa, on the Chinese coast and the Japanese home islands. Slight variations were produced as the Models 24a, 24b and 24c.

The basic Model 24 was subjected to numerous experiments. The high-altitude MK4V Kasei 27 engines were installed in one machine which became the G4M2b Model 25 while, with MK4T Kasei 25b engines it became known as the G4M2c Model 26. The G4M2d was a turbojet test-bed which, in the spring of 1945, was flown with a 1,100 lb.s.t. Yokosuka Ne. 20 mounted beneath its fuselage. One special version of the Model 24, the G4M2e Model 24-J, was built in limited numbers as a parent craft for the Yokosuka MXY8 Ohka Model 11 piloted missile. The bomb-bay doors were removed and special shackles were fitted to carry the Ohka but, despite a defensive armament of four 20-mm. cannon and one 7.7-mm. machine gun, the G4M2e proved extremely vulnerable to Allied fighter interception owing to the low flying speeds at which the Ohka could be launched. The G4M2e normally approached to within twenty-five miles of the target before launching the Ohka at approximately 175 m.p.h. Prior to the release of the missile, the parent craft was extremely unwieldy. The G4M2e was employed operationally during the American assault on Okinawa but soon withdrawn from service.

The J.N.A.F. insistence on range over protection wavered as Allied fighters took an ever-increasing toll of 1-*Rikko* bombers, and adequate protection for crew and fuel tanks was finally seen to be a necessity. The first result of this change in policy was the G7M1 Taizan (Great Mountain) which, designed to a 16-*Shi* specification, was generally similar to the G4M2 in outline. Designated M-60 by Mitsubishi, the Taizan Land Attack Aircraft was to be powered by two Mitsubishi MK10 Ha. 42/11 radials derived from the Kasei series. Design work on the airframe had commenced as early as the summer of 1942, and it was proposed that defensive armament would comprise six 13-mm. machine guns and two 20-mm. cannon, all turret-mounted in pairs. The fuel tanks were protected and adequate provision was made for crew armour. Design delays resulting from a disagreement over the design of the forward fuselage held up the Taizan and, although obviously promising, the aircraft was abandoned late in 1944 in favour of the G4M3 Model 34 which, developed in parallel, embodied certain of the Taizan's features.

The G4M3 Model 34 was a major redesign of the 1-*Rikko*, with emphasis upon fuel tank and crew protection rather than range. Initiated in November 1942, work on the G4M3 Model 34 was delayed by extensive changes to the wing structure. A single-spar structure was eventually selected, this allowing for the installation of large-capacity wing tanks containing 968 Imp.gal. The reduced radius of action offered by the G4M3 was no longer critical as, by the time production deliveries of the new model commenced, Japan was decidedly on the defensive in the Pacific, and her empire had shrunk appreciably. The initial service version was the G4M3a Model 34a, and production was assigned to both the 3rd and 7th Airframe Factories. Minor changes led to the production of the Model 36 with power ultimately changed to an improved model of the Kasei as the G4M3b. Only sixty Model 34 and Model 36 aircraft had been completed when Japan finally surrendered.

The last major development of the 1-*Rikko* series was the G4M3d Model 37 with exhaust-driven turbo-superchargers, work upon which started in August 1944. Owing to teething troubles with the super-chargers, flight trials were delayed until June 1945 and never completed. J.N.A.F. plans for an advanced version, the G4M4, as well as a wooden variant of the 1-*Rikko* were dropped with the decision to concentrate on the newer Ginga class. Thus, development of the 1-*Rikko* came to an end with the remaining air-craft of this type ending the War as short-range bombers, night patrol aircraft, maritime reconnais-sance machines, trainers and transports. For mari-time reconnaissance, the Model 24 was equipped with a Type 3 MK 6 Model 4 radar set, with Yogi antennae extending from the nose, and flat H-type antennae extending from the fuselage. sides. This was a sea-search set calibrated to a range of approx-imately ninety miles, but in fact at 10,000 feet it was effective against shipping to only some thirty miles.

A total of 2,479 bombers of the 1-*Rikko* type had been produced at the time of Japan's final defeat, and its use as a transport for the surrender delegation was without question the safest mission ever flown by a Japanese crew in an aircraft of this type. The main-stay of the Japanese Navy's long-range bomber formations throughout the Pacific War, the 1-*Rikko* joined combat in a blaze of glory but, owing to a notorious proclivity towards catching fire when hit, a high proportion of all bombers of this type termi-nated their careers in blazes having unpleasantly final results for their crews.

Mitsubishi G4M2a Type 1 Model 24

Dimensions:	Span, 81 ft. 8 in.; length, 64 ft. 4¼ in.; height, 13 ft. 5¼ in.; wing area, 840.929 sq. ft.
Power Plants:	Two Mitsubishi MK4T Kasei 25 fourteen-cylinder two-row radial air-cooled engines each rated at 1,850 h.p. at 2,600 r.p.m. for take-off, and having military ratings of 1,680 h.p. at 2,500 r.p.m. at 6,890 ft., and 1,540 h.p. at 2,500 r.p.m. at 18,040 ft.
Armament:	One 20-mm. Type 99 (Oerlikon) cannon in hydraulically-operated dorsal turret, one Type 99 cannon in each of two hand-held lateral positions, one Type 99 hand-held cannon in extreme tail, and one 7.7-mm. Type 97 machine gun on ball-and-socket mounting in extreme nose. Maximum bomb load, 2,200 lb. Alternative loads: one 1,764-lb. bomb or torpedo; one 1,100-lb. bomb; four 550-lb. bombs: clusters of twelve 132-lb., 66-lb., or 22-lb. bombs.
Weights:	Empty, 18,499 lb.; normal loaded, 27,557 lb.; maximum overload, 33,070 lb.
Performance:	Maximum speed, 272 m.p.h. at 15,090 ft., 264 m.p.h. at 6,560 ft.; cruising speed, 196 m.p.h. at 9,840 ft.; time to 9,840 ft. 7 min. 16 sec., to 16,400 ft , 13 min. 21 sec., to 26,250 ft., 30 min. 24 sec.; service ceiling, 29,360 ft.; range (with 968 Imp. gal.), 2,262 mls. at 196 m.p.h. at 9,840 ft.

Torpedoes from G4M1 bombers crippled British naval power in the Far East during the Pacific War's opening stages. Here a torpedo is being loaded aboard a G4M1.

France was the first country to place an order for the Douglas attack bomber, and the photograph above depicts the production prototype, complete with Armée de l'Air markings, five days before its first flight. The initial production model was designated DB-7.

THE DOUGLAS A-20

In some respects, the combat career of the Douglas A-20 was much less spectacular than those of many other bombers employed by the combatants. It was associated with no outstanding operations but remained in first-line service throughout the war; it did not distinguish itself on any particular battlefront, but flew with equal distinction over them all. It did as well in Russia as it did in the Pacific or the Western Desert and withal was one of the most pleasant of all combat aircraft to fly.

If for nothing else, the A-20 deserves to be remembered as a pilot's aeroplane, and its virtues were sworn in a variety of tongues, ranging from Afrikaans to Ukrainian. Its cosmopolitan nature was fundamental in its design, however, for it owed much to the Spanish Civil War and, subsequently, to the urgent need for rearmament by the French. The danger signals of the international situation in 1936 had not been ignored in the United States. Among others, a group of prominent people in American aviation were considering the future requirements of the U.S. Army Air Corps for military aircraft well in advance of the issue of any official specifications. Donald Douglas, Jack Northrop and Ed Heinemann had been concerned together in the development of the A-17 attack bomber at the Northrop Aircraft Corporation, later absorbed by the Douglas Aircraft Company as its El Segundo Division, and they turned their attention towards a possible replacement.

With the co-operation of Wright Field technicians, they drew up a set of performance requirements for an attack bomber project which bore the appellation Model 7A. This project envisaged an operating speed of 250 m.p.h. which,

with a load of bombs, three 0.3-in. machine guns and a crew of two, it was calculated, could be achieved with two 450 h.p. engines. No twin-engined attack bomber had previously been accepted for the U.S. Army, so the Model 7A had to break entirely new ground. It was a shoulder-wing monoplane with a conical-shaped fin and rudder assembly, and a semi-retractable dorsal gun turret. Before its design had been finalised, however, details of aerial combat in the Spanish Civil War resulted in its replacement by an attack project of even more advanced conception. The completed portions of the airframe of the Model 7A were scrapped and work commenced on the Model 7B.

With the resignation of Jack Northrop from the Douglas subsidiary on January 1, 1938, design work on the Model 7B was continued under the direction of E. H. Heinemann who had been Chief Engineer for

The predecessor of the DB-7, the Model 7B, is seen here with its "B Type" nose section (immediately below) and with the "A Type" nose, the latter containing four 0.3-in. machine guns.

The DB-7 Boston I (AE458) illustrated (top) was an ex-Belgian contract machine taken over by the R.A.F. for training duties. The DB-7 Boston II (AX910), immediately above, was converted for the night fighting role, under the designation Havoc I, in the winter of 1940-41.

more than a year. The Model 7B made its initial flight towards the close of 1938, and its exceptional performance became immediately apparent. Its maximum speed was more than 300 m.p.h., and its manoeuvrability was outstanding for a twin-engined aircraft. Powered by two 1,100 h.p. Pratt and Whitney Twin Wasp R-1830 engines, the Model 7B was a handsome aircraft incorporating many novel features. It retained the shoulder-wing configuration and conical vertical tail surfaces of the earlier Model 7A, and had retractable dorsal and ventral turrets mounting 0.3-in. machine guns. Four more 0.3-in. guns were installed in blisters, two on each side of the forward fuselage, and similar installations were to become a common feature of many U.S. attack bombers during the Second World War.

Another design feature to appear initially on the Model 7B which was later to be adopted on a wide scale was the provision of interchangeable nose sections to suit the aircraft for the alternative roles of bombardment or attack. As completed, the Model 7B prototype had a transparent nose accommodating a navigator and featuring an oblique optical flat panel for bomb-aiming. The entire "B" (Bombardment) nose could be detached from forward of the cockpit and nosewheel and replaced by a "solid" attack or "A" type nose housing four 0.3-in. guns for ground-strafing.

Completion of the Model 7B coincided with the arrival on the Pacific Coast, with President Roosevelt's blessing, of the French Purchasing Commission which was seeking modern aircraft for the re-equipment of the Armée de l'Air. Its members found

the performance of the Model 7B most impressive, and in February 1939 placed an order for one hundred aircraft, an order destined to be soon increased to 380. Although the prototype was flying in U.S.Army insignia, the French order was the first contract or commitment to be received by Douglas for its vast expenditure of effort. But although the French contract was based on the performance of the Model 7B, so many modifications were demanded to prevent the aircraft becoming tactically obsolete before reaching Europe, that the result was virtually a new model! The revised aircraft was designated Model DB-7 ("DB" indicating Douglas Bomber), and this was to serve as a prototype for the A-20 series.

To accommodate up to 1,764 lb. of demolition bombs and the fuel tanks for the requisite range, the fuselage was deepened. Simultaneously, the cross section was narrowed, providing a single cockpit for the pilot with no possibility of position interchange between the navigator-bombardier who was accommodated in the rounded, transparent nose, and the gunner situated in a cockpit aft of the wings. The wing position was lowered slightly, and the up-rated Twin Wasps (1,200 h.p.) were mounted in underslung nacelles. The revised airframe geometry necessitated a longer nosewheel leg, but the semi-cantilever main undercarriage members remained substantially unchanged. Armour was provided for the crew and fuel tanks, and armament comprised four fixed forward-firing French MAC (Manufacture d'Armes de Chatellerault) 7.5-mm. machine guns, and two flexibly-mounted guns of similar calibre with 500 r.p.g. firing above and below the rear fuselage.

The original work force of seventy engineers who had developed the Models 7A and 7B was increased fivefold to speed the drawings of the DB-7 to the tooling and manufacturing groups, and a production line was established before the production prototype made its first flight on August 17, 1939, at El Segundo. Development was complicated by the need to incorporate the many French requirements, including metrically-calibrated instruments and other specialised equipment. Further complications ensued following the crash of the prototype which spun in following an engine failure while carrying Captain Chemedlin of the French Air Mission, the American test pilot being killed when he baled out too low. But despite these delicate international problems, the entire batch of one hundred DB-7s was in the hands of the French by the end of 1939—a truly remarkable achievement!

Unfortunately, the Armée de l'Air was considerably slower in putting these aircraft into service.

The Douglas A-20 (39-735), illustrated at the top of this page, had turbo-superchargers. This particular machine was modified as the XP-70 for night fighting duties, and no less than fifty-nine of the sixty-three A-20s built were similarly converted. The A-20A (39-725), immediately above, was the first U.S.A.A.C. attack model.

The DB-7s were shipped to Casablanca where they were assembled and tested before delivery to conversion units in North Africa and Southern France, but only sixty-four machines had crossed the Atlantic by the time of the German offensive in May 1940. Only *Groupement* 2 became operational in time to play a small part in the Battle for France, twelve DB-7s of this unit joining operations on May 31, 1940, with a low-level attack on German columns near Saint Quentin. Five *Groupes de Bombardement* (GBI/19, II/19, and II/61 at Souk el Arba, and I/32 and II/32 at Mediouna) had a total of twenty-nine DB-7s in North Africa at the time of the French capitulation in June 1940, and these were incorporated temporarily in the Vichy Air Force, although they were later to participate in the attacks on the German strongholds on the French Atlantic Coast before France was finally liberated.

While the original order for DB-7s had been in process of fulfilment, the French government placed a further contract with Douglas for a substantial quantity of a developed version, the DB-7A. To cope with a further increase in gross weight from 14,000 lb. to 17,319 lb. which resulted from the installation of additional equipment, the DB-7A had 1,600 h.p. Wright Cyclone R-2600 engines in place of the Twin Wasps. The new power plants were accommodated in revised nacelles which had lengthened, more pointed extensions aft of the wing, and "slotted" cowlings with modified cooling gills, redesigned intake and exhaust arrangements. As a corollary to the increased power, the fin and rudder of the DB-7A were substantially increased in area by additional chord towards the tip, resulting in a noticeably less tapered outline. Even the lower-powered DB-7 had exhibited some symptoms of inadequate vertical tail surface in its directional stability and control, and as an experiment, the 131st French contract aircraft had been fitted with twin fins and rudders at the tips of the dihedralled tailplane. Serialled U-131, this modified aircraft was known within Douglas as the DB-131, and was flight tested during 1939, but the new arrangement was abandoned in favour of the larger single vertical tail.

It is not generally realised that no fewer than seventy-five Cyclone-powered DB-7As were accepted by the French government before its capitulation from orders totalling 951 aircraft, but few, in fact, reached the Armée de l'Air. The Anglo-French Purchasing Board in Washington hurriedly arranged for Britain to take over the undelivered aircraft a few hours before all French assets in the U.S.A. were frozen. Also transferred at the same time were the DB-7s of a small Belgian order, while other machines of a similar type found their way into the Royal Air Force via Free French pilots in North Africa and Metropolitan France.

Some confusion arose from the R.A.F. designation system for the various DB-7 variants, and their irregular arrival did not assist matters. About twenty of the original production DB-7s (allocated serial numbers AE457-472 and DK274-277) were the first to arrive, and these were given the designation Boston I, being employed for training and other non-operational duties on which their French instrumentation resulted in some slight complication. On arrival in the United Kingdom, their throttles were found to work backwards (i.e., forward to close) in the then-current French fashion, and these were immediately modified at Speke. In mid-1940, further small batches of ex-French or Belgian contract aircraft arrived, totalling about 150 machines. With R-1830-S3C4G Twin Wasp engines, having two-speed superchargers and Stromberg injection carburettors, in place of the original SC3G single-speed supercharged powerplants, these aircraft had been built as DB-7s, and, on paper at least, were designated Boston IIs by the R.A.F. They carried 270 gallons of fuel in protected wing tanks, and had the usual crew of three. The rear gunner had hatches above and below the fuselage for defensive armament, and as there was no possibility of changing places in the air, his cockpit was fitted with rudimentary flying controls for emergency landings.

Although procured as a bomber, the first application of the DB-7 with the R.A.F. was not directly

61

Production of the Havoc really got into its stride with the A-20G, the first of the series to have a "solid" type nose. The A-20G-10-DO (43-9929) was one of the first machines to have the wider rear fuselage and Martin turret adopted as standard by the A-20G-20-DO production batch.

marked the beginning of American daylight bombing experience which was to prove so decisive in the later offensive.

The Independence Day sortie also provided strong evidence of the Boston's capacity for absorbing punishment. One of the American-manned Bostons lost its starboard airscrew after a flak strike, and suffered severe wing damage as well as an engine fire. It actually struck the ground near its target, but its pilot brought it safely back to Swanton Morley on its remaining engine, and shot up a flak tower with his four front guns *en route*! One or two more sorties were flown with No. 226 Squadron before the American unit received its own A-20Cs in the United Kingdom.

The A-20C was the first variant of the DB-7 series to feature torpedo-carrying capability, with provision for a standard 2,000-lb. naval torpedo carried

externally below the bomb-bay. This capacity was not extensively exploited by the R.A.F. or U.S.A.A.F., but the Russian naval air arm made considerable use of the Boston as a torpedo aircraft with not a little success. Other weapon developments were explored by the R.A.F., however, Boston III W8315 being fitted with a twin-Browning Bristol power-operated turret in the mid-upper gun position, and W8269/G having four racks for 60-lb. rocket projectiles beneath each outer wing. The turret modification remained experimental on the Boston III, as did also the rocket projectile installation, but a Martin turret subsequently became standard on later A-20s.

The Martin turret was actually introduced on the next production variant, the A-20G, but before leaving the "C", the conversion of thirteen of the latter for night fighting on an experimental basis must

The XA-20B (below) was an A-20A fitted with three power-operated twin-gun turrets, above and below the fuselage, and in the nose in July 1941. The experiment was not entirely successful and was discontinued.

The R.A.F. received one hundred and sixty-nine A-20J Havocs which were known as Boston IVs. The photograph above depicts BZ403, the fourth R.A.F. Boston IV which entered service in August 1944, and operated with the 2nd Tactical Air Force in Europe until the end of the war.

be mentioned. This conversion work was undertaken in 1943, and the resultant P-70A-1-DO was fitted with six 0.5-in. Browning machine guns plus radar in a "solid" nose. Development of the next couple of stages of the A-20 was inconclusive, the A-20D being a cancelled Santa Monica project for an R-2600-7-engined variant without self-sealing fuel tanks, while the A-20E was a revised programme on seventeen A-20As with 1,690 h.p. R-2600-11 engines. Another 1941 experiment was the XA-20F-DE which was an A-20A fitted with a 37-mm. cannon in the nose, and upper and lower General Electric power turrets each mounting two 0.5-in. machine guns.

With the A-20G production had really got into its stride, and 2,850 examples of this variant were produced during 1942 at Santa Monica. Apart from the P-70 conversions, the A-20G was the first of the series to have a "solid" type nose, and the fuselage length

was increased to 48 ft. compared with 47 ft. 4 in. for the A-20C. Having R-2600-23 engines, the A-20G-1-DO had a nose armament of two 0.5-in. machine guns with 350 r.p.g., and four 20-mm. M2 cannon with sixty r.p.g. The cannon projected well forward of the nose, and were supplemented by a 0.3-in. or 0.5-in. tunnel gun with 500 rounds, and a 0.5-in. with a similar amount of ammunition in the rear cockpit. The gunner's position was no longer equipped with emergency flight controls, and provision for photographic equipment was also deleted.

Most of the early A-20Gs were passed on to the Russians, and subsequent models had the nose cannon deleted. Instead four 0.5-in. machine guns with 350 r.p.g. were mounted in the nose to supplement the existing two guns for use against ground targets during low-level attacks. Two 58 Imp.gal. (70 U.S.gal.) fuel tanks were mounted in the bomb-

The A-20H Havoc was generally similar to the G-model apart from the engines and a revised cockpit which offered improved bombing control accessibility. The accompanying photograph depicts an A-20H-10-DO (44-308).

bay to give additional range without affecting bomb capacity which remained at 2,000 lb. This bomb load was doubled from the A-20G-20 onwards which saw the introduction of underwing racks outboard of the engine nacelles and capable of carrying four bombs of up to 500-lb. each. Provision was still made for an external torpedo, although the A-20 series were no longer being used by the A.A.F. for such missions.

The A-20G-20-DO also marked the introduction of a six-inch increase in rear fuselage width to accommodate an electrically-operated Martin turret mounting two 0.5-in. machine guns with 400 r.p.g. The single 0.5-in. tunnel gun was retained for ventral defence. Bomb-bay fuel tankage was increased to a total of 270 Imp.gal. (325 U.S.gal.) which, with a 310 Imp.gal. (374 U.S.gal.) under-fuselage drop tank, gave a total fuel capacity for ferrying purposes of 915 Imp.gal. (1,099 U.S.gal.). This gave an ultimate range of 2,035 miles in 10.5 hours. The A-20G series brought the war maximum weight of the Havoc (which name, incidentally, had been adopted by the A.A.F.) up to 30,000 lb., although critical flight characteristics resulted above 27,000 lb. Combat gross weight of the later A-20Gs was 26,000 lb., which included thicker armour for increased crew protection on ground attack missions, non-ram airscoops,

carburettor anti-icers, and heaters for winterization. Better navigation equipment and Type A-2-bomb-aiming controls were added in the last production A-20Gs which were the -40 to -45-DO batches. These also embodied an improved exhaust ejector system and a modified engine cowling of the "blistered" type as used by the B-25 Mitchell.

The R.A.F. received no A-20Gs, nor any of the A-20H model which followed in 1944. These were generally similar to the A-20G except for the installation of 1,700 h.p. R-2600-29 engines, and a revised cockpit for more accessible bombing controls. Four hundred and twelve were built and, with the A-20Gs, they went into service with the U.S.A.A.F. in the Pacific, the Middle East, and the United Kingdom. The Ninth Air Force made good use of them in tactical sorties over the Continent as a prelude to D-Day, and they proved particularly successful in interdiction attacks, cutting enemy communications and pounding enemy airfields in low-level strikes. The underwing racks were also intended to accommodate chemical tanks which were used for laying smoke screens. This task was undertaken by R.A.F. Boston IIIs on D-Day, the necessary chemicals being carried in bomb-bay tanks and released from four nozzles protruding beneath the fuselage.

In July 1943, the A.A.F. requested that one out of each ten A-20Gs be modified to revert to a bombardier nose with full navigation facilities. This was to conform with the tactics of "bombing on the leader", in which only one aircraft was used to calculate the target position while the remainder of the squadron dropped its bombs at a given signal. These modifications resulted in the A-20J which had a lengthened and frameless transparent nose but was otherwise similar to the A-20G, and the A-20K which was the bombardier version of the A-20H. In all, 450 A-20J Havocs were built in 1943, and 413 A-20Ks had materialised up to the time production of the entire series was halted on September 20, 1944. By that date, 7,385 DB-7s of one sort or another had been manufactured for Britain, Russia and the U.S.A. Of these, 3,125 (including those transferred from R.A.F. deliveries) were allocated to the Soviet Union, 2,917 of these reaching their destination, and 455 were delivered to the R.A.F. under lend-lease. Twenty-eight were supplied to the Netherlands government and thirty-one to Brazil, and the peak inventory for the U.S.A.A.F. was reached in September 1944 when more than 1,700 A-20 Havocs were in service.

The R.A.F. received 169 A-20Js (BZ400-568) which were designated Boston IVs, and entered service in August 1944, and ninety A-20Ks (BZ580-669) which were designated Boston Vs. These aircraft, which had the standard twin-0.5-in. fixed nose armament, continued to operate with the 2nd Tactical Air Force in Europe until the end of the war. Eleven Boston Vs were transferred to the R.C.A.F.

To conclude the DB-7 story, it only remains to mention the odd variants not covered hitherto. An adaptation of the A-20G for night fighting resulted, in 1943, in the P-70A-2-DO. This retained the standard G-model nose armament and twenty-six were so converted, while a single A-20G-10-DO was fitted with a "solid" nose containing radar and radio equipment, and armed with three 0.5-in. machine guns in a large blister on each side of the fuselage. This became the P-70B-1. A project to use other A-20Gs and Js as night fighter trainers (P-70B-2) did not materialise. One unexplained Havoc development was the reconversion of at least one A-20J (43-9929) back to "G" standard, with the "solid" nose and six-gun armament, but this change may have been effected in the field.

A more obvious wartime modification of an A-20H was a machine adapted to take a caterpillar track main landing gear for operating from mud, snow or sand. This experiment was not developed but, like all the other thirty or so uses to which the DB-7 series was put, including strafing, low-level bombing, skip-bombing, night fighting, torpedo-bombing, observation, reconnaissance and smoke-screen laying, to mention only a few, it proved the inherent adaptability of the design.

In Europe, A.A.F. A-20s flew a total of 39,492 sorties in which 28,443 tons (31,856 U.S. tons) of bombs were dropped. They destroyed eleven enemy aircraft in the air during these raids, and lost 265 of their number. The loss rate per sortie of 0.7 per cent was the same as for the B-26 Marauder in Europe, and 0.1 per cent more than that for the B-25 Mitchell. Adaptable, dependable, tractable, and potent, the DB-7 was perhaps overshadowed in its career by the more spectacular exploits which fell to the lot of other bombers, but it ranked high among the most brilliant combat aircraft designs evolved by the U.S. aircraft industry.

Douglas A-20G-20 to -45-DO Havoc

Dimensions:	Span, 61 ft. 4 in.; length, 48 ft. 0 in.; height, 17 ft. 7 in.; wing area, 465 sq. ft.
Armament:	Six 0.5-in. Colt-Browning machine guns in fixed nose positions with 350 r.p.g.; two 0.5 in. machine guns with 400 r.p.g. in Martin power-operated dorsal turret, and one 0.5-in. machine gun with 400 rounds in ventral tunnel. Maximum internal bomb load, 2,000 lb.; maximum external bomb load, 2,000 lb.
Power Plants:	Two Wright R-2600-23 Double Cyclone fourteen-cylinder radial air-cooled engines with two-speed superchargers and driving 11 ft. 3 in. diam. three-blade Hamilton Standard Hydromatic airscrews. Each rated at 1,600 h.p. for take-off (1,675 h.p. war emergency), 1,400 h.p. at 10,000 ft., and 1,275 h.p. continuous at 11,500 ft.
Weights:	Basic, 17,200 lb.; combat, 24,000 lb.; maximum flight manoeuvre, 27,000 lb.; war maximum (ferry purposes only), 30,000 lb.
Performance:	Maximum speed, 317 m.p.h. at 10,000 ft.; maximum continuous speed, 308 m.p.h. at 10,000 ft.; typical cruising speed, 230 m.p.h.; initial climb rate, 1,300 ft./min.; service ceiling, 25,000 ft.; range (with 2,000-lb. bomb load and 604 Imp. gal. fuel), 1,025 mls. at max. cruise power at 238 m.p.h.; take-off to clear 50 ft. obstacle, 1,417 yds.; landing distance from 50 ft., 1,250 yds.

The last production variant of the Havoc was the A-20K (below), 413 examples of which had been delivered when production of the aircraft was terminated in September 1944.

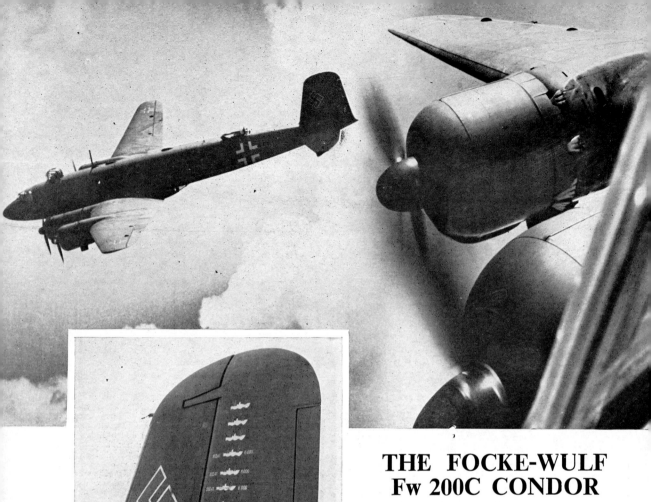

THE FOCKE-WULF
Fw 200C CONDOR

The Focke-Wulf Fw 200C Condor long-range reconnaissance bomber was purely an improvisation forced upon Germany by circumstances against which her leaders had gambled, but it was an amazingly successful improvisation. Little suited to its task, possessing a ponderous performance and extremely vulnerable to both anti-aircraft fire and aerial attack, the Condor had nothing more than a respectable endurance to commend it, yet, for some two years, it was regarded as the scourge of the Atlantic, sinking hundreds of thousands of tons of Allied shipping and giving Atlantic convoys a terrible mauling. For much of the Battle of the Atlantic, the Condor appeared ubiquitous, yet the actual number of Condors built was relatively small. Few though the Condors may have been, they demanded an inordinate effort on the part of the Allies before their menace was nullified.

The Condor was designed purely as a commercial transport, and its introduction as a combat aircraft was purely accidental. With Britain's declaration of war, the German High Command immediately realised the seriousness of its mistake in abandoning the long-range heavy bomber after the death of its leading German protagonist, the first Chief of Staff of the Luftwaffe, Lieutenant-General Wever. The need for an aircraft capable of harassing British shipping

The Fw 200C Condor, the notorious "Focke Wolf", as Winston Churchill referred to it, was the scourge of the Atlantic for a considerable period of the war, and responsible for the sinking of hundreds of thousands of tons of Allied shipping. The Condor demanded an inordinate effort from the Allies before its threat was nullified, and the first years of its operational career as a commerce raider were remarkably successful. Yet it was purely an improvisation forced upon the Luftwaffe by the lack of foresight of the German High Command.

far out in the Atlantic was obvious, and the only solution to their dilemma was to extemporize. The result was the adaptation of the Condor transport for long-range reconnaissance-bomber sorties.

The design of the Condor had been initiated by Prof. Dipl. Ing. Kurt Tank, the Technical Director of the Focke-Wulf Flugzeugbau, in the spring of 1936 as a 26-passenger commercial transport for the Deutsche Lufthansa (D.L.H.). Tank secured an official type number of his own choosing from the Reichsluftfahrtministerium (R.L.M.), the transport being designated Fw 200. This was a considerably higher type number than those being allocated to new designs at the time of the Condor's conception, but one which Tank believed to be easily remembered and ideally suited for publicity purposes.

The first prototype Condor, the Fw 200V1, later registered D-ACON and named "Brandenburg", was flown for the first time in July 1937 with Kurt Tank himself at the controls. It had been completed within twelve months and eleven days of the date that D.L.H. placed the development contract. Apart from some redesign of the tail surfaces, only minor modifications were called for as a result of initial flight tests, and two further prototypes had been flown by the following summer when planning commenced on a series of long-distance publicity flights.

The first of these flights, from Berlin to Cairo, was made on June 27, 1938, by the Fw 200V2 (D-AERE "Saarland") with one intermediate stop at Salonica, and a further long-distance flight took place on

The first operational version of the Condor was the Fw 200C-1 (illustrated at the top of the page) which was delivered to Kampfgeschwader 40 during the late months of 1940. During 1941, the two Condor-equipped Gruppen of K.G.40 became almost as serious a menace to Allied shipping as the U-boat. Later in the Condor's career it was fitted with FuG 200 Hohentwiel radar which, used in conjunction with a blind bombing procedure, enabled it to attack through cloud. The Hohentwiel array is illustrated immediately above. Some machines also had Rostock which had a wider search angle.

"Friesland") were delivered to D.L.H. for route-proving trials and crew training, and two were delivered to the R.L.M. for evaluation at the official test centre and subsequent use as staff transports. The first of these, the Fw 200V3 (D-2600), subsequently named "Immelmann III", was eventually modified for use as the official *Führermaschine*, and the second was used to transport members of Adolf Hitler's staff. The Führer's personal pilot, Hans Baur, spent several weeks at Focke-Wulf's Bremen factory familiarizing himself with the special Condor, the interior appointments of which had been given considerable thought. The apartment normally occupied by Hitler featured a large, armour-plated seat placed over an escape hatch and incorporating a parachute pack.

By this time, work had been initiated on more powerful versions of the Condor, the first of which was the Fw 200B. The Fw 200B-1 was powered by four BMW 132Dc engines each rated at 850 h.p. at 8,200 feet, and empty and loaded weights were increased from 21,560 lb. to 24,860 lb., and from 32,120 lb. to 38,500 lb. respectively. The Fw 200B-2 differed in having BMW 132H engines rated at 830 h.p. at 3,600 ft., and loaded weight was reduced to 37,400 lb. Two Fw 200B Condors were ordered by the Brazilian Sindicato Condor Limitada, with which D.L.H. co-operated closely, and these were delivered in August 1939.

The Japanese, always interested in aeronautical developments abroad, evinced a marked interest in the Condor, and on November 28, 1938, the Fw 200V1 took-off for Tokyo, stopping at Basta,

August 10, 1938, when the Fw 200V1 took-off for a non-stop flight from Berlin to New York, covering the 4,075 miles against strong headwinds in 24 hrs. 55 min., at an average speed of 164 m.p.h. The return journey was made in 19 hrs. 47 min., at an average speed of 205 m.p.h. over a slightly more southerly route. This impressive demonstration flight received considerable publicity, and Danish Air Lines (D.D.L.) placed an order for two Condors. These (OY-DAM and OY-DEM) were of the initial Fw 200A production model which, like the first prototypes, was powered by four BMW 132G-1 nine-cylinder radial air-cooled engines each rated at 720 h.p. and driving two-bladed controllable-pitch airscrews. The Fw 200A attained a maximum speed of 233 m.p.h. at sea level, and its normal range with a 6,380-lb. payload was 775 miles.

Apart from the two Condors delivered to D.D.L. all the first nine Condors were of the A-series and bore *Versuchs* (Experimental) numbers. The Fw 200V2 and five additional machines (D-AETA "Westfalen", D-ACVH "Grenzmark", D-AMHC "Nordmark", D-AXFO "Pommern" and D-ARHW

The Fw 200C differed from the B-model in several respects. It was appreciably strengthened structurally, twin-wheel main undercarriage members were adopted, and the engine nacelles were redesigned. The photo depicts an early Fw 200C-1.

The Fw 200B (right) transports unde construction for Japan and other countries were taken over by the Luftwaffe. Some Fw 200C-0 Condors were completed without the ventral tray or gondola, and operated as transports during the invasion of Norway (below right).

Karachi and Hanoi for refuelling, and arriving at the Japanese capital in slightly less than 48 hours of which 42 hrs. 18 min. were flying time. On the return flight, however, a fuel shortage resulted in the aircraft being ditched in shallow water off Manila. Nevertheless, the Condor's visit to Japan was to prove fortunate so far as the Luftwaffe was concerned. Apart from placing an order for five Fw 200B transports—which, in the event, were never to be delivered because of the start of the Second World War—the Japanese, impressed by the Condor's long range capabilities, were interested in an adaptation of the Condor for the long-range maritime reconnaissance role. This was the germ of the idea that was to give birth to the Luftwaffe's Fw 200C reconnaissance-bomber.

To meet Japanese requirements, the Focke-Wulf company began work on adapting the Fw 200B for maritime reconnaissance duties early in 1939, and the result was the Fw 200V10, destined to become the forerunner of the Fw 200C series of commerce raiders. Powered by four BMW 132H-1 engines, the Fw 200V10, which bore Werk-Nr. 0001, was essentially similar to the Fw 200B transport but had a single 7.9-mm. MG 15 machine gun in a dorsal turret mounted slightly forward of the wing trailing edge, and a short ventral gondola, offset to starboard under the forward fuselage and housing single hand-operated MG 15 machine guns firing fore and aft.

Much of the fuselage was occupied by fuel tanks, two vertical cameras were attached to the floor of the centre fuselage with the camera operator seated aft.

With Britain's declaration of war and the immediate need for a long-range aircraft for anti-shipping duties, it was decided that the Condor's airframe was the only one available remotely suitable for adaptation as an interim reconnaissance-bomber until Heinkel's He 177 became available in quantity. Germany's only other multi-engined transport, the Junkers Ju 90, was seriously underpowered already, and could not be immediately adapted for the military role, and therefore Focke-Wulf were instructed to commence work immediately on a suitable conversion.

As a four-engined transport carrying four crew members and twenty-six passengers, the Condor employed a relatively light structure totally unsuited for the military role now envisaged. The Japanese had been willing to accept the Fw 200B's structure as they envisaged using the aircraft solely for long-range

The Fw 200C-3, built in larger numbers than any other version of the Condor, embodied further structural strengthening and more powerful engines. Defensive armament was improved by the addition of lateral guns and a power-operated turret.

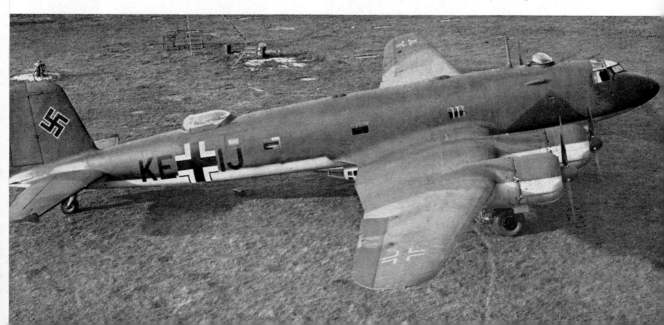

The Fw 200C-3/U2 was fitted with the Lotfe 7D bomb-sight which projected beneath the ventral gondola. A 7.9-mm. MG 15 machine gun was fitted in the nose of the gondola in place of the 20-mm. MG 151 cannon, the breach of which interfered with the bomb-sight's stowage.

reconnaissance missions at medium altitudes, but the R.L.M. demanded a commerce raider, and the basic structure therefore had to be extensively restressed. The modified Condor received the designation Fw 200C, and the construction of a batch of ten Fw 200C-0 pre-production aeroplanes began almost immediately. Power was provided by four BMW 132H-1 radials, and defensive armament comprised a hand-held 7.9-mm. MG 15 machine gun in a raised position aft of the flight deck firing forward, and a second MG 15 firing aft from a dorsal position enclosed by a sliding hood. It was proposed to fit a long ventral gondola which, offset to starboard like that of the Fw 200V10, was to house a prone bombardier's position, bomb sight and a 550-lb. bomb, and to support the greatly increased loaded weight, the main undercarriage members were fitted with paired wheels in place of the single wheels of the commercial transport. However, the pending invasion of Norway and the consequent demand for transport aircraft necessitated the hurried completion of the Fw 200C-0 Condors to participate in this campaign, and when delivered in the late spring of 1940, the majority of aircraft had not been fitted with the ventral gondola, and some lacked all defensive armament. Together with the Fw 200B transports which had been on the production line at the beginning of the war and had been taken over by the Luftwaffe, and the former D.L.H. Condors, these served in the transport role in April-May 1940.

Meanwhile, a production line had been laid down at Cottbus for the Fw 200C-1, deliveries of which commenced in the summer months, some twenty-five machines having been completed by the end of 1940. The Fw 200C-1 featured a semi-monocoque fuselage with an all-metal, two-spar wing built in three sections, metal covered to the rear spar, and fabric covered aft. Two-piece ailerons extended along two-thirds of the outer section trailing edges, and split flaps were mounted inboard of the ailerons. The Fw 200C-1 normally carried a crew of five comprising pilot, co-pilot, navigator/radio-operator/gunner, engineer/gunner and rear dorsal gunner, and defensive armament comprised a 7.9-mm. MG 15 machine gun in the forward dorsal position, an MG 15 in the rear dorsal position, a 20-mm. MG FF (Oerlikon) cannon in the nose of the ventral gondola, and an MG 15 in the rear of the gondola. The outboard engine nacelles were extended and fitted with racks to carry either a 550-lb. bomb or a 66 Imp.gal. auxiliary tank, two racks outboard of the engine nacelles each carried a 550-lb. bomb, and the ventral gondola could carry either a 550-lb. bomb or an armoured auxiliary fuel tank.

The first deliveries of the Fw 200C-1 were made to Kampfgeschwader 40 during the late months of 1940, and, after a brief period of working-up, the Condor began its relatively brief but certainly spectacular career as a commerce raider. During the months that followed, the two Condor-equipped Gruppen of K.G. 40 began to take an increasingly serious toll of Allied shipping, the inadequate anti-aircraft armament of the merchant ships, insufficient escort vessels, and an almost complete lack of long-range aircraft and escort carriers rendering their task a relatively simple one. Gruppe III based at Bordeaux-Mérignac patrolled far out into the Atlantic, while Gruppe I, based at Trondheim-Vaernes, reconnoitred beyond the Faroes, over the Irish Sea and down to the English Channel, wreaking havoc among the convoys and co-operating with U-boats under the operational control of Fliegerführer Atlantik.

The Fw 200C-1 was followed on the production line during 1941 by the Fw 200C-2 which had modified outboard engine nacelles, new faired bomb racks, and several internal modifications resulting from operational experience, but despite its operational successes, the Condor was suffering its full share of troubles which stemmed from its commercial transport heritage. Despite the fact that the military

Condor had undergone some structural strengthening, this soon proved inadequate to meet the strain of continuous operational flying at low altitudes for long periods, and the violent manoeuvres that were sometimes called for when taking evasive action. There were numerous instances of the rear spar failing and the fuselage breaking its back immediately aft of the wing on landing. These failures resulted in the hasty introduction of the Fw200C-3 during the summer of 1941, fifty-eight Condors being delivered during the course of that year. Despite the fact that the Fw 200C-3 embodied major structural strengthening of both the rear spar and the fuselage, the Condor continued to suffer structural failures, and the Focke-Wulf concern never succeeded in entirely solving the problem.

In order to maintain the performance of the Condor despite the increased structural weight, the Fw 200C-3 received four BMW-Bramo 323R-2 nine-cylinder radial air-cooled engines with methanol-water injection which offered 1,200 h.p. at 2,600 r.p.m. for take-off and emergency. Loaded weight had risen to 46,297 lb., an additional crew member was carried, and maximum bomb load was increased to 4,620 lb. (one 1,100-lb. bomb under each out-

Throughout its career the Fw 200C suffered from failures of the rear spar and rear fuselage, despite continual structural strengthening. The Fw 200C-3 in the upper photo has had a rear spar failure during take-off, and that in the photograph immediately above has broken its back.

board engine nacelle, one 550-lb. bomb on each of the two under-wing racks, and twelve 110-lb. bombs in the ventral gondola). A low-drag Fw 19 turret housing one 7.9-mm. MG 15 machine gun replaced the raised fairing immediately aft of the flight deck, and two MG 15 beam guns were mounted behind panels in the fuselage sides. As the Fw 200C-3 was intended primarily for low-altitude attack, its bombardier had to rely on a Revi sight for his bombing. The Fw 200C-3/U1 differed in having a 20-mm. MG 151 cannon in place of the old MG FF in the ventral gondola, and a large hydraulically-operated turret housing a 15-mm. MG 151 cannon in the forward dorsal position. This turret took some 20 m.p.h. off the Condor's maximum speed but the cannon was considered to be a very much more effective defensive weapon that the MG 15.

The Fw 200C-3/U2 reverted to the Fw 19 forward dorsal turret, and was fitted with the Lotfe 7D bombsight. This necessitated the installation of a 7.9-mm. MG 15 machine gun in the nose of the ventral gondola as the breach of the MG 151 cannon interfered with the Lotfe 7D's stowage. Increasingly effective Allied anti-aircraft defence was rendering the low-level attacks of the Condor's heyday extremely

hazardous, and the most satisfactory bombing altitude for the Lotfe 7D was 11,500-13,000 feet. The Fw 200C-3/U3 had an EDL 131 turret containing one 13-mm. MG 131 heavy machine gun in the forward dorsal, while the Fw 200C-3/U4 reverted to the Fw 19 forward dorsal turret but had MG 131 beam guns. The last-mentioned variant carried a crew of seven, had increased fuel capacity, and had a loaded weight of 50,045 lb.

Production of the Fw 200C-3 gave place to the C-4 early in 1942, this model being manufactured in greater quantities than any other version of the Condor. The C-3 and C-4 were basically the same aircraft, the principle differences being those associated with search radar and new radio equipment. Early production Fw 200C-4 Condors were fitted with FuG *Rostock* shipping search radar, but later machines standardised on FuG 200 *Hohentwiel* which was used in conjunction with a blind bombing procedure. Some machines were fitted with both *Rostock* and *Hohentwiel*, the double installation being necessitated by the fact that the former, although having a wider search angle and a greater range than the latter, would not give readings at a range of less than three miles and was therefore unsuitable for

Several special high-speed transport versions of the Fw 200C Condor were built for use by Germany's wartime leaders. The transport version above (Werk.Nr. 138) was the Fw 200C-4/U2, and that illustrated on the left (Werk. Nr. 137) was the Fw 200C-4/U1. The abbreviated ventral gondola is noteworthy.

connections to the engines being on the underside of the aircraft, it was extremely vulnerable to light anti-aircraft fire. The port outer engine drove the generator for the hydraulically-operated dorsal MG 151 turret and, in the event of hydraulic damage, it was extremely difficult to operate the turret by hand against a fast-moving opponent.

With the appearance of the very-long-range Liberators of R.A.F. Coastal Command, effectively closing the Atlantic Gap, Condor pilots received orders not to initiate any attack but to seek cloud cover when attacked, only offering fight if absolutely necessary. Furthermore, Condor crews had orders to return to base immediately in the event of the slightest damage rather than jeopardise the safety of a valuable aircraft, production of the Condor barely keeping pace with K.G. 40's demands. Only eighty-four Condors were produced in 1942, some of these aircraft being diverted for special transport purposes, and immediately an aircraft came off the line at Cottbus, a crew was sent specially from K.G. 40 to collect the new aircraft.

As the danger of interception by long-range patrolling Beaufighters and Mosquitos increased, the most northerly point to which Biscay-based Condors flew was 40° N, there thus being no longer any link between the Biscay area and northern waters patrolled by the Norwegian-based Condors. There were two main areas of armed reconnaissance patrol operated by Condors flying from Bordeaux-Mérignac and Cognac; one, known as the Kleine Aufklärung, or small reconnaissance, and the other known as the Grosse Aufklärung, or large reconnaissance. The dividing line between the two reconnaissance areas was approximately 45°, the smaller extending to the limit already mentioned, and the large to approximately 34° N. The westerly limit of both areas was normally 19° N, although, on special reconnaissances, Condors reached as far as 25° W. When approaching the northerly reconnaissance area, the Condors normally flew in formation at sea level for mutual protection, breaking up and proceeding singly on

blind bombing.

The 15-mm. MG 151 forward dorsal turret introduced by the Fw 200C-3/U1 was also fitted to the Fw 200C-4, and either a 20-mm. MG 151 cannon or a 13-mm. MG 131 machine gun was fitted in the nose of the ventral gondola according to the installation of the Lotfe bomb sight. The rated altitude of the Fw 200C-4 was 15,750 feet at which maximum speed was 205 m.p.h. as compared with 224 m.p.h. at the same altitude for the Fw 200C-3. At sea level, the average cruising speed was 150-168 m.p.h., with a maximum speed of 174 m.p.h. Service ceiling was 19,000 feet but at this altitude the airframe was subject to violent vibration. The basic tankage of 1,773 Imp.gal. gave a normal endurance of fourteen hours at economical cruising speed with normal safety reserves. An additional 220 Imp.gal. could be carried in an armoured tank in the ventral gondola, a 66 Imp.gal. auxiliary tank could be carried under each outboard engine nacelle, and sometimes two or three 66 Imp. gal. drums were carried to refill the fuselage tanks, thus extending the maximum endurance to some eighteen hours.

The Condor was extremely vulnerable to both anti-aircraft fire and aerial attack, and with the provision of more anti-aircraft armament on merchant ships and the introduction of CAM-ships (Catapult Air-craft Merchantmen) with their specially-strengthened Hurricane fighters, the Allies began to take the measure of the Condor. Only the first pilot of the Condor enjoyed any armour protection and, all fuel their shipping search at 11° W. Sometimes Condors *en route* for this area had to make a detour as far south as Cap Ortegal to avoid patrolling fighters. One method of shipping search frequently adopted was known as the *Facher* (Fan). A typical *Facher* search in a southerly direction starting from 15° W was to fly due West for 3°, due South for thirty miles, due East for 3°, due South for thirty miles, and so on until the allotted area had been covered.

During the early months of 1943, Condor activity fell sharply for the 2nd Staffel of Gruppe I, based at Trondheim-Vaernes, was the only unit still operating over the Atlantic, the remainder of the staffeln of Gruppe I and those of Gruppe III being scattered on various urgent transport assignments. In January 1943, the 1st and 3rd Staffeln were sent to the Russian Front where, based at Stalino, they formed a special transport unit for ferrying supplies into Stalingrad. This unit was known as the Sonder-Unternehmung Stalingrad, and received the designation K.G.z.b.V. 200. Initially, the Condors were landing supplies on an airfield in the vicinity of Stalingrad, but as the German perimeter shrank they were forced to drop supplies by parachute, each aircraft having four supply containers attached to its bomb racks. On January 18th, the Condors were transferred to Zaparozhe from where they continued their supply-dropping activities for a month before it was decided that this transport undertaking was proving too costly. For five days the Condors then confined their activities to bombing railway communications in the Stalingrad area, after which they were recalled to Staaken.

At Staaken the survivors of K.G. 40's 1st and 3rd Staffeln were amalgamated into one staffel, their aircraft were fitted with the Lotfe 7D bomb-sight and the unit was transferred to Cognac to be absorbed by Gruppe III as the 8th Staffel, and resume activities over the Bay of Biscay. In the meantime, the 7th and 9th Staffeln of Gruppe III, which had been undertaking transport tasks in Italy, had also returned to France, and once again the Condor began to appear in numbers.

The Condors now discontinued their previous practice of flying routine reconnaissance in search of shipping targets, these duties being taken over by the Junkers Ju 290A-5s of F.A.G. 5 based at Mont de Marsan. The Condors of III/K.G. 40, together with the He 177As of II/K.G. 40, and the 1st and 3rd Staffeln of I/K.G. 40 (the 2nd Staffel based at Trondheim-Vaernes being the only component of Gruppe I still equipped with the Condor), were now solely concerned with shipping attack, being sent out only when a definite target had been sighted and its position reported by the aircraft of F.A.G. 5.

The departures of Allied convoys from Gibraltar were regularly reported from Spain, and the time of arrival of the convoy in K.G. 40's sphere of operations could therefore be calculated, it only remained for the reconnaissance aircraft to establish their exact position as well as weather conditions before the Condors and He 177s took-off. The only exception to this new policy was when the total effort of all aircraft in the Biscay area was ordered by the Fliegerführer Atlantik, such as when German blockade runners were attempting to make port. On these occasions, the Condors reverted to armed reconnaissance to report the presence of any Allied warships in the area. When Allied shipping was reported, a minimum of four Condors would take-off to attack, the aircraft usually flying at sea level in line abreast in close formation to a point such as Cap Ortegal where they would fan out and fly on parallel courses at intervals of twenty-five to thirty miles. Each aircraft would periodically climb to 1,500 feet in a wide circle while making a search with its *Hohentwiel*, after which the original course was resumed. The first Condor to sight the shipping would then make R/T contact with the other aircraft. Low-level attack in conditions of clear visibility was expressly forbidden, a minimum attacking altitude of 9,000 feet being prescribed.

Some Fw 200C-3s were modified to carry two Henschel Hs 293 radio-controlled rocket-propelled bombs under the outboard engine nacelles, the wing bomb rack being removed. Condors so modified were designated Fw 200C-6, and the Hs 293 was carried operationally for the first time on December 28, 1943, when one of four Condors flying on a *Facher* search for British naval units carried two of these missiles experimentally. The Hs 293-equipped Condor encountered a patrolling Sunderland before it could make contact with the British ships, however, and was forced to ditch with the missiles still on their racks. Most of the last production variant, the Fw 200C-8, were built as He 293 carriers, but this missile was not used on a large scale by the Condor, production of which had already begun to taper off in 1943 when only seventy-six new machines were delivered, and terminated completely at the beginning of 1944 with a further eight aircraft.

By mid-1943, the He 177A was beginning to take over the roles previously performed by the Condor which, not inappropriately, was being employed increasingly for the purpose for which it had been originally designed—that of transportation. Several Fw 200C-3s had been converted for use as the personal transports of Germany's leaders, machines of this type were used on several occasions by the notorious Gruppe I of Kampfgeschwader 200 for dropping agents and saboteurs, and one special all-black Fw 200C-3 was also used for this purpose by the 9th Staffel of K.G. 40. In 1942, two special transport variants of the Condor were produced. These were the 137th and 138th production machines and were designated Fw 200C-4/U1 and U2 respectively. To reduce drag, an Fw 19 turret containing a single MG 15 machine gun was fitted in the forward

The final production version of the Condor was the Fw 200C-8. The C-8 illustrated above (Werk.Nr. 256) was the standard model with Hohentwiel radar and turreted MG 151 cannon. The aircraft illustrated below, an Fw 200C-8/U10 (Werk.Nr. 259), has the deeper outboard engine nacelles and extended ventral gondola of the Henschel Hs 293 carrier.

dorsal position, a generally similar Fw 20 turret also containing a single MG 15 was mounted in the aft dorsal position, and an abbreviated and re-designed ventral gondola mounted single MG 15s fore and aft. The Fw 200C-4/U1 and U2 differed solely in seating arrangements, the former providing accommodation for eleven passengers and the latter for fourteen, and they were appreciably faster than the standard Fw 200C-4 Condors.

The last known wartime flight of a Condor was made, perhaps surprisingly, by one of Deutsche Lufthansa's original machines. These had been handed back to D.L.H. by the Luftwaffe after the Norwegian campaign, and on the evening of April 21, 1945, one was hastily loaded with the luggage of the Berlin Headquarters Staff, the pilot, Flugkapitän Künstle, planning to fly to Barcelona via Munich. The Condor reached Munich and took-off again, heavily loaded, the pilot confident that he was un-likely to encounter Allied aircraft because of the prevailing bad weather. That was the last time the Condor was ever seen. Enquiries in Germany, Switzerland and Spain continued for years, but it was not until ten years after the end of the war that the mystery was solved when evidence was found near Munich that the plane had crashed and burned out with no survivors shortly after taking-off.

As a warplane the Condor was not a particularly brilliant aircraft, yet it established a formidable reputation. In view of the surprisingly small number of Condors built, this aircraft cost the Allies dear. For a time, co-operating with the U-boat packs, it posed one of the major threats to Britain's survival, and even though its threat had been largely nullified by the third year of the war, the Condor will always be remembered as the "Scourge of the Atlantic".

Focke-Wulf Fw 200C-3/U4 Condor

Dimensions:	Span, 107 ft. 9½ in.; length, 76 ft. 11½ in.; height, 20 ft. 8 in.; wing area, 1,290 sq. ft.
Armament:	One 7.9-mm. MG 15 machine gun in Fw 19 forward dorsal turret with 1,000 rounds; one hand-operated 13-mm. MG 131 machine gun with 500 rounds in aft dorsal position; two 13-mm. MG 131 machine guns with 300 r.p.g. under beam hatches; one 20-mm. MG 151 with 500 rounds in forward ventral position, and one 7.9-mm. MG 15 machine gun with 1,000 rounds in aft ventral position. Maximum bomb load, 4,620 lb. (comprising one 1,100-lb. bomb under each outboard engine nacelle, one 550-lb. bomb on each of the two underwing racks, and twelve 110-lb. bombs in the ventral gondola).
Power Plants:	Four BMW-Bramo 323R-2 Fafnir nine-cylinder radial air-cooled engines rated at 1,200 h.p. at 2,600 r.p.m. for take-off and emergency with methanol-water injection, 1,000 h.p. at 2,500 r.p.m. at sea level, and 940 h.p. at 2,500 r.p.m. at 13,120 ft.
Weights:	Maximum loaded weight, 50,045 lb.; landing weight, 38,800 lb.
Performance:	Maximum speed, 224 m.p.h. at 15,750 ft., 190 m.p.h. at sea level; maximum cruising speed, 208 m.p.h. at 13,120 ft., 172 m.p.h. at sea level; economical cruising speed, 158 m.p.h.; service ceiling, 19,000 ft.; endurance (with 1,773 Imp. gal. of fuel) at economical cruising speed, 14 hrs., (with 2,190 Imp. gal. fuel), 17 hrs. 30 mins.; normal range, 2,210 mls.

THE HANDLEY PAGE HALIFAX

"From Hull, Hell and Halifax, good Lord deliver us". This quotation from an old Yorkshire prayer was used by Lord Halifax in a speech before the christening ceremony for the second of Britain's wartime "heavies", the Handley Page Halifax, and Germany had ample reason to echo the latter part of that sentiment in the years that followed. No less than four out of every ten heavy bombers built in the United Kingdom during the Second World War were Halifaxes, and these shared with the Avro Lancaster the major night-bombing offensive, which, from small beginnings in 1941, built up to its tremendous crescendo in 1944. The latest in a continuous line of Handley Page bombers which had formed the backbone of the Royal Air Force's striking power since the time of that service's inception, the Halifax was not as shapely an aircraft as its Avro contemporary, but its deeper, more capacious, slab-sided fuselage rendered it suitable for a wider variety of roles, and unlike the Lancaster which was used almost ex-

clusively as a bomber during the war years, the Halifax achieved an enviable reputation as a freighter personnel transport, ambulance, glider tug, and maritime reconnaissance aircraft.

Almost since the earliest days of flying the name of Handley Page had been associated with bombers. Indeed, one was almost synonymous with the other, and it was to be expected that when, in 1936, the Air Staff outlined its requirements for a new generation of R.A.F. bombers, Handley Page would be among the companies to receive development contracts. The beginnings of the Halifax reached back further than this, however, for its starting point was to be found in the H.P.55, a projected bomber to meet the requirements of specification B.1/35. The H.P.55 design was tendered with two Bristol Hercules H.E.1SM air-cooled radials, and alternative layouts were studied with Rolls-Royce Merlin and Rolls-Royce Vulture liquid-cooled power plants, but the contract was given to a Vickers-Armstrongs design

Halifax Mk.I L9485 was employed for tests with dorsal and ventral turrets, the latter being adopted for the Halifax II.

which, developed in parallel with the Wellington, was eventually to emerge as the Warwick. A year later, a new specification was issued, P.13/36, calling for a Vulture-powered medium bomber with a greater bomb load and range than had been specified for B.1/35, and from the H.P.55, Handley Page's design team, headed by G. R. Volkert, evolved the H.P.56.

Both Handley Page and A. V. Roe (for the Type 679 Manchester) were awarded contracts for two prototypes, and both types were to be powered by a pair of Rolls-Royce Vulture twenty-four cylinder X-type engines. The order was placed in April 1937, and construction of the two H.P.56 prototypes, which were allocated the serial numbers L7244 and L7245, was put in hand immediately. At this stage, the H.P.56 had a design gross weight of 26,300 lb. Within a few months of the initiation of design work, however, Handley Page learned that production of the Vulture, which was suffering rather more than its share of teething troubles, was likely to be curtailed, and such an event would mean, of course, that the H.P.56 would not be ordered in production quantities. With official encouragement, G. R. Volkert immediately set about redesigning his bomber to take four Rolls-Royce Merlins as none of the other big engines at that time under development seemed likely to be ready soon enough to replace the

Vulture in a twin-engined layout. The redesign was, not unexpectedly, an extensive one, and although the wing and fuselage contours remained relatively unchanged, the size of the aeroplane grew appreciably, and the weight increased to a basic 40,000 lb.

On September 3, 1937, an official contract was issued to cover the construction of two prototypes of the H.P.57, as the redesigned aircraft was known, this contract replacing that previously issued for the H.P.56. The bomber was still required to meet the demands of specification P.13/36, and the serial numbers originally allocated were retained for the two prototypes. Construction began at Handley Page's Cricklewood plant in January 1938, and the first prototype (L7244) was transported to R.A.F. Station, Bicester, in the autumn of 1939 for final assembly. At Bicester, it was flown for the first time on October 25, 1939, with the company's chief test pilot, Major J. L. B. H. Cordes, at the controls. As first flown, the aircraft was powered by four Merlin X engines each rated at 1,075 h.p. for take-off and 1,130 h.p. at 5,250 ft., and driving de Havilland three-blade metal airscrews. Although the design provided for power-driven nose and tail turrets, and beam gun stations, these were not fitted for the initial trials, their positions being covered by metal fairings. Like the earlier Hampden, the prototype was fitted with

This early production Halifax I (L9515) was subsequently converted to serve as the prototype Halifax II Series IA. It tested the low-drag Boulton Paul four-gun turret and, at one stage in its career, featured extended inboard engine nacelles.

The Halifax II tended to spin uncontrollably when fully loaded, and the dorsal turret introduced on this version contributed considerably to drag. The machine illustrated (W1245) belonged to No. 233 Squadron.

automatic leading-edge slots as well as slotted flaps, the combination giving a higher lift coefficient than flaps alone, but an Air Ministry requirement for barrage balloon cable cutters in the wing leading edges necessitated the subsequent deletion of the slots. The design overload weight had now risen to 50,000 lb., and the second prototype (L7245) flew at this weight on August 17, 1940.

In the meantime, the bomber, which had already been allotted the name Halifax, had been ordered into production. Following the redesign of the original H.P.56, a production specification, 32/37, had been drawn up to cover the H.P.57, and Handley Page had been instructed to proceed with preparations for quantity manufacture, although the first contract—for one hundred aircraft—was not, in fact, formally confirmed until January 1939, despite the fact that in the previous October the Air Staff was already talking about having five hundred Halifaxes in service by April 1942—clearly somewhat optimistic but indicative of the importance already being attached to the new bomber at that early date.

The first production Halifax (L9485) flew on October 11, 1940. Powered by four Merlin X engines, it had a tare weight of 33,860 lb. and a maximum

take-off weight of 55,000 lb. Boulton Paul power-operated turrets in the nose and tail housed two and four 0.303-in. Browning machine guns respectively, Rotol constant-speed compressed-wood airscrews replaced the metal de Havilland units of the prototypes, and, for simplicity, the retractable tailwheel was replaced by one of fixed type. Maximum speed was 265 m.p.h. at 17,500 ft., initial climb rate was 750 ft./min., service ceiling was 22,800 ft., normal range with 2,242 Imp.gal. of fuel and a 5,800-lb. bomb load was 1,860 mls. From the production viewpoint, one of the Halifax's most interesting features was the method of split assembly by which it was built, this possessing the virtues of making possible the employment of more personnel in each stage of the aircraft's construction, and dividing the bomber into pieces for transportation and repair.

The initial production batch were designated Halifax B. Mk. I Series I, followed by the Series II stressed to operate at weights up to 60,000 lb., and the Series III in which the normal fuel capacity was increased from 1,392 to 1,636 Imp.gal., and the maximum fuel capacity from 2,242 to 2,326 Imp.gal. Some early machines were fitted with beam guns, and some late Series III aircraft had Merlin XX engines

The first result of the programme of divesting the bomber of its many drag-producing excrescences was the Halifax II Series I which had a "Z" fairing and, on some machines such as W7776 illustrated, the dorsal turret was removed.

which offered 1,280 h.p. for take-off and 1,480 h.p. at 6,800 ft.

All Halifax B.Mk.I production was handled by Handley Page at their Cricklewood and Radlett factories, but as part of the rearmament programme established shortly before the war, the Halifax was made the subject of a group production effort of a unique kind. Four separate assembly lines were established for the Halifax in addition to those laid down by the parent company. The first company involved in the Halifax group was English Electric, who had previously re-entered the aircraft industry to produce the Hampden. English Electric were asked to collaborate in Halifax production early in 1939, and on February 22 of that year received instructions to proceed with planning and the training of personnel for the production of one hundred Halifaxes, the first of which (V9976) was destined to fly on August 15, 1941. Next came the London Aircraft Production Group, made up of Chrysler Motors (making the rear fuselages): Duplex Bodies and Motors (forward fuselage shell and components); Express Motor and Body Works (inner wing sections); Park Royal Coachwork (outer wing sections), and the London Passenger Transport Board Works, the latter making a considerable amount of the equipment and fittings, and being responsible for the final erection and testing, at Leavesden. The first Halifax built by this group flew late in 1941. At a Stockport factory taken over for the purpose, Fairey Aviation also built Halifaxes, while Rootes Securities built others at Speke.

The R.A.F. gained its first acquaintance with the Halifax in November 1940, when the first prototype (L7244) was sent to No. 35 Squadron at Leeming for preliminary familiarisation—this machine, incidentally, ended its career in November 1941 in a crash at Boscombe Down. In December 1940, No. 35 Squadron moved to Linton-on-Ouse, and there received its operational aircraft—B.Mk.I Series Is. After a brief period of working-up, the squadron took its Halifaxes into operation for the first time on the night of March 10, 1941, when six of its aircraft (from the first twelve production machines) made a sortie against Le Havre, and two nights later, these aircraft gained the distinction of being the first R.A.F. four-engined bombers to drop bombs on Germany with an attack on Hamburg. Some three months later, on June 30, 1941, the Halifax operated for the first time by day, raiding Kiel, and in July they attacked the battlecruiser *Scharnhorst* at La Pallice.

Throughout the remainder of 1941, Halifaxes continued to operate by both day and night, frequently attacking the battlecruisers *Scharnhorst* and *Gneisenau* but, with its comparatively meagre armament, the Halifax was not entirely suited for daylight operations from which increasing losses as German fighter defences were strengthened resulted in their withdrawal at the end of 1941. Steps were already being taken to improve the defensive armament of the Halifax, however, one rather dubious scheme (the H.P.58) being a four-cannon installation in the fuselage. This project did not proceed beyond the mock-up stage as operational experience had indicated the desirability of a power-operated dorsal turret. The opportunity provided by the introduction of a new version of the Halifax, the B.Mk.II, was taken to introduce a bulbous Boulton Paul twin-gun turret similar to that installed on the Lockheed Hudson. Like late production B.Mk.I Series III aircraft, the Halifax B.Mk.II Series I was powered by four Merlin XXs and, later, Merlin 22s. The gross weight was held at 60,000 lb., and the fuel capacity was increased—normal tankage being raised to 1,882 Imp.gal. and maximum tankage to 2,572 Imp.gal.

The prototype Halifax II (L9515) was a converted Mk.I, and was first flown on July 3, 1941. On September 12, Lady Halifax undertook the official naming ceremony at Radlett, the subject aircraft being the last production Mk.I (L9608). The first production Mk.II (L9609) flew in the same month, and this was the version built initially by all the other assembly lines in the Halifax production group. The development and service introduction of the Halifax had not been without its troubles, however, for the bomber had always been slightly underpowered, and the appreciable increases in loaded weight since the basic design was frozen began to tell. The higher weights combined with the drag of the new dorsal turret seriously affected performance. When fully loaded the aircraft developed a tendency to spin uncontrollably, and losses began to grow alarmingly. A programme of divesting the Halifax of many of its drag-producing excrescences was started, and in the process many of what had previously been characteristic features of the bomber were shed.

The programme was initiated by taking a standard Halifax II (R9534) and stripping it of all equipment, replacing only essentials. It had been found on operations that head-on attacks by fighters rarely occurred, rendering the power-operated nose turret a dispensable luxury, and this was therefore removed, being replaced by a streamlined Perspex fairing, the protruding bombardier's "chin" giving place to an optically-flat panel in the symmetrical nose. A single hand-operated Vickers "K" gun on a gimbal mounting was fitted for the use of the bombardier, rather more as a gesture than a serious form of defence. A new Boulton-Paul power-operated turret of shallower type was mounted snugly on top of the fuselage, housing four 0.303-in. Brownings and offering negligible drag as compared with the two-gun turret that it replaced, and much internal equipment was omitted altogether. The tailwheel was made semi-retractable; the radio mast was eliminated, the aerial being attached to the D/F loop, and with all these modifications, the aircraft went into production as the Halifax B.Mk.II Series IA. Rolls Royce Merlin 22 or 24 engines were standard, the former offering 1,280 h.p. for take-off and 1,480 h.p. at 2,250 ft., and the latter giving 1,620 h.p. for take-off and 1,500 h.p. at 9,500 ft., and these were fitted with Morris block-

The Halifax II Series IA of No. 35 "Madras Presidency" Squadron illustrated above features the rectangular fins which were introduced to cure the rudder stalling experienced under certain conditions with the original triangular fin. The earlier fin is seen fitted to Halifax II Series IA HR679 (right).

type radiators, which permitted a reduction in the engine nacelle cross-section, in lieu of the Gallay circular-type radiators. Other changes included the provision of a shallower astro-dome, the removal of the underwing fuel jettison pipes and the cylindrical asbestos shrouds around the exhausts, and the sealing of the gap at the elevator spar and the fuselage at the rear bulkhead. The bomb-bay doors were modified to permit the carriage of larger bombs, and the overall length was increased from 70 ft. 1 in. to 71 ft. 7 in. The net gain resulting from these extensive changes was approximately ten per cent in both maximum and cruising speeds.

Before the Halifax B.Mk.II Series IA had reached the squadrons, an interim scheme had been introduced. Firstly, the nose turret was removed and replaced by what became known as a "Z" fairing on some squadron aircraft—a few new aircraft also left the factories with this nose fairing prior to the availability of the new Series IA moulded plastic nose —and these were known as B.Mk.II Series I (Special). The cumbersome two-gun dorsal turret was also removed from some aircraft to reduce drag, together with the exhaust shrouds, and the fuel jettison pipes which had projected from the trailing edge of each wing, and these aircraft joined operations with the four-gun Boulton Paul tail turret as their sole defensive armament. Later, some B.Mk.II Series I (Special) Halifaxes had the low-drag, four-gun Boulton Paul dorsal turret fitted.

At this period in the Halifax's development the bomber suffered a series of unexplained crashes in which the aircraft got into an inverted dive. Attempts on the part of Aircraft and Armament Experimental Establishment pilots to simulate the conditions under which the crashes had occurred failed to produce the desired effect. Finally, after a prolonged and worrying period of testing it was ascertained that the trouble was resulting from rudder stalling. Under certain conditions the triangular fin stalled and turbulent air passing through the gap between fin and rudder locked the latter hard over. New

rectangular fins were designed to rectify this trouble, and these were introduced as a retrospective modification during 1943.

In service, the Halifax B.II had been performing valuable work throughout 1942, and recorded several notable "firsts". Halifax B.II V9977 was the first aircraft to be equipped with the H2S radar bombing aid with the ventral radome—which was to become such a familiar sight as the war progressed—flying with this on March 27, 1942. One Halifax (W7650) flew with a ventral turret, and another (V9985) was employed for dropping trials with dummy 4,000-lb. "Block Buster" bombs. One B.Mk.II Series IA aircraft was converted by Rolls-Royce to take Merlin 65s in low mountings as the B.Mk.II Series II (HR756). The engines were fitted with four-blade airscrews, and the aircraft was subsequently employed for Merlin development flying. The Series II aircraft was part of a development programme for the Halifax IV, this mark number having been reserved for an extensively modified variant, the H.P.60A. This stemmed from Handley Page's tender, in 1939, of a Halifax derivative to meet specification B.1/39. Features of this design included a new fuselage floor, enlarged bomb-bay, and Merlin 65 engines. This development was eventually abandoned, as were plans to build a Pobjoy Niagara-powered flying scale model, but certain features of the Halifax IV design, including lengthened inner nacelles, were flown on a Halifax I (L9515) and two Halifax IIs (HR679 and HR756).

After the H2S radome had become a standard production line fitting, considerable shortages of H2S equipment manifested themselves, and, not infrequently, a 0.5-in. machine gun was mounted in the scanner fairing. Another production shortage— of British Messier undercarriages—produced the H.P.63 Halifax B.Mk.V which differed from the B.Mk.II only in having a Dowty levered suspension undercarriage. This was first flown on a Mk.I

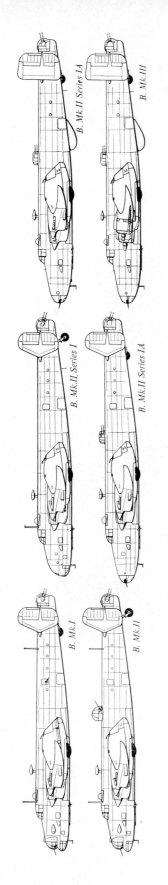

B. Mk.II Series 1A

B. Mk.III

B. Mk.II Series 1

B. Mk.II Series 1A

B. Mk.I

B. Mk.II

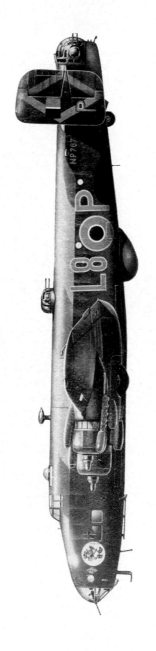

Handley Page Halifax B.VI

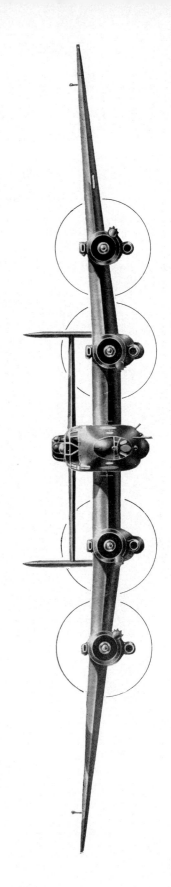

88

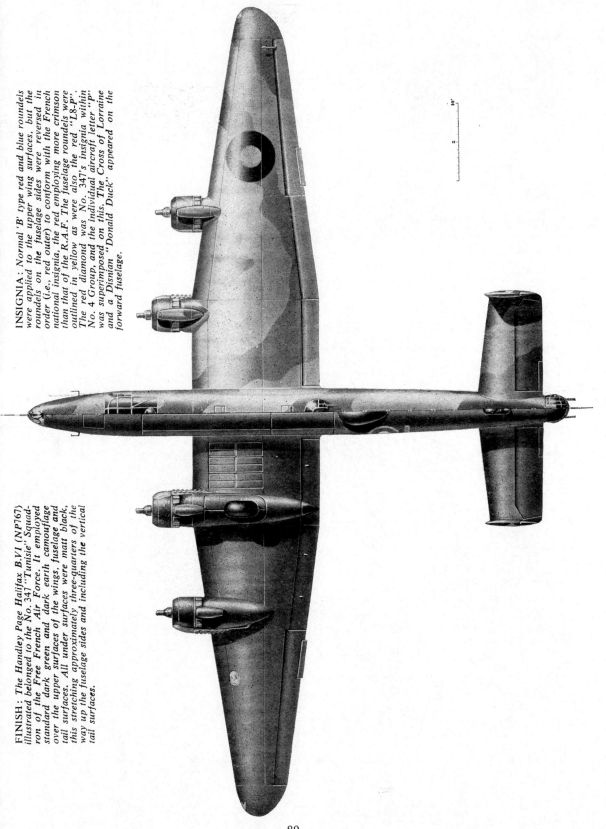

FINISH: The Handley Page Halifax B.VI (NP767) illustrated belonged to the No. 347 "Tunisie" Squadron of the Free French Air Force. It employed standard dark green and dark earth camouflage over the upper surfaces of the wings, fuselage and tail surfaces. All under surfaces were matt black, this stretching approximately three-quarters of the way up the fuselage sides and including the vertical tail surfaces.

INSIGNIA: Normal 'B' type red and blue roundels were applied to the upper wing surfaces, but the roundels on the fuselage sides were reversed in order (i.e., red outer) to conform with the French national insignia, the red employing more crimson than that of the R.A.F. The fuselage roundels were outlined in yellow as were also the "L8-P". The red diamond was No. 347's insignia within No. 4 Group, and the individual aircraft letter "P" was superimposed on this. The Cross of Lorraine and a Disnian "Donald Duck" appeared on the forward fuselage.

(Above) The Halifax II Series IA prototype (L9515) with extended inboard engine nacelles.

Some Halifax IIs were fitted with four-blade airscrews as seen on this G.R.II Series IA (JD376).

Features for the proposed Halifax IV (H.P.60A), such as lower engine thrust lines and extended inner engine nacelles, were tested on this Mk.II Series IA (HR756).

(L9520), and production Mk.Vs were built by Rootes and Fairey. The B.Mk.V Series I (Special) and Series IA corresponded to the Mk.II variants. The majority of the Halifax Vs were supplied to the squadrons of No. 6 (R.C.A.F.) Group, No. 427 Squadron based at Middleton St. George being the first unit to re-equip with these (B.Mk.V Series I (Special) being delivered early in May 1943). In the Battle of the Ruhr, from March to July 1943, Halifax IIs of No. 4 Group made no less than 2,339 sorties for the loss of 138 machines.

In 1942, Handley Page's "hack" Halifax II (R9534) was fitted with 1,615 h.p. Bristol Hercules VI air-cooled radial engines, and the company designation H.P.61 and the official designation B.Mk.III were reserved for a possible production variant employing these engines. The extra power afforded by the Hercules power plants offered significant advantages to the Halifax, and the decision was taken to place the B.Mk.III variant in production. The first production Halifax III (HX227) made its first flight on August 29, 1943, and this, and the next few production machines, were used for development purposes at the A. and A.E.E. at Boscombe Down and elsewhere. The extra power afforded by the Hercules restored the Halifax's performance, and permitted a maximum all-up weight of 65,000 lb., although much of the additional weight was absorbed by the extra fuel required for the radials, total fuel capacity being boosted to 2,688 Imp.gal. Hercules VI or XVI engines driving de Havilland hydromatic airscrews were fitted, and during production the wing span was increased from 98 ft. 10 in. to 104 ft. 2 in., the increase in wing area improving the operational ceiling.

The service début of the Halifax III in February 1944 reinstated the Handley Page bomber as a fully-operational type, for five months previously, the Halifax IIs had been relegated to less hazardous targets owing to a steep rise in the losses sustained, mostly as a result of enemy fighters which found the Halifaxes easy prey as they laboured along at moderate altitudes. The Halifax III played a prominent part in the attacks on the V-1 missile sites during 1944, and returned to daylight operations after the Allied landings in France on D-Day, attacking French marshalling yards, gun emplacements, strong points and troop concentrations. In June 1944, Halifaxes of a single Group—No. 4—set a Bomber Command record by shooting down thirty-three enemy fighters while operating over Europe. The Halifax III displayed an ability to absorb considerable battle damage for, a little earlier, in March 1944, Pilot Officer C. J. Barton of No. 578 Squadron had become the only Halifax captain to be awarded the Victoria Cross (posthumously) for his great gallantry in bringing home a crippled aircraft after a raid on Nuremberg, and there were many examples of Halifax IIIs sustaining apparently fatal punishment and yet returning to base, such as the machine which, in July 1944, returned to base with the port side of its tail assembly completely shot away by flak! In August 1944, by which time the Luftwaffe in France was putting up only token resistance, No. 4 Group's Halifaxes flew 3,629 sorties, and there were twenty-six Halifax squadrons in the line.

Closely related to the Halifax III, the B.Mk.VI was really the final bomber variant, employing Hercules 100 engines, rated at 1,630 b.h.p. at 20,000 ft. and 1,800 b.h.p. at 10,000 ft., but as airframe production outpaced the supply of the more powerful radials, some machines were completed with Hercules XVI engines as the B.Mk.VII. The Halifax VI attained a gross weight of 68,000 lb., and its prototype (NP715) was first flown on October 10, 1944. With a view to its eventual use in the Pacific theatre, it was fitted with special sand filters over the carburettor intakes, and a pressurized fuel system. The B.Mk.VI was the fastest version of the Halifax to attain operational service. Its maximum speed was 290 m.p.h. at 10,500 ft., and 312 m.p.h. at 22,000 ft. The most economical speed was 195 m.p.h. at 10,000 ft. at which range was 2,350 mls. with 2,190 Imp.gal., and 3,220 mls. with 2,880 Imp.gal. Service ceiling at 56,200 lb. was 24,000 ft., and at 68,000 lb. was 20,000 ft. Maximum bomb load was 14,500 lb., comprising two 2,000-lb. and six 1,000-lb. bombs in the fuselage, and six 750-lb. incendiary clusters in wing bays. The B.Mk.VI supplemented the B.Mk.III in service, but was too late to see widespread use. Both marks III and VI were employed by squadrons operating with No. 100 Group on radar countermeasures, and B.Mk.VIs were operated by Nos. 346 and 347 Squadrons of the

The introduction of Hercules engines in the Halifax III offered significant advantages, and the first production example of this variant, HX227 first flown on August 29, 1943, is illustrated above. The prototype Halifax III was R9534 (right).

Free French Air Force in No. 4 Group. The B.VII was used principally by Nos. 408, 420, 425 and 426 Squadrons R.C.A.F. in No. 6 Group.

By the end of the war in Europe, the Halifax II and V had passed out of service, but a lone Halifax III of No. 462 Squadron, R.A.A.F. shared with the Mosquito the distinction of being the last Bomber Command aircraft to operate against Germany—on May 2, 1945. No. 462 Squadron was one of several attached to No. 100 Group for radar jamming duties, but on this particular sortie (against Flensburg) bombs were carried. During the war, the Halifax had served with the following squadrons of R.A.F. Bomber Command: Nos. 10, 35, 51, 76, 77, 78, 102, 103, 158, 171, 190, 192, 199, 346, 347, 405, 408, 415, 419, 420, 424, 425, 426, 427, 428, 429, 431, 432, 433, 460, 462, 466, 578 and 640. The Halifax was also used on bombing operations in the Middle East, from 1942 onwards, and was the only British four-engined bomber operational in that theatre, being first used by No. 462 Squadron which was later joined by Nos. 148, 178, 227 and 614 Squadrons. Two Flights of Halifax bombers, Nos. 1341 and 1577, were also operational in the Far East, and after the termination of the war in Europe, several squadrons flew their Halifax VIs out to this theatre. These were modified to carry three 230 Imp.gal. long-range tanks in their bomb-bays, and carried special radar-detection equipment to pinpoint Japanese radar stations.

Apart from its primary role as a heavy bomber, the Halifax performed many other important tasks for which its commodious fuselage made it suitable. One of the least publicised of these was the task of dropping special agents and supplies by parachute into enemy territory, this job being undertaken by Nos. 138 and 161 (Special Duties) Squadrons. Nine squadrons of R.A.F. Coastal Command flew with the Halifax during the war, including five units—Nos. 517, 518, 519, 520, and 521—specialising in meteorological reconnaissance duties, and four—Nos. 58, 502, 546, and 547—flying anti-submarine and shipping patrols. Special equipment was carried by the Halifax for its maritime roles, the aircraft being converted from standard bombers by Cunliffe-Owen Aircraft at Eastleigh. After these modifications had been incorporated, the Halifaxes were re-designated G.R.Mk.II, G.R.Mk.V, and G.R.Mk.VI, the last-mentioned not attaining service status before the end of the war. One Halifax G.R.II, JD212, was flown experimentally with rocket projectiles mounted under the centre section, but this armament was not adopted operationally. The Halifax G.R.II first entered service towards the end of 1942.

Other specially modified versions of the Halifax served from 1942 onwards with the Airborne Forces, as paratroop- and supply-droppers, and for glider-towing. A Halifax II towed a General Aircraft Hamilcar glider into the air for the first time in February 1942, and Halifaxes first towed Airspeed Horsa gliders operationally on November 19, 1942, in an attack on the German heavy-water plant in South Norway. Variants of the Halifax separately designated for the Airborne Forces were the A.Mk.III, A.Mk.V, and A.Mk.VII, and these served extensively in the invasion of Sicily, the airborne operations over Normandy, during the ill-fated Arnhem operation, and in the final crossing of the Rhine. Developed from the Halifax A.Mk.VII to incorporate the operational experience gained during 1944-45, the H.P.71 Halifax A.Mk.IX did not reach the R.A.F. until after the war, and the A.Mk.X, which was similar to the A.Mk.IX but with Hercules 100s replacing the Hercules XVIs, was not built.

Another version of the Halifax was produced in 1944 to serve with R.A.F. Transport Command, carrying personnel, freight and casualty stretchers in the fuselage. Standard bombers were converted to operate in this role, with dorsal turrets and H2S scanner removed, and these were redesignated C.Mk.III, C.Mk.VI and C.Mk.VII. These aircraft could carry twenty-four troops, and were extensively employed during the closing days of the war and immediately afterwards to fly home released prisoners-of-war. One transport Halifax (LV838) was modified from a Mk.III to Mk.VI standard and was fitted with a pannier capable of carrying 8,000

Shortages of British Messier undercarriages resulted in the Halifax V which differed from the Mk.II solely in having a Dowty levered suspension undercarriage. A Halifax B.V Series IA (LK665) is illustrated above, and an early Mk.V (DG235) is illustrated on the left.

The final bomber variant of the Halifax was the B.VI with Hercules 100 engines illustrated above.

lb. of freight. This installation was not adopted as standard until the Halifax C.Mk.VIII came into production in 1945. This, the H.P.70, was the first transport version of the Halifax to be designed as such from the outset, and apart from the pannier, it featured fairings which replaced the nose and tail turrets. The first production C.Mk.VIII (PP225) flew in June 1945.

R.A.F. Transport Command squadrons which flew the various freighter and personnel transport versions of the Halifax up to the end of the war included Nos. 190, 295, 296, 297, 298, 620 and 644 Squadrons. No. 298 Squadron, with Halifax A.Mk.VIIs, went to South-East Asia Command in the spring of 1945, and remained there until after the end of the war against Japan.

The grand total of Halifaxes built, including those completed after the war, was 6,176 machines. Of these, the parent company built 1,590, English Electric built 2,145, the London Aircraft Production Group built 710, Fairey Aviation built 661, and Rootes built 1,070. No records are available to show a complete breakdown of production, but it is known that Handley Page built eighty-four Mk.Is, in addition to the two prototypes, and the five Halifax manufacturers built 1,966 Mk.IIs. Just over 2,000 Mk.IIIs were built—about half by English Electric—and production of the Mk.V totalled 916 from Rootes' and Fairey's factories. Most of the 480 Mk.VIs constructed were built by English Electric,

whose production terminated with this variant, and the Mk.VIIs included 161 bombers and 45 A.Mk.VIIs from Handley Page; 120 from Rootes and sixty-nine from Fairey. The balance of the total included about one hundred C.Mk.VIIIs and Mk.IXs, the last of which (RT938) was delivered from Cricklewood on November 20, 1946.

During the war years, the Halifax flew no less than 75,532 bombing sorties during which 227,610 tons of bombs were dropped. It had its vicissitudes, but by persistent improvement and judicious innovation, incorporated without disrupting the production lines, it maintained its position as one of the two principal British "heavies", and proved itself a worthy successor to that first heavy bomber of the R.A.F., the Handley Page O/400—the "Bloody Paralyser" of the First World War.

Handley Page Halifax B.Mk.III

Dimensions:	Span, 194 ft. 2 in.; length, 70 ft. 1 in.; height, 20 ft. 9 in.; wing area, 1,275 sq. ft.
Power Plants:	Four Bristol Hercules XVI fourteen-cylinder two-row sleeve-valve air-cooled radial engines rated at 1,615 h.p. at 2,900 r.p.m. for take-off, 1,675 h.p. (for five min.) at 4,500 ft., and 1,455 h.p. at 12,000 ft.
Armament:	One flexible 0.303-in Browning machine gun with 300 rounds in the nose, four 0.303-in. Browning guns with 1,160 r.p.g. in Boulton Paul dorsal turret, and four 0.303-in. Browning guns with 1,700 r.p.g. in Boulton Paul tail turret. Maximum bomb load, 13,000 lb. Alternative fuselage bomb loads, six 1,000-lb. plus two 2,000-lb., one 8,000-lb., two 4,000-lb., four 2,000-lb., eight 1,000-lb., or nine 500-lb. bombs, plus six 500-lb. bombs in wing bays.
Weights:	Tare, 38,240 lb.; normal loaded, 54,400 lb.; maximum overload, 65,000 lb. Maximum fuel capacity, 2,688 Imp. gal.
Performance:	(At normal loaded weight) Maximum speed, 278 m.p.h. at 6,000 ft., 282 m.p.h. at 13,500 ft.; maximum weak mixture cruising speed, 228 m.p.h. at 20,000 ft.; economical cruising speed, 215 m.p.h. at 20,000 ft.; range (with 1,150 Imp. gal. and 13,000-lb. bomb load), 1,030 mls., (with 1,986 Imp. gal. and 7,000-lb. bomb load), 1,985 mls.; service ceiling (normal loaded), 24,000 ft., (maximum loaded), 20,000 ft.; initial climb rate, 960 ft./min.; time to 20,000 ft., 37.5 min., (maximum weight), 50 min.

The He 177V1 (above) flew for the first time on November 19, 1939, and the engine overheating that was to plague the bomber throughout its career first manifested itself on this flight.

THE HEINKEL HE 177 GREIF

"*Bomben auf Engeland.*" So read the title of a stirring martial song which blared out of loudspeakers all over Germany and the occupied territories in those fateful autumn months of 1940. With a background of roaring aero engines and accompanied by the beating of drums, it was an impressive battle hymn ; but whatever its psychological effect on the German populace, it was hardly destined to raise the morale of the personnel of the Luftwaffe's Kampfgeschwader. They were aware that their bombers did not possess the range to attack effectively more than a small area of the British Isles. They knew that the Luftwaffe's lack of a long-range strategic bomber enabled the R.A.F. to concentrate virtually the whole of its defensive strength within the limited area to which the Kampfgeschwader were forced to confine their attentions; they saw their operational strength being sapped disastrously.

The Luftwaffe's complete lack of a long-range heavy bomber was the more surprising in view of the fact that this air arm's first Chief of Staff, Lieutenant-General Wever, had for long championed such aircraft. Wever, believing rightly that the strategic bomber would prove a decisive factor in any future European conflict, demanded bombers capable of carrying a heavy load over distances sufficient to permit an assault on any part of the British Isles; aircraft which, in view of the weakness of the German Fleet, could also harass British shipping far out in the Atlantic. Prototypes of two four-engined heavy bombers, the Junkers Ju 89 and the Dornier Do 19, were built under his aegis, but with the death of this competent and far-sighted officer in an air crash, the development of these aircraft was abandoned,

Wever's successors, Stumpff, Jeschonnek and Kesselring, favouring the smaller, medium-range, twin-engined bomber.

Lieutenant-General Wever did leave the Luftwaffe a legacy, however, in the Heinkel He 177 Greif long-range heavy bomber which was destined to provide the most dismal chapter in the wartime record of the German aircraft industry. Fires in the air, aerodynamic troubles and structural failures all contributed towards the unpopularity of this big bomber when it eventually reached the operational units. It encountered difficulties from its birth whose causes were recognised too late, and when they were recognised insufficient energy was devoted to eradicating them. Not that there was anything basically wrong with the design, which was sound and embodied as much ingenuity as any wartime German aircraft. Had effective measures been taken to solve the problems that it presented at a sufficiently early stage in its career, the Luftwaffe might have found itself possessed of a heavy bomber comparable with, if not superior to, the best of Allied machines in this category.

The Allies first became aware of the existence of the He 177 on June 13, 1940, when a Luftwaffe prisoner-of-war provided a description of the bomber's essential features which subsequently proved to be very accurate indeed, and it was feared that the appearance of this new and advanced warplane over the British Isles would not be long delayed. Had the He 177 appeared in operational service during 1940-41, it could have radically altered the picture of aerial warfare over the British Isles, but nearly four years were to elapse before, at 21.31 hours on January 21,

THE HEINKEL He 177 GREIF

1944, an aircraft of this type was shot down near Hindhead, Surrey, during the bomber's operational début over the United Kingdom.

The reasons for the He 177's prolonged gestatory period were many and varied. Only partly to blame was the German aircraft industry's failure to remove certain shortcomings, including a proclivity towards catching fire in mid-air which earned for the bomber the uncomplimentary epithet of *"Luftwaffenfeuer-zeug"* (Luftwaffe's Petrol Lighter). Major contributory factors were vacillation on the part of the Reichsluftfahrtministerium, or R.L.M. (German Air Ministry), conflicting military and political policies, and petty jealousies and commercial rivalry within the aircraft industry itself. These all conspired to prevent the co-operation and effort with which the bomber's defects could have been removed.

The He 177 was conceived early in 1938 when the R.L.M. prepared a specification resulting from Lieutenant-General Wever's energetic demands for a combined heavy strategic bomber and anti-shipping aircraft. The specification called for an aircraft capable of carrying a bomb load of at least 2,000 pounds over a range of 4,160 miles. It had to possess a maximum speed of not less than 335 m.p.h. and have the structural strength to launch its attack from a medium-angle dive.

The specification was issued solely to the Ernst Heinkel Flugzeugwerke at Rostock-Marienehe, on the Baltic Coast. At that time, the Heinkel concern was engaged in the production of the He 111 medium bomber, the He 114 reconnaissance float sesquiplane, the He 115 twin-engined torpedo-bomber floatplane, and a small batch of He 112 fighters for export. In addition to variants of these established aircraft, the drawing boards were occupied by the He 100 fighter, the He 116 long-range mailplane, and the He 119 high-speed bomber, as well as the purely experimental He 176 and He 178 rocket- and turbojet-propelled aircraft. The R.L.M. felt, with some justification, that the company was disseminating its design activities too widely and, in view of the success of the He 111, brought pressure to bear in order to force Heinkel to concentrate on bomber development. It was for this reason that the heavy bomber specification was issued only to Heinkel and not, as had been previously the practice, to several companies simultaneously.

When the Heinkel company received the specification from the R.L.M., Dipl. Ing. Heinrich Hertel had been Technical Director and Chief of Development for some four years, and the task of producing a design study to meet its requirements was entrusted to one of the most talented members of his team, Siegfried Gunter. The project, which was designated He P.1041, was submitted to the R.L.M. a few months later, and a development contract was awarded, Dipl. Ing. Hertel supervising the design, Gunter being responsible for detail design, and Ing. Schwarzler being placed in charge of construction.

The P.1041, now allocated the designation He 177 by the R.L.M., embodied many advanced and, in some respects, revolutionary features as originally conceived. These included coupled power plants (two engines paired in one nacelle and driving a common airscrew) with surface evaporation cooling. The estimated loaded weight of the bomber was 59,520 lb., and it was anticipated that its performance range would include a maximum speed of no less than 342 m.p.h. at 18,000 feet—a speed substantially greater than that attained by most contemporary single-seat fighters! Many of the bomber's features were unproven, and as work on the design progressed even Siegfried Gunter began to have second thoughts as to the wisdom of embodying so many innovations. Hertel believed, however, that all problems presented by these radical features would be successfully overcome by the time that the first prototype could be ready for testing.

The most noteworthy feature of the projected aeroplane was the use of coupled power plants—two liquid-cooled engines mounted side-by-side with a single gear casing connecting the two crankcases, the two crankshaft pinions driving a single airscrew shaft gear. The use of two engines of very large output in a heavy bomber was undoubtedly sounder aerodynamically than that of four separate engines of smaller capacity, resulting in a substantial reduction in drag and a considerable increase in manoeuvrability. The coupled engine principle also avoided the uncertainty and delay attendant upon the development of a radically new high-powered engine, and simplified production since the same basic units could serve both in orthodox single engine installations and for the coupled power plants. Gunter, always engrossed with the idea of obtaining the best possible aerodynamic form, was largely responsible for the coupled engine conception, seeing in it a means of offsetting the lack of power plants in the 2,000 h.p. category.

At the time of the He 177's conception, Gunter was already working on the designs for an extremely fast bomber, the He 119, which utilised the coupled power plant arrangement. The He 119 was powered by a Daimler-Benz DB 606 coupled engine offering 2,350 h.p. for take-off, this comprising two DB 601 twelve-cylinder liquid-cooled engines mounted side-by-side and inclined so that the inner banks of cylinders were disposed almost vertically. Installed in the fuselage near to the aircraft's centre of gravity, the DB 606 drove the airscrew by means of a long extension shaft which, housed in a tube, passed through the cockpit. The He 119 was certainly one of the fastest aircraft of its time, eventually attaining 432 m.p.h., but the overheating of the coupled engine was never entirely eradicated.

In the He 177, the DB 606 coupled engine was combined with a system of surface evaporation cooling to augment the orthodox radiators. Surface evaporation cooling was first employed on the experimental He 100 single-seat fighter, the eighth prototype of which was to capture the world's absolute speed record on March 30, 1939, by attaining 463.92 m.p.h. An immense amount of research on surface evaporation cooling had been conducted but, by the spring of 1939, the Heinkel engineers were forced to admit that it was impracticable for a service aircraft, and the first major change in the original He 177 conception was rendered necessary. The adoption of orthodox radiators of greater area naturally added to airframe drag, reducing both speed and range, and in order to maintain the latter figure as originally specified, it was found necessary to make provision for additional fuel cells in the wings. This, in turn, necessitated some increase in wing strength and, consequently, structural weight, thus further reducing the estimated speed performance of the bomber.

Another design innovation featured by the He 177 as originally conceived was the use of remotely-controlled defensive gun barbettes which offered appreciably less drag than manned turrets. Work on remotely-controlled aircraft defensive systems had reached a relatively advanced stage in Germany in the late 'thirties, but progress in this field failed to keep pace with the He 177, and the design had once more to be modified; this time to accommodate manned turrets resulting in a further increment of drag.

An even more serious problem was posed by the R.L.M. who, having demanded the ability to undertake medium-angle dives in the original specification, now insisted that the heavy bomber be capable of performing 60° diving attacks such as those for which the very much smaller and lighter Junkers Ju 88 had been designed! In order to withstand the tremendous stresses that would be imposed during the pull-out from such a dive with an aircraft of the He 177's size and weight, further structural strengthening was dictated. By now the design gross weight of the bomber had increased so alarmingly that the provision of an undercarriage of sufficient strength became a serious problem. Neither the engine nacelles or the wings, which featured a low thickness/chord ratio, provided much stowage space for the main undercarriage members, and after several extremely complex arrangements had been contemplated, a rather novel system was adopted. Two massive single-wheel oleo legs were attached to the main spar at each engine nacelle, the outboard legs with their single wheels retracting upwards and outward into shallow wing wells, and the inboard units swinging upward and inward, all units being completely enclosed by flush-fitting doors.

Aerodynamically, the He 177 was a large, well-proportioned, mid-wing monoplane which, from the structural viewpoint, offered few novelties. Conventional metal stressed skin construction was employed, the wing being built up on a single main spar.

After the death of Lieutenant-General Wever, the R.L.M. interest in the long-range bomber cooled

The He 177V5 was employed for early armament trials but both power plants burst into flame during a simulated low-level attack early in 1941.

rapidly. Germany's leaders still envisaged a limited war confined to the European continent, and Major-General Hans Jeschonnek, who succeeded Stumpff as Chief of Air Staff, was adamant in his belief that if Germany built sufficient quantities of medium bombers, Britain and France would be so impressed that Germany would be left a free hand with Poland. It was decided, therefore, virtually to abandon the further development of the heavy bomber; a gamble based on Britain staying out of the future war and one of the greatest single mistakes made by the German High Command. Construction of the prototypes of the He 177 for experimental purposes was continued, however, in view of the German Admiralty's continual representations for such an aircraft for co-operation with submarines and long-range offensive reconnaissance out over the Atlantic.

By the summer of 1939—it now becoming increasingly obvious to German leaders that Britain and France would go to the aid of Poland in the event of an attack on that country—renewed interest was being shown in the He 177, and the Heinkel company was urged to speed prototype construction. During the previous March, however, Dipl. Ing. Hertel had left Heinkel, and this did not augur well for the future of the bomber. Finally, on November 19, 1939, the first prototype, the He 177V1, was flown for the first time with Dipl. Ing. Francke at the controls. Francke was Chief of the Rechlin Experimental Establishment's E-2 flight test section, and his initial flight was terminated after only twelve minutes as the engine temperatures began to rise alarmingly. While Francke referred favourably to the take-off, general handling and landing characteristics of the bomber, he complained of some vibration in the airscrew shafts, the inadequacy of the tail surfaces under certain conditions, and some flutter which accompanied any vigorous movement of the elevators.

The He 177V1 had an empty equipped weight of 30,247 lb., and loaded weight was 52,734 lb. Overall dimensions included a span 103 ft. $0\frac{1}{4}$ in., and overall length of 67 ft. $6\frac{1}{4}$ in., a height of 21 ft. $10\frac{1}{2}$ in., and a wing area of 1,076.39 sq. ft. Although provision was made for a single 12.7-mm. MG 131 machine gun above and immediately aft of the flight deck, a similar gun in the ventral gondola and a third in the extreme tail, no armament was fitted, and only the aft bomb-bay installed. This bomb-bay projected

The He 177V7 featured a revised nose section and, together with the V6, underwent operational trials in the late Autumn of 1941 with Kampfgeschwader 40.

slightly below the lower fuselage line as a result of an increase in bomb calibres during the aircraft's construction.

The He 177V2 completed shortly afterwards was essentially similar to its predecessor and was also flown on its maiden flight by Francke. The first prototype received several modifications dictated by the initial flight tests, including a twenty per cent increase in the tail surface area, and the machine was flown to Rechlin for further testing by Francke. The second prototype, the tail surfaces of which had not been modified, was tested by another Rechlin pilot, Rickert, who performed the first diving test with the new bomber. Serious control surface flutter immediately developed and the machine disintegrated. After this incident, the tail surfaces of the third, fourth and fifth prototypes, nearing completion at Rostock-Marienehe, were modified in a similar fashion to that of the He 177V1.

The torsional vibration in the airscrew drive shafts which had manifested itself on the bomber's first flight was relatively simple of solution by comparison with the problem of engine overheating. This resulted in a notorious inflammability eventually to earn the bomber its nickname of "*Luftwaffenfeuerzeug*". The third prototype, the He 177V3 which bore the civil registration D-AGIG and had loaded weight increased to 60,198 lb., was allocated to the task of power plant development, and was flown to Rechlin in mid-February 1940. Engine tests were, unfortunately, awarded relatively low priority, for the bomber was suffering even more serious aerodynamic troubles.

The He 117V4 was retained at Heinkel's test field where another Rechlin pilot, Ursinus, undertook stability tests. While flying over the Baltic during the course of one of these trials, this prototype failed to recover from a shallow dive, crashing into the sea near Ribnitz. Attempts to salvage the wreckage in

order to determine the cause of the crash met with only partial success but it was discovered that the accident had resulted from the malfunctioning of the airscrew pitch gear.

Among the He 177's noteworthy features were its Fowler-type extensible trailing-edge flaps which occupied the entire wing trailing edges, including those portions covered by the ailerons. Each aileron comprised upper and lower portions, the latter arranged to slide rearwards with flap extension while the upper part retained its function of providing lateral control for take-off and landing. The original wing design did not take into full account the stresses caused by the Fowler flaps, however, and as a result more internal strengthening proved necessary.

The first four He 177 prototypes were essentially similar, apart from the twin bomb-bays installed in the second machine and the increased internal fuel tankage of the fourth, but the fifth machine, the He 177V5 and last of the initial prototype batch, incorporated a number of changes which were principally concerned with armament installations for trials at Rechlin. Triple bomb-bays were fitted, and hand-operated 7.9-mm. MG 15 machine guns were installed in the extreme nose, in a turret immediately aft of the flight deck, in the nose of the ventral gondola, and in the extreme tail. Early in 1941, during a simulated low-level attack, both power plants burst into flames and the He 177V5 hit the ground and exploded.

The tendency on the part of the coupled engines to ignite became increasingly serious as the test programme progressed. There were several reasons for the inflammability of the DB 606 power plants. There was a common exhaust manifold on the two inner cylinder blocks which became excessively hot and caused the usual accumulation of oil and grease in the bottom of the engine cowling to catch fire. When throttling back there was a tendency for the injection pump to deliver more fuel than the reduced requirement of the engine, and the injection pump connections leaked. In order to save weight there was no firewall, and the coupled engines were fitted so close to the wing mainspar that there was insufficient space for the fuel and oil pipelines, electrical leads, etc. This "sardine can" arrangement, as it was dubbed at Rechlin, was frequently saturated in fuel and oil from leaking connections. In addition, at altitude the oil tended to foam, partly due to the fact that the return pump was too large, and in this condition it circulated in the engines, its lubricative qualities being virtually nil. The lack of adequate lubrication resulted in the disintegration of the connecting rod bearings which burst through the engine crankcase, puncturing the oil tanks which poured their contents on to the red-hot exhaust pipe collector.

The He 177V6, like the V5, had production-type DB 606 power plants in which the maximum power for take-off was increased from 2,600 h.p. to 2,700 h.p., maximum continuous output being 2,360 h.p., and maximum cruising power being 2,080 h.p. at 18,050 ft. The empty and loaded weights of the sixth prototype increased to 37,038 lb. and 61,883 lb. respectively, and performance included a maximum speed of 289 m.p.h., a cruising speed of 263 m.p.h., a service ceiling of 22,966 ft., and a range of 3,417 mls. The He 177V6 and the similar V7 featured a revised nose section which, while following the contours of the nose section employed by earlier prototypes, was considerably reinforced and had fewer glazed panels. Whereas the V6 had 13-mm. MG 131 machine guns in the forward part of the ventral gondola, a dorsal turret aft of the flight deck, and the extreme tail, the V7 had an MG 131 machine gun in the nose, a 20-mm. MG FF cannon in the gondola and a similar cannon in the dorsal turret. From the earliest months of the War, Kampfgeschwader 40 *Wurm* had been designated the first unit to re-equip with the new

bomber, and in the late autumn months of 1941, IV/K.G.40 based at Bordeaux-Merignac received the He 177V6 and V7 for operational trials in the anti-shipping role. The two machines soon became the bane of all concerned. They were the subject of interminable modifications to both airframes and engines, and were considered totally unsuited for operational use.

In September 1941, the He 177V8, the last of the aircraft built as prototypes from the outset, all sixteen additional prototypes being conversions of pre-production or production airframes, was made available for engine tests at Rechlin, but owing to the urgency of other development work it was returned to Heinkel after only forty days, and it was not possible to resume engine tests in the air until February 1942 when the second pre-production machine, the He 177A-02, was delivered. The first He 177A-0 (Werk-Nr. 00016) of a batch of fifteen pre-production machines laid down at Rostock-Marienehe had been flown in November 1941, the second pre-production machine flying in the following month. Owing to the limited capacity of the Rostock-Marienehe plant, an additional fifteen He 177A-0 pre-production aircraft had been laid down simultaneously at Heinkel's Oranienburg factory, and Arado's Warnemunde factory initiated licence production of the bomber with a further five He 177A-0 aircraft.

The He 177A-0 had a maximum loaded weight of 66,140 lb., maximum speed was 298 m.p.h., and service ceiling was 32,800 feet. Maximum bomb load was 5,290 lb., and defensive armament comprised one 7.9-mm. MG 81 machine gun in the glazed nose, one 20-mm. MG FF cannon in the nose of the ventral gondola, twin MG 81 machine guns in the rear of the ventral gondola, a 13-mm. MG 131 machine gun in the forward dorsal turret, and a similar gun in the

The He 177A-02, the second pre-production aircraft built at Rostock-Marienehe, first flew in November 1941.

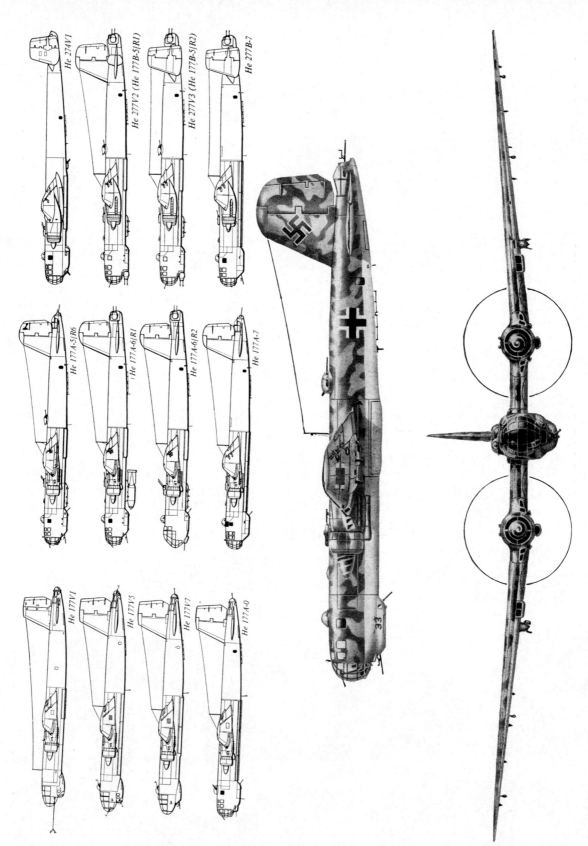

He 274 V1

He 277 V2 (He 177 B-5/R1)

He 277 V3 (He 177 B-5/R2)

He 277 B-7

He 177 A-5/R6

He 177 A-6/R1

He 177 A-6/R2

He 177 A-7

He 177 V1

He 177 V5

He 177 V7

He 177 A-0

Heinkel He 177A-5 Greif

FINISH: The aircraft depicted belonged to Group 1 of Kampfgeschwader 100, and the camouflage scheme employed differed appreciably from that of the aircraft of Kampfgeschwader 40, comprising an irregular pattern of olive khaki on bluish grey-green over the upper surfaces and standard light blue undersurfaces. Other machines employed a mottled dark blue-grey and stone grey over all surfaces, and the aircraft of K.G.40 normally employed a "splinter" camouflage pattern of dark forest green and olive over all upper surfaces with mottled pale blue-grey sides and pale blue undersurfaces.

INSIGNIA: The aircraft illustrated bore no indication of the unit but "33" appeared in black on each side of the ventral gondola. The aircraft of K.G.40 usually had the Geschwader code designation "F8" painted in small black letters and numerals ahead of the national insignia on the fuselage sides. The national insignia appeared on fuselage sides, and a black swastika outlined in white appeared on each side of the rudder. On some aircraft only the white outline of the swastika was used.

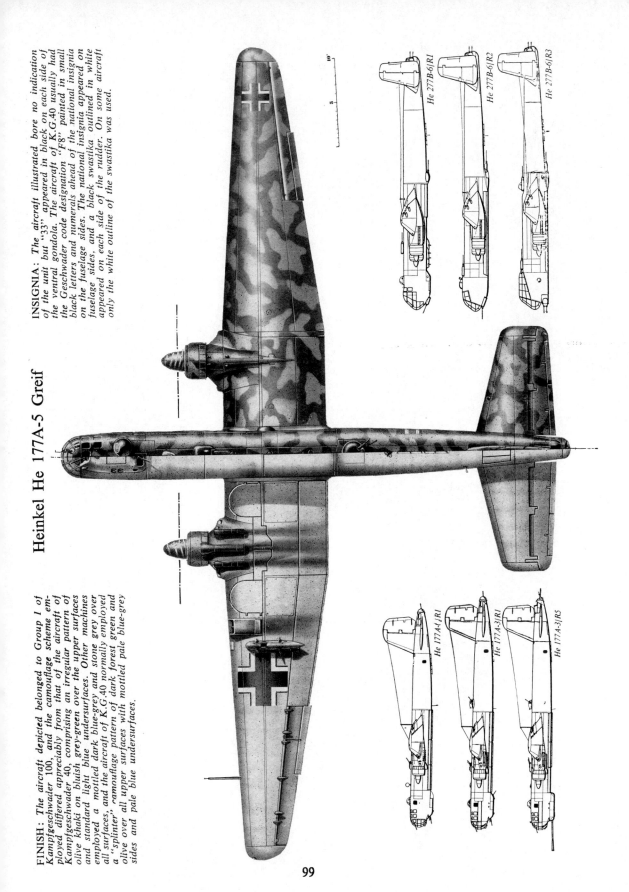

He 277B-6/R1

He 277B-6/R2

He 277B-6/R3

He 177A-1/R1

He 177A-3/R1

He 177A-3/R5

tail. The first He 177A-0 was intended primarily for armament tests, but initial trials indicated that the defensive system was unsatisfactory, and before modifications could be made the aircraft was destroyed when the engines caught fire during take-off. The second pre-production machine began engine flight trials on February 8, 1942, but a few weeks later, in May, both power plants ignited, necessitating a crash landing from which the crew escaped seconds before the plane exploded.

Tests with the He 177A-02 completed prior to its destruction had enabled the engine specialists to reach certain conclusions, however, and they recommended that the engine mounts be lengthened by some eight inches; the fuel and oil pipelines be relocated; a firewall be fitted, the oil tank be transferred to a less dangerous position, and the complete redesign of the exhaust system be undertaken. By this time the first production He 177A-1 had left Arado's Warnemunde plant, and the R.L.M. was demanding the service introduction of the bomber at the earliest possible date. Thus, only the recommendation that the oil tank be shifted was adopted as this change was thought unlikely to delay production. At a later stage, however, when service units began demanding exhaust flame dampers for night operations, the opportunity was taken to redesign the exhaust system, and with the introduction of the He 177A-3 the engine mounts were lengthened by the recommended amount.

The thirty-five He 177A-0 pre-production machines were employed for a wide variety of trials and, although the bomber was still considered to be "dangerous" because of the frequent engine fires, most experienced bomber pilots expressed favourable opinions concerning its handling qualities and general performance. Some expressed the view that the He 177 was fully as manoeuvrable as the very much smaller Ju 88, and one pilot claimed that it performed tighter turns than a Ju 88 fighter when the two machines were flown together in mock combat. However, during take-off the He 177 tended to swing badly, resulting in several accidents, and the vertical tail surfaces were therefore enlarged and the tail-wheel was modified. These changes only partially corrected the fault, and it was necessary to hold the tail down as long as possible during the take-off run. Heinkel had proposed the use of a nosewheel under-carriage, but this suggestion was turned down by the R.L.M.

The He 177-05, -06 and -07 became the He 177V9, V10 and V11 respectively, and the He 177A-012 served for trials in the "destroyer" role. The first of the five He 177A-0 aircraft produced by the Warne-munde plant was used for shallow dive tests at Lud-wigslust during which a speed of 443 m.p.h. was attained. This was the last aircraft to be fitted with the barred-gate type dive brakes for, apart from the fact that the bomber had proven incapable of withstanding the stresses imposed by a pull-out from even a medium-angle dive, Allied anti-aircraft gunners had evolved effective means of combating the dive bombers. The removal of the brakes also made room for external bomb carriers.

The first Arado-built He 177A-1 was available for testing in March 1942. Although the bomber's teething troubles remained largely unresolved, Hermann Goring was persistently demanding the quantity delivery of the He 177 to enable his Luft-waffe to "Blow the British Fleet out of the water." In these demands he was echoed by Premier-Admiral Donitz who felt that Heinkel's bomber could do a far better job against British coastal shipping than his U-boats which were encountering increasingly serious opposition around Britain's coastline. But the con-tinual modifications dictated by trials with the proto-types and pre-production aircraft, and the substantial number of these lost in accidents, necessitated the allocation of the first production batch for test purposes.

A total of 130 He 177A-1 Greif (Griffin) bombers was manufactured, all of these being produced by Arado at Warnemunde, the series being completed on June 28, 1943, and after initial attempts to employ the He 177A-1 operationally, all aircraft of this type were relegated to test, training, and special duty roles. Many of the A-1s were employed as conversion trainers at Fassberg, Lechfeld, Erfurt, Brandenburg-Briest and Ludwigslust; one was transferred to Deutsche Lufthansa (Werk-Nr. 15271) for transport duties; six were based at Fassberg for Henschel Hs 293 radio-controlled rocket-propelled missile drop-ping and control trials; one was transferred to the Junkers plant at Dessau for testing the DB 610 power plants to be installed in the Ju 288, and three were used by Rowehl's Kampfgeschwader 200 for special long-range duties. The last-mentioned aircraft were based at the Erfurt repair depot, and after each sortie the He 177A-1s were returned to their repair shops for complete overhauls!

The He 177A-1 carried 1,619 Imp.gal. of fuel for short-range operations, 1,914 Imp.gal. for medium-range operations, and 2,164 Imp.gal. for long-range operations. The fully glazed nose consisted of a series of optically flat panels and was bulged to form a ventral gondola which housed a forward-firing 20-mm. MG FF cannon with 300 rounds and an aft-firing pair of 7.9-mm. MG 81 guns (He 177A-1/R1) or a 13-mm. MG 131 (He 177A-1/R4). Additional defensive armament was provided by a hand-held MG 81 on a small spherical mounting in the glazed nose; an electrically-operated dorsal barbette con-taining an MG 131 machine gun and controlled remotely by a gunner from a sighting station in the roof aft of the pilot; and a single gimbal-mounted MG 131 machine gun immediately aft of the rudder with a rather restricted field of fire. The He 177A-1/R2 and R3 also featured a remotely-controlled ventral barbette housing one MG 131, while the He 177A-1/R4 had a manned aftdorsal turret with one MG 131. Maximum internal bomb load was 4,850 lb.

The forward fuselage provided accommodation for four crew members—the pilot, co-pilot/bombardier, navigator/radio-operator and gunner—all stationed in the extreme nose, the tail section housing a gunner. Empty weight was 35,494 lb., maximum loaded weight was 66,139 lb., and maximum landing weight was 50,706 lb. Maximum speed was 317 m.p.h., cruising speed was 267 m.p.h., service ceiling was 22,966 ft., and range varied from 746 mls. with short-range tankage to 3,480 mls. with long-range tankage.

While production of the He 177A-1 was being undertaken by Arado, the Heinkel factories had introduced an improved variant, the He 177A-3, on to the assembly lines. This differed from the initial production model principally in having the power plants mounted some eight inches farther ahead of the wing mainspar and an additional 5 ft. 3 in. fuselage section inserted aft of the bomb-bays to maintain the c.g. position. An additional dorsal turret was mounted midway between the trailing edge of the mainplane and the leading edge of the tail-plane, this being electrically-rotated and hand-elevated and containing two 13-mm. MG 131 machine guns with 1,500 rounds. The first prototype for the He 177A-3 was the He 177V15, although this aircraft did not feature the lengthened fuselage and, unlike the initial production variants of the He 177A-3 which retained the DB 606 engines, it had the more powerful DB 610 engines which had first been tested on the He 177V11. The DB 610 consisted of a pair of DB 605 engines and gave a maximum output of 2,950 h.p. for take-off and 3,100 h.p. at 6,890 ft. The second prototype for the A-3 series was the He 177V16 which was also powered by the DB 610, but the initial production model, the He 177A-3/R1 had the DB 606, and by the end of 1942 only a few had actually been delivered to the Luftwaffe, these being ferried to the Truppen-Erprobungskommando at Brandenburg-Briest for service testing.

A production rate of no less than seventy aircraft per month had been demanded but, because of the continual modifications called for, deliveries had fallen to five per month. All service reports still bitterly complained of the bomber's numerous short-comings, and the official minutes of a General-luftzeugmeister discussion held on October 15, 1942, read as follows: "He (Heinkel) is aware of the difficulties (experienced with the He 177). He has also recognised that the most important fault lies in the fact that his Technical Bureau has not carried out sufficient fundamental work to take up and carry out necessary modifications." Thus, in November 1942, Dipl. Ing. Hertel returned to Rostock-Marienehe as an R.L.M. Deputy with full powers to reorganise the development of the He 177.

In the autumn of 1942, Gruppe I of Kampfge-schwader 4, formerly flying He 111s on the Russian Front, had been withdrawn to Lechfeld where its 3rd

The He 177A-3/R3 (above) was the first version of the Greif to carry the Henschel Hs 293 missile.

Staffel commenced converting to the He 177. Training began on seven He 177A-1s but progress was extremely slow because of an acute shortage of aircraft. It was not until the early months of 1943, by which time a 1st and 2nd Staffel had been formed, that the first He 177A-3s arrived. In the meantime, the Greif had received its baptism of fire, although hardly in the way its manufacturers might have envisaged.

Kampfgeschwader 50 at Brandenburg-Briest had received twenty He 177A-1s for conversion training, and Gruppe I was hurriedly trained on the He 177A-3/R1, and redesignated Fern-Kampfgeschwader 2, before being rushed to Zaporozhe on the Russian Front where it employed its aircraft as *transports* flying supplies to the beleagured German garrison in Stalingrad. F.K.G.2 suffered an average of one loss per day in landing crashes, and the strength of the unit dwindled so rapidly that, in February 1943, after a few weeks of operations, the survivors were withdrawn to Fassberg. During the He 177's operations in the vicinity of Stalingrad, a forward maintenance unit modified several machines by installing a 50-mm. BK 5 anti-tank gun in the ventral gondola, the ammunition for the gun being housed in the forward bomb-bay. The modified aircraft were used with some success for ground attack in between transport sorties.

In April 1943, an improved variant, the He 177A-3/R2, was introduced. This featured an improved electrical system, a modified gun position in the nose of the ventral gondola, the MG FF cannon being replaced by an MG 151 of similar calibre, and a redesigned tail gun position. Prior to the introduction of the He 177A-3/R2, the tail gunner lay prone

The He 177A-5/R6 (above) was one of the principal production models of the Greif, and carried its primary offensive load externally.

in the tail, but the new position enabled the gunner to be seated and the 13-mm. MG 131 machine gun was supplanted by a 20-mm. MG 151 cannon. The He 177A-3/R3 was the first Hs 293 missile carrier, two of these weapons being mounted under the wings and one under the fuselage, and the He 177A-3/R4 had the ventral gondola lengthened by 3 ft. 11 in. to house the Kehl III control equipment for the Hs 293. The first tests with the Hs 293 had been made in 1941 with an He 177A-0 at Karlshagen. A number of difficulties had been encountered, and it was not until the summer of 1942 that the first successful dropping tests with the Hs 293 took place. The He 177A-3/R3 was used primarily for the training of crews with the Hs 293 from May 1943.

The installation of a heavy cannon in the ventral gondola of some machines during the Stalingrad fighting resulted in yet a further variant, the He 177A-3/R5, or *Stalingradtyp*, in which a 75-mm. BK 7.5 cannon was installed in the gondola. The He 177A-3/R5 switched from the DB 606 to the more powerful DB 610 power plants, but only five machines of this type were completed as the firing of the cannon resulted in severe vibration and its installation affected the flying characteristics of the Greif adversely.

Allied advances in anti-submarine warfare rendered the operation of U-boats in British coastal waters increasingly suicidal, and Donitz was particularly insistent that the He 177 be supplied as a torpedo-bomber. Thus, the He 177A-3/R7 was evolved specifically for the torpedo-bombing role and was used for trials by the Lowengeschwader K.G.26. Initially, the Italian L 5 torpedo, standard with Luftwaffe torpedo-bombing units, was used, but these, with their jettisonable stabilizing extensions, could not be stowed within the bomb-bays. Initially, two L 5 torpedoes were carried beneath the fuselage, but it was soon found preferable to carry the torpedoes beneath the wings. Unlike its predecessors, the He 177A-3/R7 had no Fowler-type flaps along the ailerons, the outer wings being similar to those of the

He 177A-5 which was being produced in parallel at Oranienburg, but only three examples of the A-3/R7 were produced, this variant being abandoned in favour of the A-5. The He 177A-3/R7 was also used for trials with the new electrically-driven LT 50 torpedo which approached the target vessel at considerable depth without revealing its track, and was exploded by magnetic force beneath the ship. The LT 50 could be dropped by parachute from an altitude of some 800 feet a considerable distance from its target.

The first He 177A-5s left the assembly lines at Oranienburg in February 1943, and, together with deliveries from Arado's Warnemunde factory, the initial delivery tempo of six machines per month had been doubled by July and stepped up to forty-two aircraft per month by the end of the year, a total of 415 machines being delivered during 1943, of which 154 were He 177A-3s. At the end of that year, however, the R.L.M., prompted presumably by the high loss rate, issued instructions that all existing He 177 bombers were to be scrapped! The engine test section had modified one machine at Rechlin to conform with recommendations resulting from the findings of the special investigation into the possible sources of engine fires ordered by Dipl. Ing. Hertel in January 1943. This investigation had revealed *fifty-six* possible causes of fire, and the machine modified at Rechlin functioned perfectly, the engines giving no trouble whatsoever over a protracted test period. The R.L.M. Technical Office was finally convinced that the solution to the He 177's engine troubles had at last been found, but the order to modify all aircraft on the assembly lines in a similar fashion came too late as it would have seriously disrupted production deliveries, while the order to scrap existing machines was tacitly ignored.

The He 177A-5 was intended primarily to carry external loads, such as the LT 50 torpedo, the FX 1400 Fritz unpowered radio-controlled armour-piercing bomb, and the Hs 293 and 294 missiles. It featured a strengthened wing, shortened under-

He 177A-5 bombers of Kampfgeschwader 40 at Bordeaux-Merignac in June 1944. K.G.40 was trained from the outset for the anti-shipping role.

carriage oleo legs, and the Fowler flaps along the outboard wing sections were removed. The defensive armament stemmed from that of the He 177A-3/R2, and thus the standard production model was designated He 177A-5/R2. The triple bomb-bay was installed but the forward bay was blanked off and an under-fuselage weapon rack was fitted. Power was provided by the DB 610 engine.

Whereas Kampfgeschwader 4 had been trained primarily as a strategic bombing unit at Lechfeld, the three Staffeln of I/K.G.50 which had operated at Stalingrad had received training with the Henschel Hs 293 and, redesignated as the 4th, 5th and 6th Staffeln of K.G.40, had been transferred to Bordeaux-Merignac on October 25, 1943 for anti-shipping duties. Gruppe I of K.G.40, the 1st Staffel of which had begun converting to the He 177A at Fassberg early in December 1942, was trained from the outset for the anti-shipping role, although training had been erratic because of a shortage of aircraft and continuous troubles with what aircraft were available. The 1st Staffel of I/K.G.40 was fully trained on the He 177A-5 by the middle of December 1943 when it was temporarily transferred to Chateaudun to join I/K.G.100 for Operation *Steinbock.*

The first major operation of II/K.G.40 (formerly I/K.G.50) took place on November 21, 1943. This unit came under the control of the Fliegerfuhrer Atlantik which co-operated closely with the Fuhrer der U-Boote. Twenty He 177A-5s carrying Hs 293 radio-controlled missiles attacked a convoy in the Atlantic, but the action was regarded as a total failure because of unfavourable conditions. Five days later, the unit again went into action with fourteen aircraft carrying Hs 293s. An Allied convoy was attacked off Bougie but four of the bombers were lost in action and three more were written off after forced landings. Fifty per cent of the attacking force was, therefore, lost as a result of this one action, and the Gruppe was left with only seven serviceable aircraft. Among the casualties was Major Mons, the Gruppenkommandeur, who had previously conceived a plan for attacking the water reservoirs in Scotland and Northern Ireland, an idea which was later toyed with by his successor, Major Rieder, but eventually abandoned.

The Hs 293 and FX 1400 were introduced operationally by the He 177 at the same time, but successes attained were of a fairly low order, and it proved difficult to guide the bombs with a high degree of accuracy. On occasions they behaved erratically, and if damaged the Hs 293 could be as much a danger to its parent as to its intended target. An example of this was given during an attack on H.M.S. *Winchelsea* and H.M.S. *Watchman* by a lone He 177A-5. The bomber released one Hs 293 at a range of 4,000 yards but this was hit by Oerlikon fire and dived into the sea. A second Hs 293 was then released but this was also hit by Oerlikon fire almost immediately it left the bomber. It then became extremely erratic, and appeared to be trying to nuzzle its parent craft, the pilot of the bomber having to resort to aerobatics in order to discourage this dangerous demonstration of affection. The Hs 293 then took station about thirty feet above the nose of the bomber which, by this time, had turned for home. For a few minutes the pair flew in this fashion, and the thoughts of the startled crew of the He 177 can well be imagined, and then the bomb dived steeply into the sea.

The heavy losses sustained by II/K.G.40 showed that daylight attacks with the Greif against convoys were impracticable, and it was decided that attacks on shipping would have to be carried out at night, either with the aid of bright moonlight or flares. New tactics were evolved, one Kette of aircraft dropping special 110-lb. flares on the beam of the convoy while another Kette attacked from the dark side, seeing their target silhouetted against the light of the flares. As the He 177s were less vulnerable to anti-aircraft fire in the darkness, they released their Hs 293s from a range of six to nine miles while flying directly towards their target, thus greatly simplifying the problem of aiming.

On October 1, 1943, I/K.G.4, which was training

(*Above*) *The He 277V1 (alias He 177B-0) was a conversion of a standard He 177A-3/R2 airframe, flying for the first time late in 1943. Only six He 177A-7s were completed, and that illustrated on the left, the fourth machine, was captured by U.S. forces.*

as a strategic bombing unit at Lechfeld, was redesignated as Gruppe I of K.G.100, and on December 18, 1943, the 3rd Staffel moved to Chateaudun where it was joined by the 1st Staffel of I/K.G.40 to participate in Operation *Steinbock* which was to mark the début of the Greif over the British Isles. Operation *Steinbock* had been conceived at the direct orders of Adolf Hitler as a reprisal against London. The Luftwaffe Supreme Command was forced to comb every operational unit in Italy and Russia for bombers to participate in *Steinbock*, and apart from the He 177s which were to form the core of the attack, some eighty He 111s, Do 217s, Ju 88s and Ju 188s were rounded up for the task.

The attack on London commenced on January 21, 1944, the Staffeln of I/K.G.40 and I/K.G.100 operating as a single unit from both Chateaudun and Rheine. After two attacks on London, I/K.G.40 was withdrawn to Germany, its place being taken by the 2nd Staffel of K.G.100 two weeks later, this unit having, in the meantime, become operational. While, as an operation, *Steinbock* could be regarded as a failure, the defences of London decimating the attacking medium bombers, the He 177s achieved some success. The more experienced crews carried maximum bomb loads and, climbing to 23,000 feet while still over German territory, approached their target in a shallow dive, attaining speeds approaching 435 m.p.h. at which night fighters could not intercept them and anti-aircraft fire could not follow them. In this way, only four He 177s were lost through enemy action, but, nevertheless, a very low degree of concentration was attained, and serviceability was invariably low because of last-minute mishaps before operations. Evidence of this was provided Major-General Pelz, appointed "Assault Leader against England" by Goring, on the night of February 13, 1944, when he witnessed the take-off and landing of the aircraft of the 2nd and 3rd Staffeln of K.G.100.

It was a cold night and the "cold start" procedure was employed. Thirteen aircraft took-off—one having come to grief with a burst tyre—but eight of these returned to base suffering from over-heated or burning engines. Of the remaining five aircraft, only four reached their target of London. The Gruppenkommandeur, finding himself over Norwich, had turned back, dumping his bombs in the Zuyder Zee. Of the four aircraft which reached London, one was shot down by night fighters. Operation *Steinbock* was called off at the beginning of March.

Several sub-types of the He 177A-5 were produced: the He 177A-5/R5 had an additional remotely-controlled gun barbette mounted aft of the bombbays but only one example of this type was completed; the He 177A-5/R6 was similar to the A-5/R2 apart from the deletion of the two forward bombbays; the He 177A-5/R7 had a pressurized cabin which increased operational ceiling to 49,870 feet, and the He 177A-5/R8, only one example of which was built, was equipped with remotely-controlled "chin" and tail barbettes, but was abandoned owing to difficulties with the control system. During 1944 a total of 565 He 177A-5s was completed, although the whole production programme virtually ground to a halt during October in favour of the "emergency fighter programme."

While production of the He 177A-5 had proceeded several improved versions of the Greif were evolved, including the He 177A-6. Work on this extensively revised model began early in 1944, and preparations were made to switch production from the A-5 to the A-6 immediately. The constant flow of modifications resulting from the complaints of frontline units delayed plans, however, and instead of fifteen He 177A-6s ready for delivery by the end of May 1944, only six were actually completed and their assembly was possible only by utilising ninety-eight per cent A-5 components. The first six He 177A-6/R1 long-range heavy bombers were conversions of standard He 177A-5/R6 aircraft and featured pressure cabins. The rear dorsal turret was deleted as an electrically-powered Rheinmetall-Borsig turret housing four 7.9-mm. MG 81 machine guns was installed in the tail, and this was considered to provide adequate rear defence. The two forward bomb-bays were deleted and the rear bay could accommodate a 1,100-lb. load, but the principle offensive load (5,500 lb.) was carried beneath the fuselage. Range was 3,600 miles, and the fuel cells were heavily armoured.

The seventh He 177A-6 was designated He 177V22 was intended as a prototype for the He 177A-6/R2 which differed from the A-6/R1 principally in having an entirely redesigned nose of improved aerodynamic form. Defensive armament comprised twin 13-mm. MG 131 machine guns in a "chin" barbette, twin 20-mm. MG 151 cannon in the remotely-controlled forward dorsal barbette, and one 13-mm. MG 131 machine gun in the rear of the central nose bulge in addition to the HDL/81V tail turret. Alternative offensive loads comprised one 5,500-lb. SC 2500 general-purpose bomb and one 1,100-lb. SC 500 general-purpose bomb; one 4,410-lb. SC 2000 bomb and one 2,200-lb. SC 1000 bomb; two Fritz-X guided bombs and one 1,100-lb. SC 500 bomb, or one Hs 293D missile and one 1,100-lb. SC 500 bomb. The whole He 177A-6 programme was abandoned after completion of the He 177V22 in favour of the He 277 (alias He 177B) programme.

The He 177A-7 was planned as a high altitude bomber making use of the additional power available from the DB 613 coupled engine which, comprising two DB 603G engines, provided 3,600 h.p. for take-off and 3,150 h.p. for climb and combat. To simplify and accelerate construction of the bomber, however, standard A-5 airframes and DB 610 power plants were employed by the six He 177A-7 bombers completed, the principal change being an increase in overall wing span to 118 ft. 1$\frac{1}{3}$ in. Empty and loaded weights were increased to 39,913 lb. and 76,280 lb. respectively, and maximum speed was increased to 335 m.p.h. at 20,000 feet.

The Japanese Navy had evinced an interest in the He 177 from an early stage in its development, and work had actually commenced on a new Hitachi factory at Chiba specifically for the quantity production of this bomber. In view of the difficulties being encountered with the coupled power plants, Professor Heinkel himself had advised the Japanese Naval Air Mission visiting Rostock-Marienehe to employ four separate engines rather than coupled units and, following his advice, the proposed Japanese production variant was to have four separate air-cooled radials. Sample tools had been delivered to Japan by submarine, and an He 177A-7 was offered to Japan for service evaluation. The third He 177A-7, completed in May 1944, was prepared for the long-distance flight, much of its armour being stripped and additional fuel cells being installed in both the wings and bomb-bays. In the late summer of 1944, the machine was readied for its non-stop flight which was to be made at extreme altitude via Siberia. However, the Japanese insisted that the aircraft be flown via Persia and India, basing their refusal to permit the aircraft to be flown over the shorter route on their neutrality pact with Russia, and maintaining this attitude even after Russia had renounced the non-aggression pact. Consequently, the He 177A-7 remained in Germany and, together with the other five He 177A-7s completed, was to

have been used to attack American targets.

An interesting experiment in aerial defence was conducted with the He 177 in the summer of 1944 by the Versuchs Jagdgruppe 10. Three He 177s were delivered to Pardubitz in June 1944, and modified for use as bomber "destroyers". Their bomb-bays were removed together with the fuel tanks immediately aft of the cockpit, and a battery of thirty-three rocket tubes was installed. The tubes were inclined to fire upwards at an angle of 60° to the horizontal axis of the aircraft and slightly to starboard. The upper section of the fuselage in which the tubes were installed was fitted with a cover containing thirty-three circular holes. For firing control purposes the battery was divided into two groups of eighteen and twenty-five rockets, and a selector switch allowed for the firing of the whole battery in groups or as single projectiles.

After flight trials, the three He 177s were flown from Pardubitz to Rechlin for firing and operational trials by V.J.G.10. It was proposed that the "destroyer" He 177s would follow an enemy bomber formation, pass below and to port of the intruders, maintaining a difference of altitude of 6,000 feet at the time of the attack from below. Some experimental daylight operations were flown by the He 177s, but no contact was made with Allied bomber formations, and as American escort fighters were becoming increasingly numerous the whole scheme was abandoned.

One of the simplest means of solving the power plant difficulties suffered by the He 177 would have been the adoption of four independent engines during the bomber's early development as was done with the Lancaster. Such a proposal was, in fact, made by Heinkel as early as 1940, and the projected variant with independent engines was designated He 177A-4. The application of cabin pressurization had already been considered, the nose section of the He 177A-1 having been redesigned to facilitate this modification, and the He 177A-4 was envisaged as a pressurized high-altitude bomber. The estimated performance of the He 177A-4 included a maximum speed of 350 m.p.h. at 21,650 feet, a maximum cruising speed of 317 m.p.h. at the same altitude, a service ceiling of 30,840 feet, and a maximum range of 2,270 miles at 258 m.p.h. There were numerous delays before the R.L.M. accepted these proposals, and then it was decided to transfer the design to the German-controlled Société Aéronautique des Avions Farman of Suresnes, near Paris, the type being redesignated He 274A.

Apart from the design study of the He 274, Heinkel's project office at Vienna-Schwechat produced a parallel study for a variant of the basic He 177 design powered by four independent engines, the He 277. Unlike the He 274, the He 277 was intended to retain the standard He 177 airframe which would enable the bulk of the existing tooling to be utilised in the event of a sudden switch to the new machine.

However, the He 277 project was turned down firmly and, indeed, pressure on the part of Professor Heinkel for the development of this bomber in favour of the existing He 177A resulted in Goring expressly forbidding any further mention of the He 277!

Despite this official opposition, Heinkel secretly continued the development of the He 277, and in all official correspondence its continued existence was disguised under the designation "He 177B". In actual fact, all drawings, calculations and works memoranda referred to the bomber as the He 277!

Until 1943, the R.L.M. remained adamant in its refusal to permit any major redesign of the basic He 177A bomber, but, on May 23, 1943, Adolf Hitler summoned a meeting at Obersalzberg of leading members of the aircraft industry, during the course of which the Fuhrer demanded a dual-purpose bomber capable of attacking London by day and night from altitudes at which interceptors would be powerless to intervene, and also suitable for attacking Allied convoys far out in the Atlantic. Heinkel claimed that the "He 177B" could fulfil these demands, and received instructions to proceed immediately with development.

A standard He 177A-3/R2 airframe was promptly modified to take four independent Daimler-Benz DB 603A engines with annular nose radiators as the He 277V1. Flight tests commenced at Vienna-Schwechat late in 1943 and, to delude Goring and the R.L.M., the machine was referred to as the He 177B-0. The second prototype, the He 277V2, referred to in correspondence between Heinkel and the R.L.M. as the He 177B-5/R1, was a conversion of a standard He 177A-5/R8 airframe and was flown for the first time on February 28, 1944, at Vienna-Schwechat. The second prototype was used for stability trials and some directional instability already experienced with the He 277V1 had resulted in the addition of small auxiliary fins to the tailplane.

In April 1944, the He 277V2 was flown to Rechlin for extensive trials where the official test pilots reported that, although the machine suffered some directional instability, the prototype handled exceptionally well. The He 277V2's armament comprised a new remotely-controlled Rheinmetall-Borsig "chin" barbette containing four 7.9-mm. MG 81 machine guns, one 7.9-mm. MG 81 machine gun in the nose, twin 13-mm. MG 131 guns in the remotely-controlled forward dorsal barbette, one MG 131 in the rear dorsal turret, and four MG 81 machine guns in the tail turret. The He 277V3 was similar to the V2 but, after the initial flight tests, a new tail assembly with twin fins and rudders was fitted with highly satisfactory results. After a conference held on May 25, 1944, Goring, declaiming that the heavy bomber "remained the kernel of aerial armament," ordered the immediate initiation of quantity production of the new bomber, the aim being a delivery rate of 200 machines per month!

The initial production model was the He 277B-5/R2 (alias He 177B-5/R2) intended for operation as a heavy bomber over medium and long ranges. It was powered by four 1,750 h.p. DB 603A engines with which it attained a maximum speed of 354 m.p.h. and a cruising speed of 286 m.p.h. Service ceiling was 49,200 feet, range was 3,728 miles, and empty and loaded weights were 48,061 lb. and 98,105 lb. respectively. The internal bomb load was 1,100 pounds and externally under the fuselage a 5,500-lb. bomb, a Hs 293 missile or two Fritz-X guided bombs could be carried. Defensive armament comprised a 7.9-mm. MG 81 machine gun in the extreme nose which was interchangeable with a 15-mm. or 20-mm. MG 151 cannon, four MG 81s in the "chin" barbette, twin MG 131s in the forward dorsal barbette, one MG 131 in the rear dorsal turret, and four MG 81s in the tail. As a result of Goring's order, which, at that stage of the war, was unrealistic in the extreme, quantity production of the He 277B-5/R2 started immediately, but, on July 3, 1944, the whole bomber programme was abandoned in favour of the "emergency fighter programme", and only eight production He 277s were completed and only two or three of these actually test flown.

Prior to the termination of all bomber development, work had started on two further variants, the He 277B-6 and B-7. The He 277B-6 had a wing span of 131 ft. 2¾ in. and four 2,060 h.p. Junkers Jumo 213F engines, and the dihedral angle of the tailplane was increased and the fins and rudders enlarged. The fuselage length was 73 ft. 2½ in. The He 277B-6/R1 was to have employed the Rheinmetall-Borsig HL/131V hydraulically-operated tail turret containing four 13-mm. MG 131 machine guns. This turret was heavily armoured but, in view of some of its features, it was fortunate for Luftwaffe air gunners that it never saw operational service. In the event of the hydraulic elevation drive failing, the top of the gunner's control stick had to be unscrewed and removed before the handle for emergency operation could be turned; the emergency firing switch had to be operated by the gunner's left knee, and the turret door was hinged at the bottom and, after locking, could only be opened in level flight, an attitude unlikely to be adopted by the bomber at the moment the gunner wanted to bale out! Other armament comprised twin 20-mm. MG 151 cannon in the remotely-controlled "chin" barbette and a pair of similar weapons in dorsal and ventral barbettes.

The He 277B-6/R2 had the width of its fuselage reduced to 4 ft. 11 in. and its length increased to 74 ft. 7¾ in., and the nose redesigned to eliminate the ventral bulge, and the He 277B-6/R3 had a deeper fuselage and manned dorsal and ventral gun positions. The He 277B-7 was a projected long-range reconnaissance aircraft derived from the He 177A-7. Featuring the same wing span, it was to be powered by the Jumo 213A, 213E or 222 engines, but only one He 277B-7 was completed, and this with DB 603A engines. This aircraft was destroyed, together with

THE HEINKEL He 177 GREIF

from maintaining any large-scale strategic bombing such as that so successfully initiated by the Allies. The Greif's chief claim to fame was the fact that it was the *only* German heavy bomber to attain quantity production during the war years. It was, in fact, one of the very few entirely new German combat aircraft designed to progress from prototype to operational service during the conflict. It was of ambitious conception, embodying as much ingenuity as any warplane to see combat, but the advances that it offered were nullified by the German aircraft industry's inability to devote sufficient effort towards its perfection.

Derived from the basic He 177 and built in France, the He 274V1, was almost ready to commence flight tests when the Germans were forced to withdraw from the Paris area

the eight He 277B-5s, just before the arrival of Russian troops.

In the meantime, work had been progressing on two prototypes of the He 274A at Farman's Suresnes plant. The fuselage was very similar to that of the He 177A and the tail assembly closely followed that finally selected for the He 277B-5. Like the latter bomber, power was provided by four independent DB 603A engines, although DB 603Gs were proposed for production machines. Although design had been initiated at Vienna-Schwechat in 1940, actual construction at Suresnes did not commence until late in 1943, by which time two prototypes, the He 274V1 and V2, and four He 274A-0 pre-production machines had been ordered.

The pressurized fuselage nose of the He 274 provided accommodation for four crew members, and immediately aft of the flight deck and divided by a catwalk was the main bomb-bay with a maximum capacity of 8,800 lb. The estimated performance included maximum speeds of 267 m.p.h. at sea level, 310 m.p.h. at 18,700 ft., and 373 m.p.h. at 36,000 ft., and range was estimated at 2,500 miles at 285 m.p.h. The He 274V1 was almost ready to fly when the Germans were forced to withdraw from Paris, and although the retreating forces took most of the design data with them, they failed to destroy the airframe which was eventually completed by French technicians and flown several months after the end of the war.

It has been said that the He 177A Greif was deadlier to the crews that flew it than to their enemies. This was, of course, an exaggeration, but the bomber undeniably suffered far more development troubles than any of its contemporaries, and these led to its failure; a failure which prevented the Luftwaffe

Heinkel He 177A-5/R2 Greif

Dimensions: Span, 103 ft. 1¾ in.; length, 66 ft. 11¼ in.; height, 20 ft. 11⅞ in.; wing area, 1,097.918 sq. ft.

Armament: One 7.9-mm. MG 81 machine gun with 2,000 rounds in the nose; one 20-mm. MG 151 cannon with 300 rounds in forward ventral gondola position; two 7.9-mm. MG 81 machine guns with 2,000 r.p.g. in rear ventral gondola position; two 13-mm. MG 131 machine guns with 750 r.p.g. in remotely-controlled dorsal barbette; one 13-mm. MG 131 machine guns with 750 rounds in rear dorsal turret, and one 20-mm. MG 151 cannon with 300 rounds in tail position. Offensive load: (Internally) Sixteen 110-lb., four 550-lb., or two 1,100-lb. bombs. (Externally) Two FX 1400 Fritz radio-directed armour-piercing bombs, two Henschel Hs 293A-D radio-controlled rocket-propelled missiles, two LMA III parachute sea mines, or two LT 50 torpedoes. Maximum bomb load, 13,200 lb.

Power Plants: Two Daimler-Benz DB 610A-1/B-1 (A-1 port and B-1 starboard) twenty-four cylinder liquid-cooled engines each rated at 2,950 h.p. at 2,800 r.p.m. for take-off, 3,100 h.p. at 2,800 r.p.m. at 6,890 ft. for emergency, and 2,750 h.p. at 2,600 r.p.m. at 6,800 ft. maximum continuous.

Weights: Empty (equipped), 37,038 lb.; normal loaded, 59,966 lb.; maximum loaded, 68,343 lb.

Performance: Maximum speed (normal loaded weight), 303 m.p.h. at 20,000 ft., 248.5 m.p.h. at sea level, (maximum loaded weight), 273 m.p.h. at 20,000 ft.; maximum cruising speed, 258 m.p.h. at 20,000 ft., economical cruising speed, 210 m.p.h. at 20,000 ft.; range (with two Hs 293 missiles), 3,417 mls., (with two FX 1400 bombs), 3,100 mls.; initial climb rate, 620 ft./min.; time to 10,000 ft., 10 min., to 20,000 ft., 39 min.; service ceiling, 26,250 ft.

The third Seattle-built Boeing XB-29 Superfortress prototype (41-18335) flew for the first time in June 1943, and embodied extensive engine and equipment revision.

THE BOEING SUPERFORTRESS

While the Boeing Superfortress gained for itself undying fame as the first aircraft to drop an atomic weapon, thus bringing about the sudden termination of hostilities in the Pacific, it is also deserving of a place in the history of aerial warfare as one of the principal Allied weapons in the war against Japan. The laborious and costly island-hopping campaign conducted in the Pacific by the Allied forces was undertaken largely to seize bases for Superfortress operations against the Japanese homeland. Once bases had been established, the Superfortresses of the United States' 20th Air Force systematically and inexorably erased the industrial cities of Japan one by one with the terrible weapon of fire. The closely packed and lightly constructed Japanese buildings were extremely vulnerable to incendiary attacks, and the destruction wreaked by Superfortresses in some built-up areas amounted to as much as 99.5 per cent.

In addition to these devastating blows against strategic targets, the Superfortresses were simultaneously employed on a highly successful campaign of minelaying in Japanese home waters, thereby applying an economic and logistic stranglehold to the islands of Nippon. The delivery of the two atomic bombs against Hiroshima and Nagasaki was, therefore, in the nature of a *coup de grace*, although essential to shorten the war. The Superfortress was, thus, largely responsible for the final defeat and surrender of Japan without invasion, and the instrument which provided the ultimate vindication of the American visionaries of strategic air power.

After the successful outcome of the struggle by the few proponents of strategic air power to procure the B-17 Fortress—the first U.S.A.A.F. strategic bomber —the way for the introduction of very much larger bombers was appreciably smoother, but the Superfortress was not to be the result of a single specification or design development. It was the product of a continuous series of design studies stemming from

the experimental XB-15 of 1937. Such a machine as the Superfortress was first envisaged in the late 'thirties when U.S. military thinking turned to the possibility of an Axis invasion somewhere in the Americas with subsequent enemy air attack against U.S. industrial centres. This concept of "hemisphere defence" called for the production of several types of long-range bombers with operating radii between 1,500 and 4,000 miles, but the 2,000-mile radius bomber specified by the Kilner Board in mid-1939 was perhaps the true starting point for the bomber which was to achieve fame as the Superfortress, although its design origins stretched back even further.

Boeing's design team had included pressurization as an essential in a series of design studies undertaken long before any appropriations were made for a pressurized bomber. The first of these studies, the Model 316, was derived directly from the XB-15, from which it differed primarily in the relocation of the wing from a low to a high position, and the installation of a nosewheel undercarriage—the first to be contemplated for a Boeing design. As the XB-15 had proven seriously under-powered, the Model 316 featured four of the new 2,000 h.p. Wright Duplex-Cyclone R-3350 eighteen-cylinder radials which, it was anticipated, would be more than adequate for the projected bomber's 89,900 lb. gross weight. In March 1938, Boeing had been asked to submit a design study for a pressurized version of the B-17 Fortress with a view to taking maximum advantage of this bomber's high-altitude capabilities. Known as the Model 322, this study resembled the commercial Model 307 Stratoliner in some respects, combining a new, large-diameter circular-section fuselage with standard Fortress wing and tail assemblies. The Model 322 also featured a nosewheel undercarriage and four Pratt and Whitney R-2180 radial engines. Only four gun positions were provided owing to pressurization difficulties, but the bomber had an estimated maximum speed of 307 m.p.h. at 25,000 ft., and a maximum bomb load of 9,928 lb. However, at that time, the Air Corps was receiving insufficient funds for the purchase of adequate quantities of the existing Fortresses, and the project was not taken up officially, although Boeing continued design development as a private venture.

In the next series of studies, Boeing proposed the use of the new liquid-cooled Allison V-1710 engine of 1,150 h.p., and in the Model 333, these engines were installed in tandem pairs. The significance of this project in the subsequent development of the Superfortress was that, for the first time, it was proposed to utilise two pressurized sections in the fuselage linked by a small-diameter tunnel, and this feature was to be retained in all subsequent design studies up to and including the Superfortress. The Model 333A differed from its predecessor primarily in the relocation of the engines, but because of the low-altitude characteristics of the V-1710 power plant, variations of the project were proposed with the new flat-mounted Wright and Pratt and Whitney radial engines. In February 1939, the Model 333B project was finalised, with four 1,850 h.p. Wright R-1800 engines buried in the thick, 111 ft.-span wing, and with a gross weight of 52,180 lb., its maximum speed was estimated at 364 m.p.h. at 20,000 ft.

Because of the restrictions on wing space resulting from the buried engines, the Model 333B would have had a range of only 2,500 miles when carrying a 2,000-lb. bomb load, and this was inadequate for the "hemisphere defence" concept. Thus, a month later, the Model 334 was projected, the wing span being extended to 120 ft. in order to provide sufficient fuel capacity for a range of 4,500 miles. The power plants —this time Pratt and Whitney radials—were still buried in the wing, a twin fin-and-rudder assembly was selected to facilitate the installation of tail armament, and gross weight was increased to 66,000 lb. to permit a maximum bomb load of 7,830 lb. The Superfortress began to take recognisable shape in July 1939, however, with the appearance of the Model 334A project in which both the buried engine installation and the twin fin-and-rudder assembly were rejected in favour of conventionally-mounted Wright R-3350 radials and a single vertical tail surface. The Model 334A featured a high aspect ratio wing of 135 ft. span, and such was the promise of the project that Boeing built a mock-up of the bomber at their own expense in December 1939.

Although these design projects had grown steadily in size, one more step was necessary in order to produce a bomber within the scope of the so-called "Superbomber" specification which was to be issued in January 1940, and this step was taken with the Model 341, design of which was initiated in August 1939. The Boeing Aerodynamics Unit had developed a new high-lift aerofoil for a high aspect-ratio wing of 124 ft. 7 in., and this offered the Model 341 an estimated maximum speed of no less than 405 m.p.h. at 25,000 ft., despite the proposed use of the smaller Pratt and Whitney R-2800 engines of 2,000 h.p. Weighing 85,672 lb., this bomber was expected to have a range of 7,000 miles with one ton of bombs, or a maximum load of 10,000 lb. over shorter distances.

On November 10, 1939, General H. H. Arnold, then Chief of the Air Corps, asked the War Department for permission to issue a specification for a "Superbomber" to replace the B-17 Fortress and the B-24 Liberator, and the necessary authority was granted on December 2nd. As Data R-40B, the specification was circulated among the Boeing, Lockheed, Douglas and Consolidated companies on January 29, 1940, calling for a bomber with a speed of 400 m.p.h., a range of 5,333 miles, and the ability to deliver a 2,000-lb. load over this range. In the light of early wartime experience in Europe, the original specification was almost immediately modified with regard to defensive armament, and in order to incorporate self-sealing fuel tanks, additional armour, etc.

In order to meet the requirements of the specification, the Boeing engineers scaled up the overall dimensions of the Model 341 project, replaced the R-2800 engines with the more powerful Wright R-3350s, and came up with the Model 345 which was submitted to Wright Field on May 11, 1940. The Model 345 had a 141 ft. 3 in. wing, and a double-wheeled tricycle undercarriage, the main members of which were designed to retract into the engine nacelles instead of sideways into the wing as in previous projects. The projected bomber possessed a similar range to that of the Model 341, but the maximum bomb load had been increased to 16,000 lb. The estimated speed of 382 m.p.h. at 25,000 feet was slightly lower than that of the smaller project, but the defensive armament had been substantially increased from six manually-operated 0.5-in. guns to ten guns of the same calibre plus one 20-mm. cannon. These were all mounted in Sperry retractable power-operated turrets above and below the fuselage, and in the tail, operated under remote control by gunners looking through periscopes at strategic points.

Evaluation of the preliminary designs submitted by Boeing, Lockheed, Douglas and Consolidated placed them in that order of preference, and contracts for preliminary engineering data issued on June 27, 1940, designated the bombers XB-29, XB-30, XB-31, and XB-32 respectively. The Lockheed and Douglas designs were subsequently withdrawn from the competition, but development of the Consolidated XB-32 continued as a safeguard against the failure of the favoured Boeing XB-29. On August 24, funds were appropriated for the construction of two XB-29 prototypes, and two XB-32s were also ordered. On December 14, a third XB-29 was ordered, together with a static test airframe.

THE BOEING SUPERFORTRESS

In the event, the rival Consolidated XB-32 was the first of the two bombers to fly—on September 7, 1942—but the teething troubles suffered by this aircraft were such that relatively few had attained service status by the closing months of the war. Backing of the Boeing XB-29 was something of a gamble, since under the normal procurement policy existing in 1940, the bomber could not have been delivered until 1945, and it therefore had to be ordered in quantity before ever the prototype became airborne. Large-scale production was authorised on May 17, 1941, when the U.S.A.A.F announced that an order would be placed for 250 machines to be built at the Government owned Wichita factory. This contract, which was signed in September, was doubled in January 1942, and in the following month, the U.S.A.A.F. announced that the new bomber was also to be built by Bell Aircraft, North American Aviation, and the Fisher Body Division of General Motors. Thus, by the time the first XB-29 made its first flight on September 21, 1942, tooling was well advanced for orders totalling no less than 1,664 machines.

Although each B-29 Superfortress bomber necessitated diverting the material sufficient to build eleven P-51 Mustang fighters, with the corresponding production facilities, the U.S.A.A.F. gamble was based upon the reputation gained by the B-17 Fortress, and the experience of the Boeing company in the construction of large, multi-engined aircraft. These included, of course, the pre-war Model 307 Stratoliner which had been the first pressurized aircraft to enter commercial service, and which gave Boeing a head start with the incorporation of this radical feature in the XB-29. Although strikingly clean in design, the Model 345 was further refined, particular attention being paid to fuselage shape and engine nacelle fairing. The forward fuselage was extended, resulting in an increase in length from 93 ft. to 98 ft. 2 in., and the contours of the streamlined transparent nose was rounded off. The shape of the inner engine nacelles gave cause for particular concern since they each had to house two turbo-superchargers with their intercoolers, plus the twin-wheeled main undercarriage units. The final nacelle shape was one of the cleanest ever produced, although passing more cooling air through than any previous type.

The rear portions of the inner engine nacelles were extended aft of the wing trailing edges which were modified to improve the flap characteristics, and a large dorsal extension was added to the vertical tail surfaces to improve asymmetric handling, but the tailplane and elevators remained exactly the same size and shape as those of the B-17 Fortress, although they were of different section and construction. They were, in fact, flight tested on a B-17 which was also used to develop servo-tabs to lighten the load on all the controls of the Superfortress. Redesign of the bomb bay allowed a large number of small bombs to be carried in addition to the 1,000-lb. and 2,000-lb. bombs originally planned, and at the same time the maximum capacity was increased to 20,000 lb.

Final armament modifications resulted in the Sperry remotely-controlled gun turrets becoming permanently external instead of retractable, but despite this modification, the Superfortress suffered no more drag than the Fortress, although being one-third as large again and, at 114,500 lb., almost twice the weight. Design estimates then indicated a reduced maximum range of 5,333 miles with one ton of bombs which was that originally demanded, and the finalised aircraft met with the complete approval of the U.S.A.A.F., although some service technicians were concerned over the bomber's high wing loading. At one time, some pressure was applied to Boeing to reduce the wing loading by increasing the bomber's wing area, but Boeing engineers succeeded in convincing the critics that any increase in wing area would seriously reduce the machine's performance. Fowler flaps reduced the high wing loading problem during the critical take-off and landing phases of a flight, increasing the lift coefficient of the wing and adding some twenty per cent to the overall area when extended.

A full-scale wooden mock-up of the XB-29 was made available for U.S.A.A.F. inspection from April

The first XB-29 Superfortress prototype (41-002), flown for the first time on September 21, 1942, was completed without the remotely-controlled armament system.

The first Wichita-built Superfortress, B-29-1-BW (42-6242), delivered deficient from the combat-readiness viewpoint and subsequently modified during the "Battle of Kansas".

7, 1941, and a month later the first engineering drawings were released for prototype construction. On June 16, 1941, production engineering began for fourteen YB-29s for service evaluation and 250 B-29s, the first twenty-five machines being required by February 1943. As the Boeing plants were entirely occupied with B-17 Fortress orders, a completely new factory for Superfortress production had to be built at Wichita, and after Pearl Harbour, it was obvious that further facilities would be required. Superfortress production was therefore planned at other plants, including a new Boeing factory at Renton; a factory to be operated by Bell Aircraft and to be built at Georgia, and a Glenn Martin factory at Omaha which was selected to replace the Fisher Body plant at Cleveland originally designated as a Superfortress production source. It was planned that Boeing's Seattle plant would also produce the Superfortress as Fortress production tapered off, and in addition to the airframe assembly plants, the most widespread sub-contracting programme ever planned was established, and such companies as Fisher Body, Chrysler, Hudson, Goodyear, Briggs, Murray and Cessna produced major airframe components.

Powered by four 2,200 h.p. Wright R-3350-13 engines driving three-bladed airscrews, the first XB-29 (No. 41-2) made its first flight from Boeing Field, Seattle, on September 21, 1942, with Edward Allen at the controls. The first airframe was completed without the remotely-controlled armament system in order to accelerate flight testing, but this programme suffered a serious set-back when the second XB-29 (No. 41-3), which had flown for the first time on December 28, 1942, developed an unextinguishable engine fire while making a landing approach on February 18, 1943, plunging into a nearby factory, killing eleven of Boeing's most experienced Superfortress specialists, including test pilot Edward Allen, and a score of workers on the ground.

Some delay was then encountered in the development programme while fire hazards in the XB-29 were reduced, but in June 1943, the third Seattle-built prototype (41-18335) began its flight tests. This third machine embodied extensive engine and equipment revision which resulted from experience gained with its two predecessors, and was soon handed over to the A.A.F. at Wichita for armament and accelerated flight testing. This prototype also crashed, but not before the potential of the design had been indicated. Among the principal changes required for production B-29s were the introduction of four-bladed Hamilton-Standard airscrews, and the replacement of the periscopically-sighted Sperry gun turrets by a completely new system of General Electric turrets controlled from adjacent astrodomes. This change in armament caused considerable delay in the B-29 programme, although the first YB-29 (41-36954) with Wright R-3350-21 engines, left the line at Wichita on April 15, 1943, flying for the first time on June 26, 1943.

By July, seven YB-29s had been delivered to the

The B-29A differed from the B-29 in having a stub wing centre section resulting in a one foot increase in overall wing span. The aircraft illustrated here is a B-29A-5-BN.

A.A.F., and, as representative operational aircraft, they were used to equip new training groups categorised as VHB (Very Heavy Bomber) or VLR (Very Long Range) units. The application of these units had changed considerably from the original conception of hemisphere defence, and eventually differed substantially from the 1940 plan of having twenty-four B-29/B-32 groups to bomb Germany from the United Kingdom and North Africa, plus a possible further two groups operating against Japan from Luzon. It was not until December 1943 that the decision not to use the B-29 against Germany was finally taken, but in the meantime, Brig.-Gen. K. B. Wolfe had been given the task of setting up Super-fortress combat training units for operations in 1944 against Japanese targets from bases in China. This was done simultaneously with the service testing of the YB-29s, and on June 1, 1943, the first Super-fortress unit—the 58th Bombardment Wing (VH)—was activated at Marietta, near Bell's Superfortress plant. One hundred and fifty Superfortresses had been promised for early 1944, enough for four VHB groups, and on September 15, 1943, the Wing Headquarters was re-established at Salina, Kansas, with some of its groups near the Wichita factory. The first Superfortress Wing initially comprised five groups—the 40th, 444th, 462nd, 468th and 472nd Bombardment Groups (VH)—but the last of these was scheduled to remain at Smoky Hill Field, Salina, as an operational training unit. On November 27, 1943, the XX Bomber Command was formed at Salina for overall control of the Superfortress units, and another Very Heavy Wing, the 73rd, was formed with four more groups to absorb the second batch of 150 Superfortresses.

At that time, however, there was only one Super-fortress for each twelve crews, since it was not until October 7th that the flight characteristics of the air-craft received A.A.F. approval, and all initial crew training had to be conducted on Martin B-26 Marauders and Boeing B-17 Fortresses. At that time, much of the Superfortress's equipment had not been perfected or, indeed, tested on the prototype or pre-production aircraft, and rather than delay production by stopping the assembly lines to in-corporate modifications and equipment, the first production aeroplanes were leaving the lines at Wichita deficient from the combat-readiness view-point. The A.A.F. had established modification centres to bring the Superfortresses up to combat standards, but the programme was seriously hampered by the need to work in the open air in inclement weather, delays in acquiring the necessary tools and support equipment, and the A.A.F.'s limited experience with the B-29. Such were the delays that Boeing personnel had to be drafted from the Wichita and Seattle factories to reorganise the programme and assist with the modifications. The period from March 10—April 15, 1944, when the first Superfortresses for combat duty were passing through the modification centres, became known as the "Battle of Kansas".

Towards the end of 1943, the Bell-Marietta and Boeing-Renton plants began turning out production Superfortresses, which, from the former factory, were like the B-29-BW and later B-29-MO aircraft in being powered by R-3350-23, -23A or (when modified) -41 engines, having a war emergency rating of 2,300 h.p. Maximum permissible weight of the first Super-fortress series was 138,000 lb., although the normal gross was 133,500 lb. There were slight differences in equipment among the various sub-contracted aircraft, but they all started off with the same armament and fuel capacity. The Superfortress was the first production aircraft to make extensive use of remotely-controlled armament. While manned turrets had been contemplated during early stages of the Superfortress's design, they had been rejected as unsuitable for the altitudes at which the bomber was designed to operate. Four barbettes, each containing two 0.5-in. guns, were, therefore, installed at strategic positions in the fuselage, two on top and two underneath, and controlled remotely from sighting stations in the pressurized areas of the fuselage. These twin-gun barbettes, each with 1,000 r.p.g., could be controlled from a primary or a secondary station, and, in addition, a tail turret under the direct control of a tail gunner, housed two 0.5-in. machine guns and a 20-mm. M-2 Type B cannon with 100 rounds. Fuel was stowed in fourteen outer-wing, eight inner-wing, and four bomb-bay tanks, to give a maximum capacity of 6,801 Imp.gal. (8,168 U.S.gal.), but an early modification added four tanks in the wing centre-section, bringing the total to 7,896 Imp.gal. (9,438 U.S.gal.).

This fuel load gave the Superfortress a maximum range of well over the 5,000 mile figure of the original Project "A", but this was only possible for ferrying purposes, a more normal range being about 3,700 miles with up to 12,000 lb. of bombs. Maximum internal bomb load was 20,000 lb. (for 2,850 miles), with provision for alternatives of four 4,000-lb., eight 2,000-lb., twelve 1,600-lb., twelve 1,000-lb., or forty 500-lb. bombs. Later production versions of the Superfortress had the front upper turret armament increased from two to four 0.5-in. guns, each with 875 rounds, and the last batches (B-29-25 to -65-BA*; B-29-50 to -100-BW, and B-29-20 to

---

* BA=Bell (Atlanta); BW=Boeing (Wichita), and MO=Martin (Omaha). Other manufacturers were BN=Boeing (Renton) and BO=Boeing (Seattle).

-60-MO) lost the 20-mm. cannon from the tail position. Lingering doubts as to the practicability of the remotely-controlled armament system, however, resulted in the completion of one B-29-25-BW (42-2444) with manned turrets. This aircraft featured two power-operated dorsal turrets and two central "ball" turrets each containing two 0.5-in. machine guns, one 0.5-in. gun in each of two beam positions, and two additional 0.5-in. guns in a blister on each side of the fuselage nose.

The Martin-Omaha plant turned out its first B-29 in mid-1944, and completed 536 of the 2,774 Superfortresses of the first series to be built. Effort at the Boeing-Renton factory was devoted entirely to the slightly modified B-29A (production blocks -1 to -75-BN) of which 1,119 were produced. The B-29A differed in having R-3350-57 or -59 engines of the standard 2,200 h.p., and only three centre-wing tanks in all but the first few machines, giving a maximum fuel capacity of 7,734 Imp.gal. (9,288 U.S.gal.). They also lost the single tail cannon (before the four-gun upper turret was introduced), and had a 1 ft. increase in span, to 142 ft. 3 in. as the result of the adoption of a stub wing centre section, the wing of the B-29A being built in seven major pieces as compared with the six pieces of the B-29's wing. Three B-29A-BN Superfortresses were converted by the Pratt and Whitney company to take 3,000 h.p. R-4360-33 engines, and redesignated XB-44, to become test-beds for the later Boeing B-50. This followed an earlier conversion of a YB-29, which was fitted with four 2,600 h.p. Allison V-3420-11 liquid-cooled inline engines for experimental purposes, and became the XB-39. In both cases, the maximum speed was increased to more than 400 m.p.h., despite the increased gross weights of 145,000 and 142,000 lb., and the potentialities of bigger power plants convincingly demonstrated.

One of the biggest drawbacks of the Superfortress was its tendency towards being underpowered at high gross weights, resulting in a certain amount of engine trouble throughout its service life. This was a small price to pay for the truly remarkable rapidity of its

One B-29-25-BW Superfortress (42-2444) was completed with twin manned dorsal turrets and two "ball" turrets, each with two 0.5-in. guns, and a similar gun in each of two beam positions and on each side of the nose.

FINISH AND INSIGNIA: The Boeing B-29-45-MO illustrated is probably the most famous of all Superfortress bombers, being Colonel Tibbets' "Enola Gay" from which the first operational atomic weapon was dropped. This aircraft, which belonged to the 393rd Bombardment Squadron (VH) of the 315th Bombardment Wing, was non-standard insofar as the fore and aft dorsal and ventral gun barbettes were removed, although the manned tail turret was retained. Whereas early production Superfortresses had matt olive drab upper surfaces with grey under surfaces, in common with all aircraft of this type operational with the U.S. Twentieth Air Force in the Far East, "Enola Gay" employed a natural metal finish over all surfaces.

The national insignia, which comprised a white five-pointed star on a dark blue circular field superimposed on a white bar which, in turn, was outlined in dark blue, appeared on the upper surface of the port wing, the lower surface of the starboard wing, and on each side of the fuselage. When delivered from the factory, the serial number normally appeared on the tail fin in black, but this was invariably deleted in the field to provide space for the group symbol. The Bombardment Group letter "R" appeared in black on the vertical tail surfaces, this being enclosed in a black circle indicating the Air Division. For the atomic strike, the group letter was replaced by a black arrowhead in a circle (this insignia being illustrated by the photograph on page 116). The individual aircraft number "82" appeared in black aft of the national insignia on the fuselage sides, and was repeated above and ahead of the nosewheel housing. The name "Enola Gay" was painted in black below the transparent panels of the flight deck.

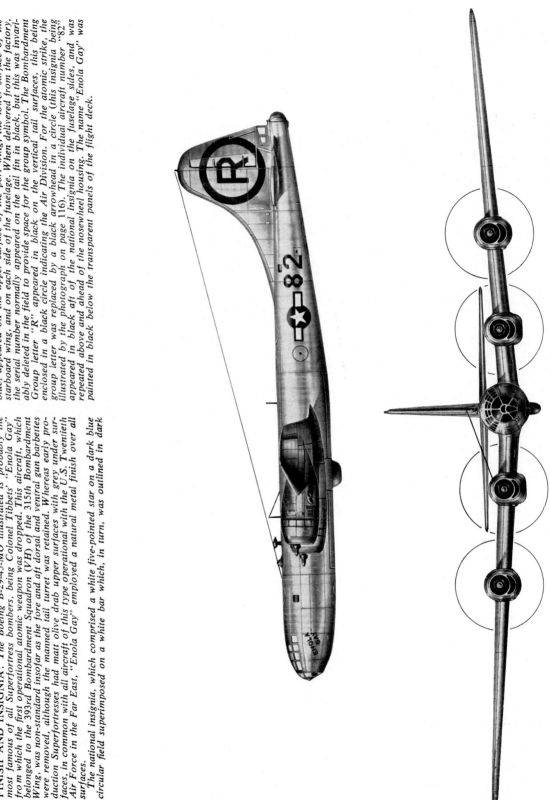

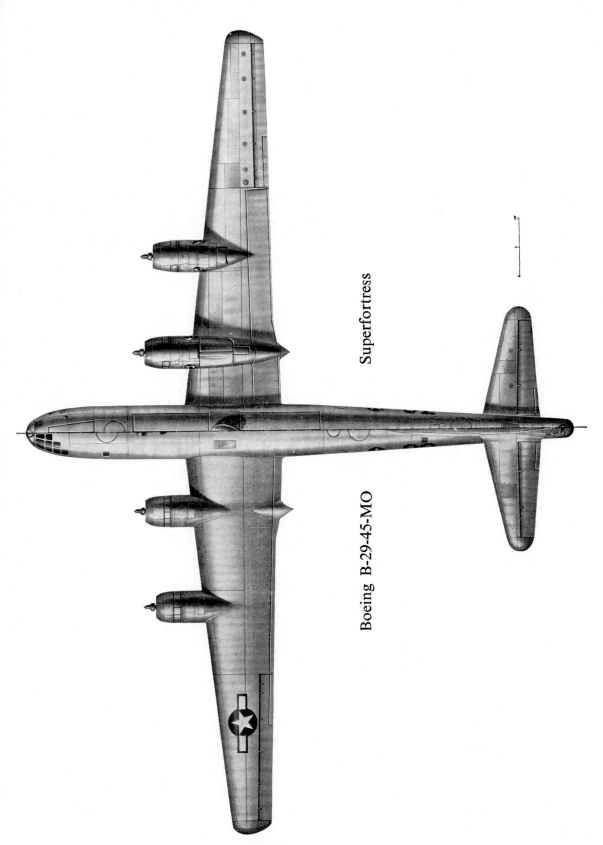

Superfortress

Boeing B-29-45-MO

The B-29-45-MO "Enola Gay" which, piloted by Colonel Tibbets, dropped the atomic bomb on Hiroshima. The aircraft was accompanied on its mission by six other Superfortresses carrying observers and survival equipment.

development, and the Superfortress's operational efficiency far outweighed the inevitable shortcomings. It was little more than eighteen months after the first flight of the XB-29 that the first Superfortress landed in China, on April 24, 1944, at Kwanghan, supported logistically by C-46, C-54, C-87 and C-109 transports, and it is a little-known fact that one of the first Superfortresses to go overseas was flown to the United Kingdom in March 1944, to be demonstrated to the 8th Air Force before proceeding to the main Far Eastern Superfortress base at Calcutta. The use of this somewhat devious delivery route was intended to delude the Axis powers into believing that the B-29 was to be used against Germany.

Despite the secrecy with which the Superfortress bases had been prepared, and the various deceptions practised, the Japanese had no difficulty in identifying the Superfortresses as soon as they arrived in the Far East; an arrival delayed by a week due to the aircraft being grounded after several accidents on the ferry route. Five B-29s were lost through engine failures, and four seriously damaged out of the initial batch of 150 sent to India, but when the ferry trips stopped, in March 1945, only three more had been lost out of the overall total of 405 despatched.

Before the Superfortresses began bombing operations from their Chinese bases, they had to assist in airlifting all necessary supplies and fuel over the "Hump". For this task, some were stripped of nearly all combat equipment and, used as flying tankers, each carried seven tons of fuel. This transport role, while vitally necessary, prevented further operational training from being completed, and when the first mission was scheduled—against railways shops at Bangkok, Thailand—most of the 240 crews in XX Bomber Command had an average of less than two hours' B-29 combat training each. A short and intensive training programme was, therefore, instituted, before the combat schedules were planned. Bomb loads were to be 10,000 lb. per aircraft, and with 5,700 Imp.gal. (6,846 U.S.gal.) of fuel, the

aircraft were to weigh 134,000 lb. About one hundred Superfortresses were despatched in daylight from bases in India to attack Bangkok on June 5, 1944, and most of these bombed their targets by radar owing to the bad weather—the latter largely accounting for the five aircraft lost on this initial mission. Somewhat surprisingly, in view of the Japanese awareness of the existence of the Superfortresses in the theatre, Radio Tokyo reported that the Bangkok raid had been made by B-24 Liberators.

All the aircraft of the 58th Bombardment Wing (VH) were Wichita-built B-29-BWs, which were, therefore, the first to bomb enemy targets. From the outset, they made good use of the extensive radar and electronic equipment with which they were provided, which included Loran, BTO, "H2X" (later "Eagle"), "Raven" electronic countermeasures on occasions, and "Ella" IFF. To relieve Japanese pressure in Eastern China, where Brig.-Gen. Claire Chennault's forward airfields were threatened, the next Superfortress mission was scheduled against Japan, where, on June 15th, about fifty B-29s bombed the steel mills at Yawata by night. This operation cost seven Superfortresses, only one due to enemy action, but, like the Bangkok raid, little damage was sustained by the targets.

From thence onwards, the build-up of Superfortress missions was slow and widely scattered until the capture of the Mariana Islands of Saipan, Guam and Tinian in July and August 1944 permitted the construction of five great airfields, each accommodating a wing of 180 Superfortresses and 12,000 men. under the newly formed 20th Air Force. These bases enabled the VHB offensive to be concentrated on Japan, after a series of training missions by additional B-29 groups which arrived in the Marianas from October 12th onwards. The first Marianas-based attack against the Japanese homeland took place on November 24th when eighty-eight Superfortresses bombed Tokyo, but the success of this and subsequent daylight attacks was limited.

This B-29-30-BW (42-24473) was the fifty-fourth Wichita-built Superfortress of the second production order (calling for five hundred aircraft) allocated to this plant.

The U.S.A.A.F. was attempting to use the Super-fortresses on similar operations to those of the 8th Air Force over Germany (i.e. daylight precision raids in formation at high altitudes). This resulted in poor bombing accuracy, small bomb loads to ensure altitude performance, and considerable engine trouble because of the prolonged climbs required at high gross weights. Maj.-Gen. Curtiss E. LeMay, who had been given the B-29 command in the India-China theatre, took over the Marianas-based Super-fortresses in January 1945, and was immediately keen to try the effects of incendiary attacks against Japanese cities. He also decided, in March, to change the Superfortress's role to that of low-altitude night bomber. This greatly increased the available bomb load of the B-29, and simultaneously decreased its vulnerability over the target since the Japanese possessed little or no night defence organisation.

In the first of these attacks, on March 9th, 334 Superfortresses burned out some sixteen square miles of the heart of Tokyo, killing more than 80,000 people—the greatest destruction of any single raid of the war. Within a few days, four more major cities had been attacked, and thirty-two square miles of destruction added to the score of the Superfortresses. Having met virtually no aerial opposition during their nocturnal attacks, the A.A.F. decided to strip its B-29s of all defensive armament except the two 0.5-in. machine guns in the tail, thus permitting the maximum load of bombs to be carried. In addition to B-29s and B-29As stripped in the field, the Bell-Atlanta plant built 311 Superfortresses with only tail armament and two 0.5-in. guns on special hand-held mountings in the waist positions of the pressurised gunners' cabin, as B-29Bs. With R-3350-51s, or similar series engines to earlier B-29s, these had their maximum speeds increased by 10 m.p.h. to 367 m.p.h. at 30,000 ft. At the same gross weight of 135,000 lb. as earlier B-29s, and carrying a similar fuel load of 5,764 Imp.gal. (6,923 U.S.gal.), the B-29B could carry 16,000 lb. of bombs instead of 12,000 lb. over a range of about 2,600 miles.

As the Pacific War drew towards a conclusion, rapidly accelerated by the depredations of the Super-fortresses, about one thousand B-29s were opera-tional in twenty-one combat groups of the 20th Air Force out of a total of forty VHB groups which had by then been formed. In addition to devastating bombing attacks by as many as 600 aircraft in a day, the Pacific-based Superfortresses flew 1,528 mining sorties around Japan in 1945, planting by parachute more than 12,000 mines. These are estimated to have resulted in the sinking of about 800,000 tons of Japanese shipping. Another important task per-formed by the Superfortresses was photographic-reconnaissance. As no other aircraft had the range to survey B-29 targets for damage reports, a few Superfortresses were modified in the field to carry cameras in mid-1944. The first of these crashed during the initial B-29 mission against Japan in June 1944, but others later photographed Okinawa for airfield sites and as a prelude to the island's invasion.

Meanwhile, technicians at Wright Field were developing an extensively modified Superfortress expressly for photographic-reconnaissance duties, with long-range fuel tanks in the bomb-bay, and numerous K-18 and K-22 cameras to cover oblique, tri-metrogen, and vertical survey. As the F-13A, a number of Superfortresses were converted from B-29-BWs and B-29A-BNs, and were sent to the Pacific in November 1944. In the following month, when seven F-13As had arrived in the China-Burma-India theatre, "C" Flight of the 1st Squadron, 311th Photo-Reconnaissance Wing, was established with them, and missions were soon flown to Penang, Bangkok and Saigon. More F-13As later arrived, and these continued to operate on vital photo-reconnaissance sorties until the end of the Pacific War.

The final Superfortress offensive was undertaken mostly at night, but occasionally by day, with P-51D Mustang escort from Iwo Jima, and by May 1945, Tokyo, Nagoya and Yokohama had been virtually burned out. Bombing techniques employed path-

117

This B-29A-30-BN (42-94106), like all A-model Superfortresses, differed from the initial production model in having a four-gun forward turret and a stub wing centre section.

finder lead ships, carrying 180 70-lb. M47 Napalm-filled bombs each, followed by the main force with each Superfortress dropping twenty-four 500-lb. clusters of M69 oil incendiaries in a pattern, distributing 8,333 of these bombs per square mile. On some occasions, the attacking Superfortresses suffered heavy losses, not usually through direct combat, and in the Tokyo raid of May 25th, twenty-six B-29s were lost of the 502 despatched. The overall loss rate, nevertheless, at this stage of the offensive, was only 1.9 per cent.

When the B-29-45-MO (44-86292) "Enola Gay" ushered in the atomic age over Hiroshima on August 6, 1945, this was the climax of the most memorable chapter in the development of the Superfortress. From 1943 onwards, when much scientific effort was concentrated on producing an atomic bomb, it was obvious that such a weapon would be very large, and it was realised that the Superfortress would be the only aircraft capable of carrying it. The A.A.F. was made responsible for modifications to the aircraft to render it suitable for ballistic tests on the bomb, and for organising a special operational unit, and work began early in 1944 to produce fifteen Superfortresses capable of carrying the nuclear weapon. The modifications involved were fairly extensive, but the atomic bomb was tailored as closely as possible to fit the B-29.

The unit selected to work up with the new weapon, in mid-1944, was the recently-formed 393rd Bombardment Squadron (VH), within the specialist 509th Composite Group, which was taken over at Wendover Field, Utah, by Colonel Paul W. Tibbets on December 17th. The Squadron's Superfortresses then dropped inert experimental versions of the weapon to test its ballistics, and their training was completed by long-range practice flying from Batista Field, Cuba. In May, the Composite Group, with its parent 315th Bombardment Wing, took its Superfortresses, which were stripped of all turrets and guns except in the tail, to Tinian in the Marianas, where training and conventional bombing sorties over Japan for target familiarization soon began.

Simulated atomic missions were also flown, usually at about 29,000 ft., but dropping T.N.T.-filled, light-cased, 10,000-lb. missiles with similar ballistics to the nuclear bomb. By the end of July, soon after the first test weapon had been exploded in New Mexico, the Group was ready, and two operational bombs had been ferried to the Pacific by air and sea transport. The first target had eventually been selected as Hiroshima, as the largest un-bombed Japanese city, and seven Superfortresses were designated for the mission. Of these, one was a spare to stand by at Iwo Jima; three were weather reconnaissance aircraft to survey the primary, secondary and tertiary targets, and two were observation aircraft carrying cameras, recording equipment, scientists and technicians to accompany the single strike aircraft, Colonel Tibbet's "Enola Gay". Two F-13As were laid on for subsequent target reconnaissance, and other specially-equipped B-29s, carrying survival equipment, and known as "Superdumbos", were arranged to provide air-sea rescue facilities as in the case of normal Superfortress missions. These "Superdumbos" were, incidentally, the predecessors of later lifeboat-carrying Superfortresses designated SB-29s.

The seven Superfortresses on the first atomic strike had their group insignia and aircraft names painted over for the mission, but wore special so-called "vistory" numbers. The crews concerned were given some indication of the power of their special weapon, but not its precise nature. The atomic bomb itself, which had been nicknamed the "Little Boy", was a cylindrical device measuring 129-in. in length by 31.5-in. in diameter. Four antennae bristled from its tail, and, weighing 9,700 lb., it contained 137.3 lb. of Uranium 235. "Enola Gay" took-off from Tinian at 02.45 hours on August 6, 1945, and as the aircraft approached the Japanese coast, the primary target was reported relatively clear for attack. At 09.15 hours, Major T. W. Ferebee released the nuclear bomb at an altitude of 31,600 ft., and a ground speed of 328 m.p.h. At 800 ft. above Hiroshima a powder charge sent one Uranium mass through a hollow shaft into the other mass, and one fifteen-hundredth of a microsecond later fission commenced. With the equivalent force of 20,000 tons of T.N.T., it devastated 4.7 square miles of the city, and killed more than 70,000 people.

Three days later, on August 9th, a second atomic force attacked Nagasaki. Deletion of the aircraft markings resulted in some confusion in official reports of this raid which initially credited one of the observation aircraft, "The Great Artiste" of Major Charles W. Sweeney, with having dropped the second atomic weapon. In fact, this aircraft, which Major Sweeney had flown on observation duties on the Hiroshima strike, was exchanged for another Superfortress, Captain F. Bock's "Bockscar" in order to obviate the necessity of removing the special scientific equipment installed in "The Great Artiste" for the previous strike. Captain Bock took over Major Sweeney's aircraft, and the latter officer released the atomic bomb from "Bockscar". It was only after the war, when it was planned to preserve "The Great Artiste" as a museum piece, that a check of serial numbers in the mission reports revealed the error. In very poor weather conditions, the Nagasaki bomb was dropped largely by radar, but again the results were devastating. When the Japanese

The first YB-29 Superfortress (41-36954) was fitted with four Allison V-3420-11 liquid-cooled engines for experimental purposes and redesignated XB-39.

surrender followed, on August 14th, no fewer than 828 Superfortresses were airborne on conventional bombing missions. The massive force was then transferred to transport and supply dropping operations, although 462 Superfortresses were mustered to fly over the U.S.S. *Missouri* during the surrender ceremonies on September 2nd.

During the Pacific War, Superfortresses dropped 171,060 tons of conventional bombs on Japanese territory, compared with 6,781 tons for all other aircraft combined. In addition to atomic weapons, some of the Superfortresses were equipped to carry a 22,000-lb. "Grand Slam" or "earthquake" bomb of British design under each inner wing, between the engine nacelle and the fuselage, giving a short-range offensive load of 44,000 lb. These weapons were not used operationally, although after the war some Superfortresses modified to carry a single 22,000-lb. bomb half-buried in the bomb-bay were used in extensive tests against German defences on deserted Baltic islands.

With the termination of the Second World War, development of the B-29C (with improved Wright R-3350 engines) by Boeing-Seattle was cancelled, and the re-engined B-29D-BN, with four 3,000 h.p. Pratt and Whitney R-4360 power plants, was subsequently developed into the newer B-50. When production ceased at Renton on May 28, 1946, V-J Day having resulted in the cancellation of 5,092 Superfortresses still on order in September 1945, although a small number well advanced on the assembly lines were completed, 3,970 Superfortresses had been built, including 2,766 by Boeing at Seattle, Renton and Wichita; 668 by Bell and 536 by Martin. On V-J Day, the U.S.A.A.F. had 2,132 Superfortresses on hand, and many of these were subsequently cocooned for long-term storage.

It makes an interesting tailpiece to the wartime story of the Superfortress to recall the admiration for this splendid bomber evinced by the United States' erstwhile allies, the Russians. In fact, such was their interest in the B-29 that the Russians sequestrated three Superfortresses that, short of fuel after bombing missions against Japan, were forced to land at Vladivostok, the nearest "friendly" territory. The first B-29 to land at Vladivostok was piloted by

Captain Howard R. Jarrell; the second was the "General Arnold Special", the most famous Superfortress produced by the Boeing-Wichita plant, and the first aircraft over the target on the first B-29 mission of the war, and the third was piloted by 1st Lt. William J. Mickish. The crews were eventually returned to the United States, but their aircraft were retained by the Russians who eventually produced copies of the B-29 under the designation Tupolev Tu-4 as the standard long-range heavy bomber of the Soviet Air Forces. The adoption of this aircraft by the Russians in 1947 was a strange tribute to the soundness of the Superfortress's 1940 conception., but imitation *is* the sincerest form of flattery.

The Superfortress made an immense contribution to subsequent bomber design. It was the Second World War's heaviest production warplane, and the first pressurised aircraft to attain large-scale production. It was also the first to make extensive use of remotely-controlled armament, but perhaps the most remarkable feature of its history was the fact that it was designed, built, tested, and placed in operational service within four years.

Boeing B-29 Superfortress

Dimensions:	Span, 141 ft. 3 in.; length, 99 ft. 0 in.; height, 27 ft. 9 in.; wing area, 1,736 sq. ft.
Armament:	Twelve 0.5-in. machine guns in four remotely-controlled turrets and in the tail, each with 1,000 rounds of ammunition, plus a single rearward-firing 20-mm. M2 Type B cannon with 100 rounds. Maximum internal short-range bomb load, 20,000 lb.
Power Plants:	Four Wright Cyclone R-3350-23 eighteen-cylinder air-cooled radial engines, each with two General Electric turbo-superchargers, rated at 2,200 h.p. at 2,800 r.p.m. for take-off, and with a war emergency rating of 2,300 h.p. at 25,000 ft.
Weights:	Empty, 74,500 lb.; normal useful load, 45,500 lb.; maximum useful load, 60,500 lb.; normal loaded, 120,000 lb.; maximum overload, 135,000 lb.
Performance:	Maximum speed, 357 m.p.h. at 30,000 ft., 306 m.p.h. at sea level; maximum continuous cruising, 342 m.p.h. at 30,000 ft.; economical cruising, 220 m.p.h. at 25,000 ft.; initial climb rate (at combat weight), 900 ft./min., service ceiling, 33,600 ft.; range and endurance (at 10,000 ft. with 5,585 Imp. gal. of fuel) with 4,000-lb. bomb load, 2,650 mls. in 8.9 hrs., with 10,000-lb. bomb load, 3,250 mls. in 16.4 hrs.

The Ki.67-Ib Type 4 Model 1B Hiryu illustrated above was the standard production model of what was undoubtedly the finest Japanese Army Air Force bomber encountered in combat. Originally flush-mounted lateral gun positions were used but these were replaced by blister-type positions as shown in the photograph on the left.

THE MITSUBISHI KI.67 TYPE 4 HIRYU

The job of intelligence officer is no simple task. An intimate knowledge of aviation is necessary in order to correctly evaluate combat reports, and it is inevitable that, at times, mistakes are made; errors which may not be corrected for many months and which may well prove costly in terms of lives and material. Such a mistake was made with the first identification of the Mitsubishi Hiryu (Flying Dragon), the finest Japanese Army Air Force bomber to be encountered in combat. When torpedo-carrying Hiryu bombers made their début in October 1944, during the second battle of the Philippine Sea, with an attack on the American Fleet, the type was promptly recorded as "a new Naval attack bomber". The conclusion was logical enough, for the new aircraft was indeed acting as a naval bomber in co-operation with Japanese Naval Air Force units operating from Formosa, and it was not until the Hiryu was met over China, far beyond the operating range of the nearest naval air units, and the wreckage of crashed Hiryu bombers had been analysed in the Philippines, that the truth was discovered.

The discovery was alarming. For three years the Allies had been at war with Japan and, although Japanese capabilities in the design of combat aircraft had been seriously underrated, it had been discovered that the Japanese Army bombers were exceptionally vulnerable to fighter attack. The appearance of the Hiryu signified an end to this vulnerability, and the rapid replacement of the obsolete Mitsubishi Ki.21-II

and Nakajima Ki.49-II bombers was ominous. The J.A.A.F. bomber force, hopelessly outclassed and believed largely impotent, was being revitalised with an aircraft far superior to any it had previously possessed.

The events leading up to the initial use of the Hiryu off Formosa created a paradox of genealogy and operational demand. Originally evolved as a high-performance bomber to meet an Army specification, the Hiryu owed much to the standard G4M naval bomber, and was superficially similar in configuration. Adopted as a standard J.A.A.F. bomber type in 1944, and produced exclusively for the Army, the urgent need for attack bombers for use against the American Fleet off the Philippines led to the Hiryu's baptism of fire as a naval attack aircraft flown by J.A.A.F. crews in consort with J.N.A.F. units. Following this operational initiation, the Hiryu was assigned to its basic Army mission, only to be returned to naval co-operation later in the war when, once again, the J.N.A.F. had insufficient attack bombers to handle the situation that had developed.

The most advanced Japanese Army bomber of the war to see operational service, the Hiryu was designed by the Mitsubishi Jukogyo K.K. in response to an Army heavy bomber specification issued in February 1941. In spite of the limited design personnel available, a situation that became progressively worse after Japan embarked upon the Pacific war, the Mitsubishi staff undertook the design and development of the new

120

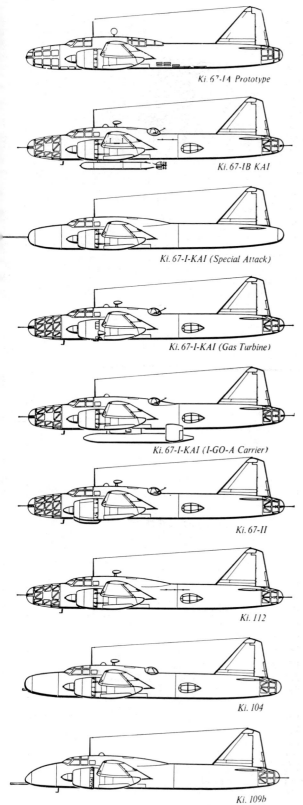

Ki.67-I4 Prototype

Ki.67-IB KAI

Ki.67-I-KAI (Special Attack)

Ki.67-I-KAI (Gas Turbine)

Ki.67-I-KAI (I-GO-A Carrier)

Ki.67-II

Ki.112

Ki.104

Ki.109b

THE MITSUBISHI Ki. 67 TYPE 4 HIRYU

bomber with enthusiasm. The new aircraft presented a challenge, for it provided Mitsubishi with the opportunity to create a replacement for their earlier K.21-II Type 97 heavy bomber, as well as regain the profitable position of the leading J.A.A.F. heavy bomber designers and manufacturers, a position which was being threatened by the Nakajima Hikoki K.K. with their Ki.49 Donryu Type 100 bomber series. The J.A.A.F. specification called for a bomber that could carry a bomb load appreciably farther, faster and higher than the standard Ki.21 and Ki.49 bombers. It was to represent a major step forward in J.A.A.F. bomber equipment, providing equality with the bombers of the western nations, and offering an effective weapon for use against Russia in the event of an open conflict with that country. The specification called for an operational altitude of up to 23,000 ft., a tactical radius of 620 miles with a 1,100-lb. bomb load, and a maximum speed of at least 310 m.p.h. in order to bring J.A.A.F equipment into line with Naval bomber projects then under development. The specification recommended the use of the most dependable power plants available, such as the Mitsubishi Ha.101 Type 100 air-cooled radial of 1,450 h.p., then being employed by the Ki.21-II bomber; the successful Nakajima Ha.109 radial of similar power, later adopted as the Type 2 and used in the Ki.49-II bomber, or, if development progressed favourably, the unproven Nakajima Ha.103 radial engine of 1,800 h.p. The new bomber was to carry nine or ten crew members and an effective defensive armament comprising six 7.92-mm. machine guns in nose, dorsal, ventral, waist and tail positions.

With Mitsubishi's acceptance of the specification, and the J.A.A.F. assignment of the experimental Ki.67 project designation to the bomber, work began in earnest late in 1941 at Mitsubishi's Nagoya plant, Kumishiko Kono, General Manager of the Nagoya Works and Chief of the Engineering Department, being appointed Chief Project Engineer. Kono's position and acclaimed success with the Ki.15, Ki.30 and Ki.51 series of J.A.A.F. light bombers gave considerable stature to the Ki.67 project, and he was assisted by Chief Engineer Ozawa Kyunosuke, well-known in Japan for his work on the standard Ki.21 bomber, and earlier work on the Ki.2 Type 93 light bomber, a type based on the Junkers K-37. Early in 1942 the design team was augmented by the addition of Yoshio Tsubota, a young engineer who had received his degree from the California Institute of Technology, and possessed a background of practical training in the U.S.A. Free rein was given to the Ki.67 design team in order to encourage new ideas, and, as a result, the bomber project became a showpiece of advanced thinking on the part of Japanese engineers, incorporating an advantageous blend of combat-tested innovations and contemporary Western ideas as a result of American-oriented training and the analysis of captured Allied aircraft obtained during the opening months of the war. Crew safety was

THE MITSUBISHI Ki. 67 TYPE 4 HIRYU

The Mitsubishi Ki.67-Ib Hiryu was used by the Japanese Navy as a torpedo bomber in a desperate bid to stem the Allied invasion of the Philippines. External torpedo racks were fitted as seen in the photograph.

awarded higher priority than previously, with ⅝-in. three-ply rubber protection for most fuel and oil tanks, and armour protection for the crew members. Other advanced ideas incorporated in the design included fully-feathering airscrews, radio altimeter, etc.

The first prototype Ki.67 was completed at Mitsubishi's 1st Airframe Works at Nagoya in December 1942. An unusually slim and clean mid-wing monoplane, the Ki.49 was beautifully proportioned, and when the prototype entered its flight test programme at Mitsubishi's Kagamigahara airfield in Gifu soon after the first of the year, it was soon discovered that the aesthetic qualities of the Ki.67 did not belie its performance, and despite the size of the aircraft, it was found to be highly manœuvrable, and could effect loops and vertical turns with ease. The J.A.A.F. was highly enthusiastic regarding the test results, and made immediate preparations for the mass production of the new bomber, anticipating that the first deliveries would be made in little more than a year's time.

The Ki.67's excellent performance was no accident, for the design team had quietly side-stepped the original specification in order to provide the aircraft with as much power as possible. Coincident with the design of the Ki.67, Mitsubishi were also engaged in a programme of boosting the power ratings of existing engines. The most promising Army engine in the programme was the new Ha.42/11, designed by Diploma Engineer M. Shomura, and based on the successful Kasei series of radials. Experimental work had commenced in 1942 at Mitsubishi's 2nd Engine Works, part of the Nagoya factory complex, and the designation Ha.104 was applied to the developed engine. An eighteen-cylinder twin-row radial incorporating such innovations as a two-speed supercharger and fan-assisted cooling, and rated at 1,900

h.p. for take-off, the Ha.104 was incorporated into the Ki.67's design, the bomber becoming the first service type to use the new engine. Development work progressed rapidly, and the Ha.104 was placed in production in 1943 at many Mitsubishi factories.

Completed as a six- to eight-seat bomber with a defensive armament of four 12.7-mm. machine guns and one 20-mm. cannon, the Ki.67 experimental heavy bomber underwent an intensive test programme under J.A.A.F. direction, a second prototype being completed in March 1943, a third in May, and one or two additional aircraft were completed each month throughout the remainder of the year, and absorbed by the test programme, fifteen machines being completed by the end of 1943. In its original form as the Ki.67-Ia, or Model 1A, the bomber had flush-mounted gun positions in the waist of the fuselage. During the test programme these were replaced by blister-type positions; the nose and tail gun positions were modified; the engine cowlings were improved, and changes were made in the equipment and instrumentation. Although the numerous revisions improved the performance and operational capability of the bomber, the seemingly endless series of changes called for by the J.A.A.F. seriously delayed the Ki.67 programme, and by April 1944 only twenty-one machines had been completed, including the prototypes. The urgent demand for such bombers as the Ki.67 at the front owing to the worsening war situation dictated an immediate agreement on a basic production model if the J.A.A.F.'s production programme was to be realised, and, caught between the desire to incorporate the latest developments in the bomber and the need to finalise the design for production, the J.A.A.F. finally gave its approval for quantity manufacture of the type early in 1944 as the Mitsubishi

FINISH AND INSIGNIA: *The Mitsubishi Ki. 67-I Hiryu illustrated on the opposite page employed, like virtually all Hiryu aircraft that entered J.A.A.F. service, dark olive green upper surfaces with medium sea grey under surfaces. In view of the haste with which the Hiryu bombers were introduced into operational service, many standard service markings, such as "combat stripes" and colourful squadron insignia, were ignored. The sole identifying markings carried by the Hiryu illustrated comprised a Japanese Kana*

character identifying the Buntai (Squadron) followed by the individual aircraft number (i.e., "148") which appeared in white across the vertical fin. Other aircraft of the same unit included "346," "135" and "146".

The circular red national insignia, or Hinomaru, appeared on the upper and lower surfaces of both wings, and on the fuselage sides. On some aircraft this insignia was outlined in white, but most Hiryu bombers did not have the national markings outlined.

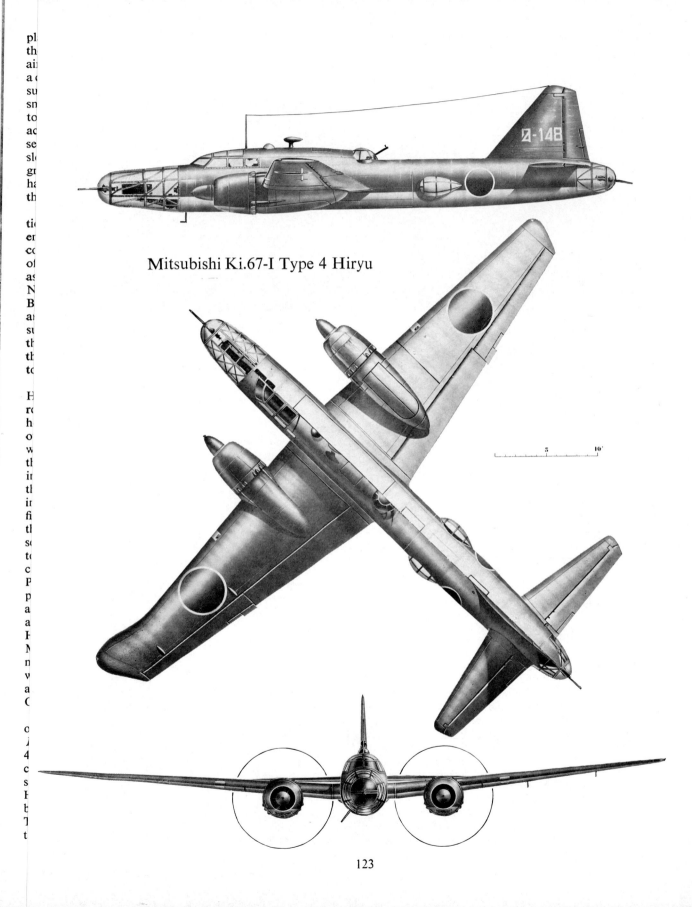

Mitsubishi Ki.67-I Type 4 Hiryu

123

The Ar 234V14 was generally similar to the pre-production Ar 234B-0, and was used principally for testing equipment to be installed in series aircraft. Of the twenty pre-production Ar 234B-0 aircraft, thirteen were sent to the Rechlin Test Centre.

held on continuously, and the brakes were frequently burned out after two or three landings.

Production tempo of the Blitz began to mount during the Autumn of 1944, and approximately one hundred and fifty machines had been delivered by the end of the year. At a meeting held on November 21, 1944, the highest priority was given to the Ar 234B as one of four key production types (the others being the Dornier Do 335, the Heinkel He 162, and the Messerschmitt Me 262), and aircraft were delivered direct to K.G. 76 from the Alt Loennewitz assembly line, but a relatively small proportion of these saw operational use because of the high rate of training accidents, shortages of pilots, and other causes. Nevertheless, the Ar 234B-2 began to appear in increasing numbers over the Allied lines and on at least one occasion reconnoitred over the British Isles.

While production had been gaining momentum, Arado had been busily engaged in the development of more advanced versions of the basic design. The Ar 234V13, which had commenced tests on August 30, 1944, reverted to a similar engine arrangement to that first tested by the Ar 234V8—four BMW 003A-1 units in two paired nacelles. The Ar 234V14 was powered by two Jumo 004B turbojets and was generally similar to the Ar 234B-0 and used for equipment testing; the Ar 234V15 was powered by two BMW 003A-1 engines, and the Ar 234V16 was a particularly interesting experimental model intended for research at high subsonic speeds. It was to have been powered by two BMW 003R composite power plants, each consisting of a BMW 003A-1 turbojet and a BMW 718 bi-fuel rocket motor which augmented thrust by 2,700 lb. for three minutes. Tail surfaces were swept, and four different sets of wings were built for flight testing by this prototype. The first set were of wooden construction and similar planform; the second set

were unswept metal wings of laminar profile; the third set were exceptionally thin swept metal surfaces, and the fourth set were also metal swept surfaces but of laminar profile. Unfortunately, the BMW 303R power plants were not delivered, and, in consequence, the Ar 234V16 was not tested. Neither the Ar 234V17 (two BMW 003A-1 turbojets and pressurized cabin) or V18 (four BMW 003A-1 turbojets and swept wing and tail surfaces) was completed.

The next Versuchs type, the Ar 234V19, was the first real prototype for the more powerful C-series which was entering production during the closing stages of the war. Development of the Ar 234C was seriously hampered by the fact that the experimental assembly plant had to be dispersed to different regions over a period of fifteen months, and shortages of fuel frequently delayed the flight test programme. The Ar 234C was essentially similar to the B-series apart from the fact that it was powered by four BMW 003A-1 turbojets in two paired nacelles. Several detailed modifications were made, including changes in aileron design and skin contours, the nosewheel was enlarged, and air brakes were experimentally fitted. The Ar 234V19 flew for the first time on September 30, 1944, and was intended to serve as a prototype for the proposed Ar 234C-1 production model. This was to have been a high-speed reconnaissance aircraft with a pressure cabin, two cameras in the rear fuselage, and two rearward-firing 20-mm. MG 151 cannon in a pack beneath the fuselage. The estimated performance of the Ar 234C-1 included maximum speeds of 515 m.p.h. at sea level and 542 m.p.h. at 19,700 ft., a range of 920 miles and the ability to climb to 32,800 feet in 11 min. 54 sec.

The Ar 234C-2 was a proposed bomber generally similar to the C-1 capable of carrying one 2,200-lb.

The first production model was the Ar 234B-1 (above) which began to appear over the Allied lines on reconnaissance sorties in the autumn of 1944. It carried no defensive armament or bombs, and was used solely for photo-reconnaissance.

bomb and two 1,100-lb. bombs over a range of 472 miles, or one 1,100-lb. bomb over a range of 995 miles. Maximum speed in clean condition was estimated at 555 m.p.h. at 19,700 feet. Various schemes were proposed for towing a 3,086-lb. bomb or a Fieseler Fi 103 flying bomb, and one project entailed the transportation of a Fi 103 on a cradle on the back of an Ar 234C-2. For launching, the missile was to be raised on the cradle by a series of hydraulically-operated arms to clear the top of the parent aircraft.

The Ar 234C-1 and -2 were abandoned in favour of the multi-purpose Ar 234C-3 for which the Ar 234V20 served as a prototype. It was intended that the Ar 234C-3 be fitted with four BMW 003C turbojets each rated at 1,980 lb.s.t., but the non-availability of these units necessitated the retention of the BMW 003A-1 in the prototype and the initial batch of production machines. The cockpit roof of the Ar 234C-3 was raised to improve visibility, and armament comprised two rearward-firing 20-mm. MG 151 cannon in the fuselage with 250 r.p.g. For the night-fighting role, it was proposed to carry a twin 20-mm. cannon pack beneath the centre fuselage, this being replaced by AB 500 cluster containers of anti-personnel bombs or other weapons for the ground attack role, and the standard range of 550-lb., 1,100-lb., and 2,200-lb. bombs could be carried for level- or dive-bombing attacks. The Ar 234C-3 had empty and maximum loaded weights of 14,400 lb. and 24,250 lb. respectively, maximum speed ranged from 496 m.p.h. at sea level to 532 m.p.h. at 19,700 ft., and range was 765 miles. Only nineteen production Ar 234C-3 aircraft were completed before the end of hostilities, and these were never issued to an operational unit. A reconnaissance aircraft essentially similar to the C-3 was the C-4 which was to have been delivered at a rate of thirty machines per month by June 1944. Like its immediate predecessor, the Ar 234C-4 was to be powered by BMW 003C engines as soon as these became available for installation.

The Ar 234V21 which appeared on November 30, 1944, and the V22, V23, V24, and V25 which were all tested during the following three months, were all prototypes for the Ar 234C-5 single-seat bomber with a pressure cabin and powered by four BMW 003C units, a reconnaissance version being designated Ar 234C-6. The Ar 234V26, completed on March 20, 1945, was built to test laminar-flow aerofoils at high speeds, while the V27 was a test-bed for air brakes.

In view of Germany's concentration on fighter production and development during the closing months of the war, it is hardly surprising that the Ar 234 should be considered for this role, particularly in view of its fine performance. A few weeks before the end of the war in Europe, the Ar 234V28 and V29 appeared, these being prototypes for the two-seat Ar 234C-7 night fighter. Whereas the prototypes were each powered by four BMW 003A turbojets, the proposed production model could be powered by two 2,860 lb.s.t. Heinkel-Hirth HeS 011 or two 2,200 lb.s.t. Jumo 004C turbojets. Armament was to comprise one 20-mm. MG 151 cannon with 300 rounds in the fuselage and two 30-mm. MK 108 cannon with 100 r.p.g. in a pack beneath the centre fuselage. The Ar 234C-8 was a proposed bomber variant powered by two 2,310 lb.s.t. Jumo turbojets.

Evolved in parallel with the later C-series variants was the Ar 234D, ten prototypes of which were, under construction and scheduled for completion by the end of 1945. These were all to have been powered by the Heinkel-Hirth HeS 011, but only two of the prototypes, the V31 and V32, were actually completed before the final collapse. Two D-series variants were proposed, the Ar 234D-1 two-seat reconnaissance aircraft, and the Ar 234D-2 two-seat bomber. A projected night fighter based on the D-series was the Ar 234P, the nose being modified and lengthened to accommodate radar interception equipment, but no prototype had been completed by the end of the war.

The only version of the Blitz to see operational service was the Ar 234B, and only 210 examples of this aircraft had been completed at the time of

135

The Ar 234C-3 was a multi-purpose aircraft which could be used for close-support, level- and dive-bombing, and night and bad weather fighting. Only nineteen Ar 234C-3s were completed before the end of hostilities.

Germany's final defeat despite the very high priority allocated to the production of this aircraft by the R.L.M. Only a small proportion of these reached K.G. 76, and while they undertook a certain amount of photo-reconnaissance and bombing, their operations being an annoying thorn in the Allies' side, they were too few to seriously affect the issue. The Blitz was thus just another extremely advanced German weapon that arrived too late.

Arado Ar 234B-2 Blitz

Dimensions: Span, 46 ft. 3¼ in.; length, 41 ft. 5½ in.; height, 14 ft. 1¼ in.; wing area, 284.167 sq. ft.

Armament: Two rearward-firing 20-mm. MG 151 cannon with 200 r.p.g. Maximum bomb load, 3,300 lb. Alternative loads: Three 1,100-lb. SC 500J or SD 500 bombs; one 2,200-lb. SC 1,000 bomb or SD 1000 bomb and two 550-lb. SC 250J bombs; one 3,085-lb. PC 1,400, or three AB 500 or AB 250 anti-personnel bomb clusters.

Power Plants: Two Junkers Jumo 004B turbojets with eight-stage axial-flow compressors and single-stage turbines each rated at 1,980 lb. s.t.

Weights: Empty, 11,464 lb.; loaded (clean), 18,541 lb; maximum loaded, 20,613 lb.

Performance: Maximum speed, 461 m.p.h. at 19,685 ft., 460 m.p.h. at 26,250 ft., 435 m.p.h. at 32,800 ft.; time to 19,685 ft. (with 1,100-lb. bomb load), 12.8 min. (with 3,300-lb.), 17.5 min., to 26,250 ft. (with 1,100-lb.), 21.6 min. (with 3,300-lb.), 34.1 min.; maximum range (with 1,100-lb. bomb load), 967 mls. (with 3,300-lb.), 683.5 mls.; maximum endurance (at sea level), 1.25 hrs. (at 33,000 ft.), 3.25 hrs.

The Ar 234 V 21 was the first prototype for the proposed Ar 234C-5 single-seat pressurized bomber powered by four BMW 003C turbojets. The V 21 (below) and the similar V 22, V 23, V 24 and V 25 were all tested during the last months of the war.